Gender and
the Journal

SUNY Series, Literacy, Culture, and Learning:
Theory and Practice
Alan C. Purves, Editor

Cinthia Gannett

Gender and
the Journal

Diaries
and
Academic Discourse

State University of New York Press

Published by
State University of New York Press, Albany

For information, address State University of New York
Press, State University Plaza, Albany, N.Y., 12246

Library of Congress Cataloging-in-Publication Data

Gannett, Cinthia, 1951-
    Gender and the journal : diaries and academic discourse / Cinthia
Gannett.
        p.   cm. — (SUNY series, literacy, culture, and learning)
    Includes bibliographical references and index.
    ISBN 0-7914-0683-0 (cloth : alk. paper). — ISBN 0-7914-0684-9
(pbk. : alk. paper)
    1. English language—Rhetoric—Study and teaching. 2. Diaries-
-Authorship—Sex differences. I. Title. II. Series

PE1404.G36 1991
828'.03—dc20   90-10138
                                                                    CIP

10 9 8 7 6 5 4 3 2 1

To my family,
who have loved and listened.

Contents

Preface

Every seed destroys its container or else there
would be no fruition.
        —Florida Scott-Maxwell,
            The Measure of My Days

Florida Scott-Maxwell's metaphor, which I have borrowed from her diary (Scott-Maxwell 1979, 65), aptly describes my sense of both the process of this work and its contents. The first seed was sown several years ago when a male student came to my office one day and told me he didn't like writing the journal that had been assigned in my composition class. He said it was too much like a diary and that the "girls" did a better job because they kept diaries at home.

Although I dismissed the comment at the time, it ultimately germinated when I went back and reread all the journals from that class. I discovered that the forms and functions of the journals did tend to vary according to the gender of the writer. For one thing, the women's journals were, on average, more than twice as long as the men's. More striking was my finding that most of the women were keeping—or had kept—personal journals outside of the academy, while only two of the men reported keeping anything like a journal. Even then they were careful to label their writing a *writer's journal* and not a *diary*.

But that brief blossom of understanding left me with several new questions such as "Why?" and "So what?" that needed to be cultivated. So, the next year, I surveyed several sections of composition classes about their experiences with and attitudes toward journal keeping. That larger plot of information yielded considerable confirmation of my first study and suggested that my students had gendered perceptions of the forms and functions of journals and diaries. Those perceptions were clearly grounded in their own experiences with keeping and reading journals and diaries long before they reached college. I also began to consider for the first time the complex relations between my own diary keeping, begun at age thirteen, and the types of diaries I had read in school or, later, had asked students to keep in composition, linguistics, and women's studies courses. I also started reading "the catalogs" and became fascinated by what I was discovering about the historical and cultural traditions of journal and diary keeping both inside and outside of the academy. That fascination resulted in a dissertation (Gannett 1987).

After leaving it fallow for a year, I have gone to work on it vigorously—reseeding, pruning, and picking the dead blossoms so that new ones could grow. For example, while the work was originally motivated by classroom research and the dissertation itself centered on the student journals, with the discussion of the gendered history toward the end, I have refocused the book so that the discussion of the social and historical traditions of journal and diary keeping can be offered as context for the gender differences which continue to surface in academic student journals today.

I have also added an introductory discussion of some of the theoretical contexts which inform, explicitly and implicitly, the writing of this book—specifically, the infusion of social constructionist perspectives and feminist perspectives which have burst open the traditional boundaries of literary and literacy studies and have asked important new questions about the relationship between gender and language.

Throughout the book, I explore that relationship both explicitly, through the content of specific claims, and implicitly, by employing the increasingly common rhetorical strategy of interpolating alternate voices or discourses into what is otherwise a very traditional academic text. This strategy will be discussed more fully in chapter 1.

Perhaps the most interesting thing I discovered is that the types of writing referred to by the cover terms *journal* and *diary* have repeatedly broken free from the verbal vessels designed to categorize and contain them. Shuttling to and fro between domains of discourse, journals and diaries have operated as the verbal vehicles for the sober and serious chronicling of business activity or public affairs in one incarnation, court scandal and witty gossip in another. They have provided an outlet for the reflective scrutiny of one's spirituality, a scorecard for the conscience. They have acted as primary agents for self-education and for formal public education. In the university, the journal can be found at one moment in the library, trying on the mantle of art, loosely draped in the genre of autobiography by literary scholars,[1] or in one of the offices checking in with its other kindred forms; the epistolary tradition, the essay, and the novel. A few moments later, it can be located in a class-room, being exercised as a utilitarian tool for the development of critical thinking or prose style. Victorian etiquette books prescribe the keeping of a proper journal or diary as an important part of becoming a proper young lady. Yet once started, many diaries have the intriguing tendency to stray toward more subversive ends. Thus, as chimeric sites of writing which move between dominant and muted discourses, between writing and literature, between convention and self-construction, journals and diaries offer a singular occasion for tracing the inflections of gender and other social constructions through discourse.

Following are the questions which I have used to develop each of the major chapters in turn. Chapters 1 and 3 both offer theoretical con-texts or background which some readers may already have. Readers are welcome to follow their individual inclinations in deciding how to make use of this book.

1. What theoretical conversations and actual situations of the writer frame and inform this work on journals and diaries?
2. What do we know about the journals or diaries in composition stud-ies? What are the similarities and differences between the various types of writing that we identify as journals or diaries?
3. What do we know about the relationships between gender and writ-ing, or gender and language, that might offer an explanation or descriptive framework for studying gender similarities and differ-ences in journal or diary keeping?
4. What forms and functions have journals and diaries taken histori-cally, and how has gender shaped the development of these tradi-tions?
5. How does this complex and gendered legacy of journal and diary keeping inform the practice of journal writing and the perceptions of journal keeping that our students bring with them to school?
6. Finally, how do these issues illustrate the importance of understand-ing the social and historical contexts and the gendered politics of lit-eracy research and instruction both inside and outside of schooling?

As in many New England gardens, the weeds grow as luxuriantly as the flowers in this book. Yet, I hope the reader will be able to pick out cosmos and marigold, poppy and peony, bachelor's button and snap-dragon, and choose to save some seeds for future planting.

Acknowledgments

Possibly the most important lesson people learn when they write their first book is that producing three hundred pages of words and writing a book are very different projects. Writing a book requires, in addition to a writer with an idea or two and a pen or word processor, the combined resources of family, friends, and professionals over a long stretch of time. I would like to thank my husband, Timothy, who is my constant source of comfort and joy, as are my children, Benjamin and Molly. My larger family, both my various parents, Joy, Paul, Howard, Ted, and Liz, and the Gannett and Finnegan siblings, have supported me as well, offering child care and other material and mental assistance, in addition to excusing my absences from family gatherings (or my appearance with a set of notes in hand).

Since this book began as a dissertation, it is important to acknowledge the influence of my graduate advisors, Robert Connors, Tom Newkirk, Donald Murray, Donald Graves, and Karl Diller, on my life and work. Also, I would like to acknowledge the Graduate School and the English Department of the University of New Hampshire, under whose auspices the dissertation was written, and those who have offered technical assistance.

In the process of revising the dissertation, I was given several other kinds of support. My thanks to Alan Purves, Priscilla Ross, and the several other editors and reviewers who saw merit in the project and saw me through the complex process of editing and publishing. The University of New Hampshire libraries in Manchester and Durham provided gracious and timely assistance; the Humanities Center and Vice President's Office provided funds for technical assistance; and Deans

Roberts, Resch, and Haebler at my home campus provided essential course releases, summer fellowship money, and the necessary encouragement and nudging for me to finish. Joan Howard provided invaluable technical and stylistic expertise. My colleagues at Manchester, particularly those on the composition staff, have also supported and nurtured me through this process.

Very special thanks must go to the women I write, think, laugh, and weep with: Sharyn Lowenstein, Elizabeth Chiseri-Strater, Sherrie Gradin, Bonnie Sunstein, Donna Qualley, Pat Sullivan, Hildy Crill, and Carol Barringer. I owe an enormous debt to all those journalers whose collective efforts have created a rich tradition of writing to enjoy and to study, and to all the students who let me read, learn from, respond to, and write about their journals.

1

The Book and the Writer:
The Convergence of Composition Studies, Social Constructionism, and Feminist Criticism

Any fool can generalize.
> —Florida Scott-Maxwell,
> *The Measure of My Days*

Think of writing as a social practice and its study becomes an inquiry into the circumstances under which people read and write.
> —Linda Brodkey,
> *Academic Writing as Social Practice*

The image of a seed bursting its container also suggests the dynamic and recursive tension between structure and limitation on the one hand and change or growth accompanied by the breaking of form on the other hand. Much of the current theoretical work on reading and writing—and in the humanities in general—is undergoing just such a transformation; questioning, discussing, debating the very nature of knowledge, language, and the notion of the self, that is, the relationships between life, language, and text. And, while I want to keep Florida Scott-Maxwell's maxim on the generalizing capacities of fools clearly in mind, I feel that it would be useful to review and comment on some of the debates and discussions which helped shape the writing of this book.

In fact, one of the critical reasons why this type of book on the gendering of journals or diaries, both as literary forms and as sets of literacy practices which occur both in academic and nonacademic settings, can be written right now has to do with the serendipitous breaking or opening of the disciplinary containers which we usually call Composition Studies, Literary Studies, and Language Studies.

Indeed, many scholars have begun to shift their focus from the study of the products of writing and reading in order to consider jointly the dynamic and interactive processes of reading and writing, and the social and historical contexts of all acts of discourse, including literacy practices which are often classified as outside the domain of "literature" and/or which are generated outside academic cultures. In so doing, they have challenged traditional notions about authors, texts, reading, writing, canonicity, and above all, language (Berlin 1988; Bizzell 1982; Bizzell 1986; Brodkey 1987; Bruffee 1986; Cooper 1986; Faigley 1986; and LeFevre 1987). Drawing on the methods and metaphors of such diverse enterprises as philosophy (Rorty 1979), sociolinguistics (Heath 1983), psycholinguistics (Vygotsky 1962), anthropology (Geertz 1973; Geertz 1983), Marxism (Bahktin 1981), and from poststructuralism/deconstruction/French feminisms (Cixous 1986; Derrida 1972; Foucault 1980; Irigaray 1985; Kristeva 1981; Lacan 1977; and Marks and Courtrivon 1981), these widely ranging and exuberantly disarrayed theoretical conversations frequently align themselves both with what are coming to be known as social-constructionist views and with much feminist work.

This current set of ideas argues, among other things, that no act of writing or reading is completely personal or private, and that the "self" itself is partly or wholly a social construction. Since journals and diaries have often been associated with descriptions such as *private writing*—writing that has no audience—and *personal writing*—the book of the self—these views radically challenge our traditional ideas about the very nature of the journal. At the same time, these new ideas about the self and discourse can be seen as offering us interesting possibilities for reconceiving, or reinventing, the idea of the journal.

Composition, Social Constructionism, and Feminism

Both feminist and social-constructionist views have recently entered the composition conversation, and both refer to a wide variety of perspectives on language and writing. If I may play Florida Scott-Maxwell's "fool" momentarily, I want to try to summarize some of the claims which I see as common to many social constructionists' and feminists' views and consider the convergence or consonance between those overlapping perspectives because it is that intersection of theoretical frames which informs the perspectives I am trying to bring to this discussion of the journal.

In the article "Competing Theories of Process: A Critique and a Proposal," Lester Faigley offers one perspective on social views of writing by describing three "competing" perspectives on the writing process, which he calls expressivist, cognitive, and social. The social view, he observes:

> is less codified and less constituted at present than the expressive and cognitive because it arises from several disciplinary traditions. . . . Statements that propose a social view of writing range from those urging mere attention to the immediate circumstances of how a text is produced to those denying the existence of an individual author. (Faigley 1986, 534)

Indeed, Karen Burke LeFevre, in her *Invention as a Social Act*, identifies and discusses several possible overlapping perspectives or levels of perspective on writing as a social activity.

> Invention may first of all be seen as social in that the self that invents is, according to many modern theorists, not merely socially influenced but even socially constituted. Furthermore, one invents largely by means of language and other symbol systems, which are socially created and shared. . . . Invention often occurs through the socially learned process of an internal dialogue with an imagined other, and the invention process is enabled by the internal social construct of audience, which supplies premises and structures of belief that guide the writer. . . . Invention becomes explicitly social when writers involve other people as collaborators, or as reviewers whose comments aid invention, or as "resonators" who nourish the development of ideas. . . . Finally, invention is powerfully influenced by social collectives, such as institutions, bureaucracies, and governments which transmit expectations, and prohibitions, encouraging certain ideas and discouraging others. (LeFevre 1987, 2)

A central claim which most social constructionists and feminists share is that language and discursive practice is constitutive. Thus, a critical theme common to these enterprises is that language not only conveys social reality, but is also one of the prime elements in its construction and maintenance.

> First, language should be viewed as an active force in the way we constitute—not simply copy—reality; language thus plays an active role in how we perceive and think and invent. Second, language should be viewed in its development and its use as a dialectic between individuals and social realms. Invention that occurs with language has often been understood as a principally intrapsychic event that goes on privately in the individual. Yet language is inevitably social as well. It is what we inherit from previous generations, what we learn from others, what we share with others. Language is itself the result of ongoing social process. (LeFevre 1987, 2)

Viewed this way, language is both the seed and the container, and therefore it can be used to contain or burst open our various perceptions of reality. As Linda Brodkey writes: "Whoever uses language creates a world and a world view in words. To say that language is a material resource is to argue that we fabricate culture as a matter of course in narratives, which can be seen then both as cultural practices and cultural artifacts" (Brodkey 1987, *Academic Writing*, 105). No longer seen as the transparent reflection of an objective reality, nor the passive vehicle for the conveyance of ideas, language and discourse are now clearly seen to have the power to marginalize or empower, mute or magnify, hurt or heal. In short, language, the social codes it embodies, and the discursive forms that it employs all write us into the social and cultural positions that we, as we write, experience as intrinsically ours.

Indeed, probably the most interesting and provocative set of debates percolating for those interested in social-constructionist and feminist views of language has to do with specifying the relation between "self" and "language," has to do with asking questions like: How much of the self is socially or linguistically constructed? or Does saying that the self is multiple and socially constructed mean there is no "self"?

John Clifford, in a recent review of works on the theory and politics of composition studies in *College English*, describes the debate as follows:

> In its present incarnation, the debate rages around the decentered subject and the traditional individual. In Lacanian psychology and structural Marxism, for example, the subject is conceived of as either a fragmented and structured illusion or the site of powerful

sociohistorical forces beyond anyone's control. In the thinking of the traditional humanist, however, the individual possesses a coherent consciousness that fulfills its intentions and acts purposefully in the world. (Clifford 1989, 527-28)

Many thinkers have moved away from the traditional humanist notion of the "self" as an autonomous, coherent, and completely individual entity and toward the view that the self is partially socially constructed through language and other forms of social organization, a "self formed through social negotiation, through a dialectic between a temporary self-in-process and society" (Clifford 1989, 528). However, some, whose views are grounded most fully in poststructural perspectives, tend to view the self as completely socially constituted. Such a position would, indeed, deny the "existence of the individual writer."

Thus, some would grant language far more power, and far more control, espousing a view that we are not agents in the generation of meaning, but rather, "the prisoners of language." We are thus simply recipients of language and social codes. Freed and Broadhead, for example, link poststructuralism with the following view of the author: "No longer an author, the writer is, instead, authored by language. Not a manipulator of signs, the writer is manipulated by them, subjugated by 'the prison house of language'" (Freed and Broadhead 1987, 156).

Bruffee also summarizes the strong variant of the social-constructionist perspective as claiming not only that texts and knowledge are socially and linguistically constructed but that the writers themselves also are:

> A social constructionist position in any discipline assumes that entities we normally call reality, knowledge, facts, texts, selves, and so on are community-generated and community-maintained linguistic entities—or more broadly speaking, symbolic entities—that define, or "constitute" the communities that generate them. (Bruffee 1986, 774)

Faigley, too, sees a social view of writing as moving beyond both the expressivist and cognitive views of writing in terms of its focus on the social construction of the writing self. According to him, expressivist views of composing see the individual as using language as a means for self-discovery, while cognitivists would claim that individuals use language to configure and construct reality. However, "in a social view, any effort to write about the self always comes in relation to previous texts" (Faigley 1986, 536).

But many social constructionists—and most feminists, I suspect—hold a view related to that of Linda Brodkey, who draws on both
social-constructionist and feminist ideas in her work. She focuses on the
social situation of writing and reading and sees the relations between
writers and texts as reciprocal and dynamic. Thus, while she describes
her view as one in which writing is seen as a "socially constituted act
whose meaning and value to writers and readers depends on contingent
social arrangements," she notes that "the practices of writers and readers are seen as social and thereby material enactments of their collective
as well as individual understanding of what can and cannot be done in
writing" (Brodkey 1987, vii. Emphasis added). Even more to the point,
she writes:

> There is always a context, for writing as speaking, consisting at the
> very least of a writer, a reader, a text, and a situation. In order to
> understand variation in writing, one would need to explore how
> textuality, the meaning and value of a text, is created in the recip-
> rocal social relations that writers and readers construct in their lan-
> guage. (Brodkey 1987, *Academic Writing*, 96)

Similarly, Marilyn Cooper employs the phrase "the ecology of
writing" to discuss her notion of a dialectic process whereby discourse
communities, and individual speakers and writers, act on each other to
change or maintain discursive practice and the linguistically-con-
structed reality that underlies it (Cooper 1986). Karen Burke LeFevre
sums it up nicely when she writes that the terms *individual* and *social* are
not mutually exclusive categories. Rather they are "dialectically connected, always co-defining and interdependent" (LeFevre 1987, 37).

While I spent much of the summer, spent much of my writing
time thinking, indeed, worrying, about the issues of language and the
social construction of self, I know these issues are not fully resolvable.
What follows is an excerpt from my journal that catches what I was
thinking about that subject on 20 July at about ten o'clock in the morning.

*[Thinking thinking thinking about what to say—what I know—what I
can discover by writing. My brain wants to pull so many many—too many??
strands together. I was never any good at French braiding. Worried about
voice—subjectivity—who is the I that writes—how do I connect the postmod-
ern, deconstructive nonself inscribed only by other voices, with me, a multiple,
changing, person in process, but an I nevertheless. The I who has dirt under her
fingernails from weeding the garden and a cat sleeping next to her, who worries*

about showing the house to prospective buyers and whether or not she can afford to buy a Cross pen to write. A permeable I—inside and outside, but unified over time, which she knows by many things—like by keeping and reading her journals.

I guess I'll just have to be comfortable with the fact that the discussion of these issues will take place throughout the text I write. Certainly, however, some form of dialectic and reciprocal view of the relation between self and language is the one that I find most compatible at present (whoever I am), and this certainly informs my perspectives on gender, journals and diaries.]

Also, some composition scholars, like Lester Faigley and James Berlin, see social-constructionist views as incompatible with a process view of writing because of the latter's acceptance of and pedagogical emphasis on the idea of a genuine voice or a personal voice which they claim assumes the traditional notion of the self as authentic and individual. But Linda Brodkey suggests that social views of writing are generally compatible with, and indeed build on, current models of writing as a set of processes.

> Any notion of writing process presumes implicitly or explicitly, that writing is best understood as a set of observable human practices. Thus, any attempt to study writing, even writing as literature, would necessarily entail situating writers and writing practices with a social, psychological, historical and political context. (Brodkey 1987, *Academic Writing*, 80. See also Knoblauch 1988)

A second critical constructionist claim is that reading and writing take place in the context of—although not necessarily in the presence of—historical and current communities of other readers and writers who share essential, although often invisible, literacy habits, conventions, and discursive models. Thus, the concept of community, borrowed from linguistic notions of speech community, has become an increasingly important idea in social-constructionist views of literacy. "However unseen they may be, the norms define the writer's community, a context that conditions, governs and constrains, not just the message, but the writer producing it" (Freed and Broadhead 1987, 162-63). Or, as Brodkey writes: "All writers use the language of a community, and all must write in ways deemed appropriate to and by a community" (Brodkey 1987, *Academic Writing*, 12).

Even though the idea of a discourse community sounds relatively simple and positive, much recent work has shown that language communities are structurally and ideologically complex. Joseph Harris, in his recent essay on the notion of plurality within and between discourse communities, "The Idea of Community in the Study of Writing," comments:

> We write not as isolated individuals, but as members of communities whose beliefs, concerns, and practices both instigate and constrain at least in part the things we can say. Our aims and intentions are thus not merely personal, idiosyncratic, but reflective of the communities to which we belong." (Harris 1989, 12)

Close examination of the workings of these multiple communities and networks, according to Harris and others, however, reveals not only plurality, but along with it, issues of power, dominance, privilege, and marginalization.

Consider the critical and frequently invoked term, the *academic discourse community*. The term was first employed in composition in a rather global, presumably neutral, and definitely benign way to capture the significant distinctions between the language habits and conventions of entering or marginal students and those of the university community to which students were to be "initiated" (Bruffee 1986, 783). However, it has become apparent that a simple dichotomous set of "communities"—the academic and the nonacademic—do not sufficiently represent the complexity of discursive practices and discursive politics within and between disciplines or within the academy as a whole. Thus, a central task of social-constructionist work is to explore the convergences, coalitions, and tensions between and among varieties of discursive networks (some deriving from disciplines, others from particular methodologies, such as deconstruction, or from interdisciplinary enterprises, such as feminism) which collectively compose the academic discourse "community," and to explore the critical connections between academic literacy communities and the host of other discursive communities to which people belong or which condition people's uses of language (Bizzell 1982, "Cognition, Convention"; Bizzell 1986, "Composing Processes" and "What Happens?"; Bartholomae 1986; Brodkey 1987 *Academic Writing* and "Modernism"; Bruffee 1986; Chiseri-Strater 1991; Freed and Broadhead 1987; Harris 1989; Heath 1983; Myers 1985; Odell and Goswami 1985; and Neilsen 1989).

For example, Shirley Brice Heath, in her landmark ethnographic and sociolinguistic study, *Ways with Words*, probes the connections and discontinuities among home, community, and school literacies in the communities of "Roadville" and "Trackton" (Heath 1983). She finds that nonacademic, often oral discourse traditions which vary according to region, race, gender, and class, are primary influences in the developing literacies of children, even though they are often ignored in school .

More recently, Joseph Harris has provided another illustrative example of the multiple and shifting relations between speech and writing communities which are stratified by class through an examination of his own discursive position in the academy. He reports that after he reached college, he realized that his coming from a working-class background, from a radically different discourse community, had had profound consequences for him in the university. "This sense of difference, of overlap, of tense plurality, of being at once a member of several communities and yet never wholly a member of one, has accompanied nearly all the work and study I have done at the university" (Harris 1989, 11).

Issues of plurality and power in academic discourse are also thoughtfully considered in Lu Min-zhan's autobiographical essay, "From Silence to Words: Writing as Struggle," in which she explores the difficult negotiations she had to make as she moved among English, French, and Chinese and their respective ideologies at home, in the classroom, and in the world (Min-zhan 1987). Yet, shuttling to and fro among languages or language communities is not the same as moving from one clearly marked linguistic territory to another. As Harris observes astutely, "the borders of most discourses are hazily marked and often traveled and . . . the communities they define are thus often indistinct and overlapping" (Harris 1989, 17).

In sum, although methods of inquiry range widely in the investigation of the reciprocal and complex relations among language, epistemology, individual speakers and writers, and the contexts and communities in which they speak and write, James Slevin identifies some of the common origins and concerns of social constructionists as follows:

> The social origins and contexts of writing are a common interest of many scholars and teachers influenced by current theories of discourse and ethnographic studies of actual textual production. These influences lead to a concern with how writing is produced and, more specifically, with conditions that enable it *or* (especially in some feminist and pedagogical studies) those conditions that *dis*able it. . . . Scholars and teachers with these different interests share in common such questions as the range of discursive forms available to a writer, the ideological dimensions of these forms, the nature of authorship, and even the availability of a readership. (Slevin 1986, 549)

Like social-constructionist perspectives, feminist theory and practice have also been "bustin' out all over," proliferating and permutating at an amazing rate, and producing a rich ecosystem of both ordinary and exotic theoretical varieties of description and explanation of gender, sexuality, and sexual difference, and other sources of social and textual difference. It is impossible to review adequately the development or the current state of feminist theory and practice here, but detailed treatment is available in several new book-length collections.[1]

First—and at the very least—scholars, researchers, and teachers with this perspective tend to recognize that discourses and the people who generate them are always socially and historically situated, and thus have both historical and social contexts, constraints, and consequences, and that gender has historically played a critical role in situating all writers and readers. For example, in response to the traditional, modernist view of the writer as a solitary genius who works alone in what is invariably *his* garret producing original *master*pieces unaffected by material, social, or historical contexts or conditions, Brodkey and many others have pointed out that historical, material, and quotidian conditions have always differently affected the type, quality, and quantity of the writing and reading that women have done. She suggests that the scenes of writing for women are often rooms that are leased, not purchased, and sparsely furnished. Both the literal and figurative houses women write in are filled with many rooms and many people and multiple obligations (Brodkey 1987, "Modernism"). Naturally, therefore, feminists are interested in such material and historical conditions as access to literacy, schooling, and publishing, since for centuries, many women were explicitly denied access, solely on the basis of their gender, to literacy generally or to specific types of literacy, which were usually the most public and powerful forms.

In "Composing as a Woman," an important new article which signals the increasing interest in feminist perspectives in composition research, Elizabeth Flynn agrees that such issues are critical to a feminist understanding of composition. "A feminist approach to composition would focus on questions of difference and dominance in written language" (Flynn 1988, 425). She suggests that teachers "ought not to assume that males and females use language in identical ways or represent the world in a similar fashion" (Flynn 1988, 431).

Indeed, for many feminists, understanding the complex historical and social relationships among gender, language, and discursive practice is critical to their practice as feminist scholars and teachers. One important strand of feminist thought has concerned itself with the ways in which women as a group have historically been muted, silenced, and marginalized by language and language use. I will explore this claim throughout this work, as I try to document and understand the profound social and epistemological consequences of discursive marginalization.

As a corollary, many feminists are concerned with notions of discourse community, having always been in or around multiple discourse communities, and they have recognized that those communities that have far more public power than others have tended historically to be male-constructed or male-affiliated. They recognize that some discourse communities are voluntary or elective while others are not. Like Joseph Harris, they feel their own "tense plurality," their own multiple, marginal, and often restricted memberships in most public and dominant discourse communities.

Similarly, feminists are also interested in exposing the processes of literary and curricular canonization, the mechanisms whereby certain powerful discourse communities determine which types of literacy practices or instances of writing will accrue literary, academic, or pedagogical value. Feminists have also identified the generic and aesthetic categories which sustain the canon as historically the products of male manufacture and therefore not representative of all human experience, but rather representative primarily of the perspectives of white, elite, heterosexual, Western males.

Finally, most feminists recognize the enormous power of language which, as a social construction, continues to reflect and reproduce a world in which asymmetrical subject positions are ascribed according to gender, inflecting all our perceptions of the world and of our places in it. Language affects not only our perceptions of each other as gendered beings, but also our perceptions of ourselves, and of gender itself.

Certainly, it is important to acknowledge the critical insight that women are not all alike—there is no "transhistorical changeless, feminine essence" (Clifford 1989, 531)—and that race, class, ethnicity, sexual orientation, and religion are also important determinants in the social construction of the self. Nevertheless, gender as a social construct powerfully writes itself onto all of our lives and we must try to decipher its inscriptions and revise them, rewriting them as we see fit.

Of course, a woman remembered only as Aunt Jane of Kentucky had this notion of the social construction of the self all figured out a long time ago when she wrote this passage in her journal:

How much piecin' a quilt's like a life. . . . The Lord sends us the pieces but we can cut 'em out and put 'em together pretty much to suit ourselves, and there's a heap more in the cuttin' and the sewin' than there is in the caliker. (Bank 1979, 76)

The Situation of a (Feminist Academic) Writer in 1991

It is impossible to do anything without telling a story.
—Marilyn French, "Text as Context"

The Academy has a limited tolerance for lived experience, which it easily dismisses as "stories."
—Linda Brodkey,
Academic Writing as Social Practice

The theoretical claims in the previous section are important, but they do not, by themselves, provide the entire context for this text. Indeed, since, as both a social constructionist and a feminist, I have just spent the last several pages discussing the importance of placing writers and writing into social and historical context, it is only fitting for me to locate some of the critical contexts and communities which inform my own writing generally, and this writing specifically, as a preliminary and prefigurative illustration of the central claims and methods of this book.

Several factors influence the personal and social situation from which I write. I am 39, a baby boomer, and an assistant professor of Composition/English at a small branch of a larger state university. As a white, middle-class child growing up in Ohio in the 1950s, I lived in relative comfort and emotional security. My parents were college-educated—my father worked in public relations, my mother was a social worker—and so I learned to value literacy and schooling in general. That envelope of protection and security was torn open when I was sixteen and my father, quite suddenly, died. I tried to staple it shut by marrying a disabled Vietnam veteran at the age of eighteen, one week after receiving my high school diploma and one week before I graduated from Girl Scouts. I began working on my Master's degree only because my first husband went to England to do a pottery apprenticeship and told me to find something else to do. My interest in graduate school was considered selfish by many friends and relatives and it dealt a final blow to my first marriage. We separated during the first semester of my Ph.D. work.

I was married for the second time in 1981, after my second year of doctoral study. My husband and I are raising two children, one from each of my marriages, who are fourteen and seven years old. We feel lucky to have survived the Ph.D. process, which took eight years. During that time, I started one dissertation and abandoned it after three chapters; I was morning sick—all day—from September to April (when my daughter Molly was born) the year I had my dissertation fellowship. Naturally, I always worked full time, or nearly full time, in addition to my academic and domestic responsibilities. Later, when I was writing the second dissertation, we were faced with a protracted custody battle over the older child, Benjamin.

Not surprisingly, my "professional life" has been filled with gaps: work unwritten, or unfinished, or unpublished. All those years, I subscribed to the "fluke theory" of success. When I did well, it was an accident; when I did poorly, it was my fault. I clearly wanted both a family and a career, but often felt as though I was succeeding at neither of the two. I believed that if I were only smarter, better organized, more supportive, or more productive, I would be able to successfully integrate both sets of roles.

What I am finally beginning to understand, however, is that my personal situation as an academic woman is not unique, but rather common, and is directly related to the issues of marginalization, muteness and empowerment which are among the central themes of this book. In *Women of Academe: Outsiders in the Sacred Grove*, Nadya Aisenberg and Mona Harrington interviewed thirty-seven "deflected" academic women (women who had been deflected from a regular professional academic career) and twenty-five tenured academic women, who represented a variety of institutions, regions, and disciplines (Aisenberg and Harrington 1988). Collecting more than fifteen hundred pages of transcription, they found several critical recurring patterns of response. Surprisingly, the deflected and tenured women's stories were far more similar than distinct in that both groups had, indeed, been marginalized professionally and economically.

As women rise in the professions, they are stymied at a certain level by the remaining force of old social norms that, in the past, barred women from public life generally. The old norms buttressed the division of responsibility—public roles for men, private for women—with a variety of assumptions about male and female natures, drawing natural connections between given proclivities and given roles. Women's identity was located in the body and in the emotions, men's in the mind. Women gave birth, suckled infants, nursed the sick, cleaned homes, cooked meals, provided sympathy, enchantment, and inspiration. Men learned, calculated, bought, sold, fought, wrote, painted, philosophized. (Aisenberg and Harrington 1988, 4)

Aisenberg and Harrington suggest that these inequalities are in large part sustained by the force of what they call "the marriage plot"—which applies to all women, whether married or not—the central tenet of which is that "women's proper goal is marriage, or, more generally, her primary sphere is private and domestic. Her proper role is to provide support for the male at the head of the household [or, one might add, the male-run institution] of which she forms a part" (Aisenberg and Harrington 1988, 6).

Most of the women in the study reported, in varying permutations, enormous difficulties in trying to negotiate both the supportive roles of "the marriage plot" and the "adventure plot" of their own professional development. They told of handling a disproportionate amount of domestic work and child care; of having less financial support for their educations than their male counterparts; of having to subordinate their professional interests and development to those of others. While the women, as a group, often felt both exhilarated and transformed by learning and teaching, and they often felt simultaneously excluded from full participation in academic culture. As I read, I kept hearing voices again and again that could have been mine:

Graduate Student in Humanities
    I felt that some day they were going to find me out. You know the feeling that it's not quite true, that my I.Q. was really 60. (Aisenberg and Harrington 1988, 67)

Graduate Student
    I was teaching two freshman sections while I was taking courses for the master's. And then I fell ill, I was quite seriously ill not long after I was married, and had to drop a whole semester really. . . . It may have been pure exhaustion. (Aisenberg and Harrington 1988, 44)

Language Scholar writing dissertation
    The baby was due in January, came in February. . . . And I was serving on three or four faculty committees, and teaching and advising thirteen students. So I just got tired all the time. (Aisenberg and Harrington 1988, 45)

Classicist
    They're not going to like it. I'm not doing good enough work. They think I'm not really serious because I have a family and I have other obligations. My career pattern isn't like theirs. I'm too old. (Aisenberg and Harrington 1988, 68)

Issues of Voice and Discourse Community

Many of the issues these women raised centered precisely around problems of voice, of knowing, of language, and of discourse community. Indeed, Harrington and Aisenberg had to add a whole new category they called "voice" after they started analyzing their interview data because it was such a recurrent theme in women's stories about academic life and about the tensions they felt in their relationships to academic discourse communities. Continuing the metaphor of the "adventure" and the "quest" plot, the authors explain that speaking, particularly, speaking with public and academic authority, is associated with the quest plot, while silence is better suited to the marriage plot.

A strong clear voice is necessary to the practice of the profession, both literally in the classroom and figuratively in written research. But our stories demonstrate that women trained or training in specific disciplines—that is, following the quest plot—still report feeling "inadequate," "uncomfortable," "an imposter," "mute." To state views boldly in public debate, to challenge the intellectual views of others, still pose problems for professional women.

Why should this be so? Why do women find persistent difficulty with forms of public assertion? Why do they refer to silence, apology, diffidence, hesitancy, as characteristic of their discourse? One powerful reason is that a voice of authority is exactly the voice the old norms proscribe. . . . To be loveable, the goal of the marriage plot, a woman must be silent. To express professional knowledge and wisdom, a woman must speak and speak with authority. To presume that, as women enter the professions in ever greater numbers, the injunctions of the marriage plot will simply fall away, is to indulge in wishful thinking. (Aisenberg and Harrington 1988, 64-66)

Even before my specialized graduate training in applied linguistics and composition theory and pedagogy I knew how important, how central, language is to the shaping of our everyday experience, how critical it is to every social interaction or educational enterprise. I knew somehow that words were powerful; they could help or hurt. I must have known something about the power of naming, as I remember naming my two dolls with wonderful sounding words I had heard on the radio: Diarrhea and Polio. I got in trouble in school more than once for making up words, and was scolded by a teacher who asked the scathing rhetorical question: "Who do you think you are? A dictionary?"

I know I loved writing. I wrote reams of poetry. I even wrote my classmates' compositions—often in homeroom—just for the fun of it. Most importantly for my purposes here, I was an intense, albeit sporadic, diary keeper from junior high school on.

Yet in college and graduate school, I found I often had difficulty both with the topics I chose and with finding an appropriate voice or style in which to write about them—another common problem for women writers and academics, according to Aisenberg and Harrington. For example, although I did well in school, I had certain so-called *problems* with my writing, particularly in graduate school. I was told more than once to stop apologizing. I was told that my claims weren't strong enough; or that my criticisms were too qualified. When I spoke in class, I found that while I would try to hold my ideas in, they would build up pressure to the point that they would erupt in a great gush of words. One professor called me "hyperfluent"—ambivalent praise at best.

When it came time to write my dissertation, I started the wrong one. It was an important topic and an ambitious one, but not compelling enough to force me to write it in addition to all my other responsibilities. All along I wanted to write about the relationships between gender and language but felt I had already used up my feminist option by writing about gender, language, and brain laterality for my master's thesis (Gannett 1976). I can clearly remember people asking me if I was *still* working with that gender stuff.

But the critical problem in writing that work, as in writing this one, was the problem of finding a voice or voices with which I could express myself as a woman, as a feminist, and as an academic.

> Writing, as it has been traditionally required in college, can be understood to be a "male" establishment form, in as much as the aims and modes of scientific, informative, exploratory and persuasive discourse, even until recently, literary discourse, have been defined and developed by men heading intellectual institutions and by the predominantly male writers whose ideas the professors have valued. College writing trained and still does train students to use their minds in time-hallowed ways. For female students, this still, I suspect, means straining to attain a style, voice, and role that is hard to integrate with sexual and domestic success. (Goulston 1987, 21-22)

Given the difficulties that academic women, myself included, often have with academic writing, deciding how to write this book was not easy. As Mary Jacobus explains:

Utterance, though, brings the problem home for women writers (as for feminist critics). The options polarise along familiar lines: appropriation or separatism. Can women adapt traditionally male dominated modes of writing and analysis to the articulation of female oppression and desire? Or should we rather reject tools that may simply re-inscribe our marginality, and deny the specificity of our experience, instead forging others on our own—reverting perhaps to the traditionally feminine in order to revalidate its forms (formlessness?) and preoccupations—rediscovering subjectivity; the language of feeling; ourselves. (Jacobus 1979, 14)

I have tried to resolve this dilemma by inscribing the issue of academic women's multiple voices stylistically throughout the text, as the reader will have already noticed. That is, since the focus of the book is precisely the set of tensions among traditional academic and literary discourse communities, women as marginalized users of discourse within those communities, and the marginal discourses of journals and diaries, I have decided to open up this particular academic discourse to those other voices and discourses to explicate some of these points of connection and disconnection. To converse with the traditional academic voices of objectivity, authority, abstraction, and/or agonism, I have invited some individual voices, some openly subjective, even passionate voices; some hesitant, wondering-aloud voices. I have also welcomed the myriad voices of journal keepers, female and male, student and professional, famous and anonymous, to this colloquium.

Thus, the diaristic, the anecdotal, the quotidian, the material conditions of writing, the immediate and seemingly random evidence from popular culture—both my own lived experience and that of those around me—all accompany and inform my work here. I do not intend a simple equation of masculine and feminine voice here, but rather a colloquy of public and private voices, academic and not-so-academic voices, which have often been linked to the masculine and feminine worlds of discourse.

These issues of canon and curriculum, marginalized and multiple memberships in various discourses, self and voice, are not only central to my writing, they also prefigure the central issues my students face in their journal writing and those that men and women have faced in their attempts at public and private forms of writing throughout the centuries. Their voices are the heart of this piece, the life of this text.

As for me, I feel somewhat like Wendy Goulston, who writes in her resonant essay on women writing in and for the academy:

Whenever I pursue ideas about women in depth, I wonder to
what degree and for whom they are true. While skepticism can
sharpen understanding, the self-doubt lurking behind my skepticism often blocks my thinking. Theories that suggest that women's
socialization produces internalized oppression explain this
dilemma: women are often not sure of their own ideas, especially
when asked to express them in rhetorical forms that have traditionally been used exclusively by men. This is my thesis and my
situation. (Goulston 1987, 19)

But as I plunge ahead into the wilderness of this text, I also feel
just like Mollie Dorsey Sanford, who left Indianapolis in March of 1857
for the Nebraska Territory and who kept a journal of her westward travels and pioneer experience. Mollie understood the intellectually transforming power of writing when she penned this entry in her diary on 10
September 1860. "I know I shall never pose as an author or writer. But I
do often wish I might be something more than a mere machine" (Sanford 1976, 98).

2

Academic Journals: Panacea or Problem

A journal is like a cave. What will we find there?
—Ken Macrorie, *The Journal Book*

Almost everyone knows what a diary is until it
becomes necessary to define one.
—Steven Kagle, *American Diary Literature*

Academic uses of journal writing are enormously popular right now, not only in the composition classroom, but across all the disciplines and across all educational levels. Innumerable articles and several books testify to the value and currency of these academic journals, which are used often as prewriting, or heuristic, tools for developing fluency and generating meaning. Journals are also used as a means of personalizing and synthesizing knowledge and as an aide-mémoire, among other things.

Together, the ERIC (Educational Resources Information Center) Index and the Education Index show at least one hundred articles published in the last decade on the pedagogical uses of journals. I found articles on using journals with almost every school population conceivable, almost everywhere on the globe. From gifted children to the learning disabled and the hearing impaired, from ESL (English as a Second Language) students in Saudi Arabia and Micronesia to bilingual Spanish students who write their journals in both languages, from Japanese children who write "life-experience composition books" to five-year-olds in Oregon who begin their formal schooling by learning to write journals as they learn the alphabet, journals have become a significant part of many children's formal schooling experiences. Navajo and Australian children alike have learned to keep journals for school. Journal applications have also been found for peer tutors, graduate students, teachers in training, and experienced teachers.

Yet, teachers who have assigned academic journals—particularly freewriting or prewriting journals—repeatedly discover that journals work perfectly, or at least well, for some students, but seem perilous to others. Some students take to them like trout to streams, finches to the big blue, or—even better—as canaries to song. They learn through writing. They discover connections. They are stimulated by language and acts of generating meaning. They connect, through writing, to much larger intellectual domains. For these students, teachers need practice almost no pedagogy. They can provide such students with a notebook and the encouragement to write.

But for many other students, keeping a journal can be a miserable experience. Some students are bewildered by the assignment; others are downright bored. For these students, to varying degrees, the journal as a writing experience may contribute little to their understanding or skill in writing. For the teachers of these students, finding an effective journal pedagogy poses a real challenge.

Journals are clearly powerful writing instruments. Yet, for all the array of available material on their use as prewriting tools, we know very little about them simply as writing. Most of the articles offer descriptions of very specific, often overlapping, pedagogical applications or conversion narratives which testify to the value of journals in the classroom. While these articles are both important and valuable, they don't explain why journals (more than other kinds of assigned academic writing) act as an intellectual panacea for some students, but are problematic for many others. They offer little theoretical perspective or understanding of the place of academic journaling in its larger historical and social contexts.

Just the sheer number of names currently used to describe academic journals is daunting: learning log, daybook, dialogue journal, word-processed journals, think books, notebooks, personal journal, literary logs, classroom diary, double-entry journals, process journals, language logs, and so on. Worse, there has been little concerted effort to sort out the similarities and differences in form or function among these various descriptors. As for pedagogy, we just don't know why some students find journals so compelling, while other students find them repellent, difficult, intimidating. As Ann Berthoff cautions, "journals can be just as deadly as any other heuristic if we don't think about what we are doing with them" (Berthoff 1987, 12).

Ironically, even as the value of academic journals is being increasingly acknowledged, their educational uses are being challenged from several directions. Some fear that journal writing may not foster the same quantity or quality of complex intellectual thought as other kinds of academic writing tasks, while others assert that journals are "dangerous" because they can be used for political indoctrination, or because their so-called personal nature constitutes an "invasion of privacy." In fact, some individuals and groups are trying to ban their use entirely in school settings (Macrorie 1987; Schinto 1987).

In order to understand why the use of journals inspires such extreme and contradictory responses from students, teachers, parents, and school boards, we need to consider the complex public and private, as well as the academic and nonacademic lives that journals and diaries have led. In particular, we need to consider the tension that has developed around the issue of public/academic and private or personal writing captured in the tense relation between the term *journal*, which in composition and education parlance has become the preferred term, the generic name, and the term *diary*, which is denotatively similar, but which has come to be associated with connotations such as overly personal, confessional, trivial, and, as I will argue, feminine. Let us start the discussion of these issues by tracing what is often assumed to be the introduction of the journal as a pedagogical tool in the composition curriculum in the 1960s.

Journals and the Process Movement

Journal writing, as it has been represented in much of the current literature, is usually depicted as a classroom composing activity which entered the curriculum as part of the writing-process movement of the 1960s and 1970s. With the shift from product-oriented pedagogies to process-based teaching came the new emphasis on prewriting—that is, writing and thinking which one did before the drafting of an entire composition. Prewriting activities include discovering meaning, finding a focus for a subject, generating specifics, discovering the structure of ideas and information, and experimenting with language and voice—very useful preliminaries to writing formal discourse for an audience or teacher. The journal, daybook, writing diary, or whatever else it might be called, was identified immediately as a locus for a variety of prewriting activities, because of its informal, personal, and reflective nature, as well as its structural capacity to handle frequent, regular, and short practice writings.

D. Gordon Rohman and Albert O. Wlecke were among the first to acknowledge the potential of the journal as a prewriting tool during this period in their work, *Prewriting: The Construction and Application of Models for Concept Formation in Writing* (Rohman and Wlecke 1964). Addressing the question of why students write so "poorly," so "indifferently," Rohman and Wlecke suggested that "it is just possible that much writing fails because it is conceived within what Bruner calls the 'expository mode,' and the student-writer, as a result, is never given the chance to participate in the essentials of the process which he is being called to master" (Rohman and Wlecke 1964, 24). In order to engage students more fully in the process of discovering ideas—or better, discovering new connections between concepts which would allow them to compose interesting and engaged essays—Rohman and Wlecke encouraged students to use various prewriting techniques, such as meditation, analogy exercises, and most importantly, a writing journal, which they introduced as follows:

> Because we assumed that the process of assimilation and transformation was nothing if not personal, we began our course by asking students to keep a journal. We defined a journal as a record of the mind to distinguish it from the diary which is a record of what one does. Although the distinction is not absolute, we emphasized that we were more interested in what students thought than in what they did. . . . We sought to drive them back and away from the merely automatic language they had inherited from their culture. We encouraged them to practice thinking less generally and more concretely, stressing the value of achieving a personal sense of what is real. (Rohman and Wlecke 1964, 24-25)

Another early herald, Dan Fader, argued in 1966 in *Hooked on Books* that the student journal should be a key component to getting English into every classroom (see Fulwiler 1982, 30).[1]

Models of the writing process, and the actual composing processes of experienced and novice writers were researched in the early and mid-1970s, and new interest was given to the multiple functions and stages of writing as defined by several major figures, such as James Britton, Peter Elbow, Janet Emig, Ken Macrorie, James Moffett, Donald Graves, and Donald Murray. Writing pedagogy based on the heuristic and expressive functions became increasingly important. As Janet Emig put it in the title of an important early article, writing and its associated processes needed to be considered as "a mode of learning" (Emig 1977). For these scholars and teachers, the writing journal has become a valuable and, in some cases, central part of their pedagogical repertoire, and they each have contributed important descriptions of the academic journal.

Ken Macrorie, for example, has contributed the famous metaphor of the journal as a "seedbed" for developing ideas and germinating writing which ultimately will become a final, formal product. In *Telling Writing*, he devotes an entire chapter to "Keeping a Journal." Macrorie also uses the metaphor of the journal as a "practice ground," which can be "intensely personal," but must "record telling facts which take the reader through the door into some essences" (Macrorie 1970, 123). He sees journaling as a means for students to consider an experience or set of ideas over time. "Keeping a journal forces a writer to put something into the sock every day or so. Often when he reviews what is there, he sees materials that fit together and build. He can work with them" (Macrorie 1970, 129. Note that the writer is a "he"). Keeping a journal, therefore, is critical if one wants to become a better writer, according to Macrorie.

In *Writing without Teachers*, Peter Elbow promotes the use of "freewriting" or "automatic writing" as a way to generate more writing, create fluency, and prevent premature editing. He advocates the use of a "freewriting diary" as the locus for these short, frequent writing activities:

> If you are serious about wanting to improve your writing, the most useful thing you can do is keep a freewriting diary. Just ten minutes a day. Not a complete account of your day: just a brief mind sample for each day. You don't have to think hard or prepare or be in the mood: without stopping just write whatever words come out—whether or not you are thinking or in the mood. (Elbow 1973, 9)

Don Murray is another important theorist and teacher who sees the journal as an essential writing tool. A professional writer as well as a teacher, he has studied the writing practices of professional writers for many years and has documented the many ways in which writers use journals. He has also discussed the wide array of writing activities that comprise his own "daybook." Murray's professional and pedagogical use of the journal amply demonstrates the extraordinary flexibility of the journal as a compositional tool which can be used for one kind of writing activity, as with Peter Elbow's "freewriting diary," or for several activities in combination.

What distinguishes Murray from the other important process-movement purveyors of the journal, however, is the extent to which he explicitly grounds his journal pedagogy in his own journal-keeping practices and his heightened awareness of some of the critical historical traditions of journal writing which inform his own understanding and use of the journal today (Gannett 1988). As he writes, "My journal is first cousin of the eighteenth century Commonplace Book, in which people copied down observations, reflections, and pieces of wisdom from what they had read in a lifelong self-education plan" (Murray 1985, 68).

The journal—or "daybook" as Murray calls his version of it—is the core around which Murray builds all his writing, as he explains in *A Writer Teaches Writing*. In the excerpt from that work which follows, note also how he grapples with the issue of naming the journal, sensing the tensions among various terms and their powerful historical connotations.

THE DAYBOOK

I am able to make use of fragments of time because my tools, first and foremost my daybook, are with me at all times. My daybook—or writer's log—is what some writers call a journal. When I wrote in a journal, I would swell up like rice in water and fill the space with wordy pronouncements. I tried to be Camus or Gide or someone famous and probably secretly imagined students reading my journal after I was dead. I was unbearable, unreadable—even by me. I'd write for days, read it over and laugh. I lost years, whole decades, when I could not keep a journal. I also tried to keep a diary, but the trivial events of my life were so trivial I was embarrassed reading them. The term "daybook," however, freed me. It was a working document, a sort of lab notebook, and since I have called it a daybook, it has become the most valuable resource I have. . . .

It takes me about six weeks to fill a daybook, and when I'm finished with one I go back through it and pick out anything that I need to work on in the next book. Usually this means a page or two of notes at the most. I keep the daybooks on a shelf, and since everything is entered by date I can usually remember about when I wrote something and go back to it if I need to. The fact is I don't go back that much, but the process of writing down is vital. I'm talking to myself, and the daybook is a record of my intellectual life, what I'm thinking about and what I'm thinking about writing. I use little code words in the lefthand margin. The initials for this book were AWTW *(A Writer Teaches Writing)* and that was the code I put next to notes about what might be in this book. It's easy for me to review the daybooks to see what I've written on a particular project. Many of my articles and books evolve over a period of years, and the daybook both stimulates and records my thinking.

   If you decide to try a daybook, or a log, remember that it does not contain finished writing. It can be a place for writing, a draft, but my book at least, has all sorts of other writing that doesn't even look like writing. (Donald M. Murray, *A Writer Teaches Writing*, Second Edition, 68-69. Copyright 1985 by Houghton Mifflin Company. Used by permission.)

   Murray's list of the varied content of his journals is impressive, and, having had the chance to read through several of them, I can testify to the accuracy of his list. In addition to the brainstorming, prewriting, listmaking, and drafting, Murray interpolates lists of jobs (domestic and professional), planning for writing work, self-exhortation on his progress, talks, single lines, multiple leads, whole poems, and occasional drawings. But Murray's many voices are only a fraction of what is contained in the journals, because Murray really does use his journal as a "common place." There are literally thousands of quotes and anecdotes, often—but not always—about writing, which create a chorus that moves across time and space on the pages of the more than sixty-five volumes of his daybook. He even pastes in bits of social correspondence, postcards, letters to and from friends, a wedding invitation, a eulogy (Gannett 1988, 8).

   Murray's journal, then, seems to operate as a tracking device for the myriad forms of his intellectual life, both inside the academy and outside—his writing, his writing about writing, and his writing about teaching about writing. Murray also reported to me that he does include other, more personal material in his journals, but in a compressed, indirect, and "coded" form. While he doesn't often write extended reflective entries on many of his immediate personal experiences, he will enter a phrase or name, a cryptic reference or remark which will conjure up for him an entire experience or set of feelings. This "coding" allows him access to this repository of information, while preventing accessibility to other readers.

   As representatives of a process approach to the teaching of writing, people such as Rohman and Wlecke, Macrorie, Elbow, and Murray have described journals with several important metaphors which suggest a variety of overlapping intellectual purposes. The journal is a seedbed where ideas can be planted; it is a mine where precious concepts or images lie in wait for excavation; it is a practice ground where one works out—prewrites or drafts—as a preliminary to formal writing.

Inducing fluency and intellectual discipline, the journal offers an invitation to serve as the record book of the mind's life—the hard disk for the soft human memory.

Interestingly, each writer or theorist discussed above seems to conceive of the journal as accommodating somewhat differing proportions of personal—in contrast to intellectual—content, in his own journals or in the journals of his students, and each finds this distinction sufficiently significant to require discussion. With the exception of Elbow, who uses the modified form "freewriting diary," each one has felt it necessary to make some type of distinction between the diary and the journal, characterizing the diary either as trivial (the rote recording of everyday events) or as the more personal of the forms.

Rohman and Wlecke, for example, as I noted earlier, favored the term *journal*, which they defined as a "record of the mind," over the word *diary*, which they felt was simply a record of "what one does" (Rohman and Wlecke 1964, 24). While Murray was uncomfortable with the term *journal* because it made him too self-conscious as a writer, he was even more uncomfortable with the term *diary*. In the long quote about the daybook, Murray explained that when he called his journal by the name *diary*, he found he was writing too much about his day-to-day life. "I also tried to keep a diary, but the trivial events of my life were so trivial I was embarrassed reading them" (Murray 1985, 68). Murray was also careful to report that he "coded" personal information in his journal, rather than writing about it directly.

Macrorie, on the other hand, started off his chapter on journal keeping in *Telling Writing* by trying to persuade students that a journal is not just "a square idea" (Macrorie 1970, 122). But in the introductory passage, he addresses two different audiences—a female, who has kept a personal diary of the dreamy, confessional type, and a male, who has briefly attempted to log his external activities, and then stopped.

> "What a square idea," you may have said to yourself when you read the title of this chapter. A journal! You kept a diary in high school and took it out the other day and looked away in embarrassment—
> "This was the greatest day of my life. I met Tim. He was standing outside the dime store, this tall, handsome boy—a dream that's what he was—and I thought—'He ought to be on TV'—and then Jeannie introduced me and I thought I'd die. I couldn't believe it. Before I knew what was happening I found myself being walked home by him. He's just absolutely—I can't say what he means to me."

Or if you're a man, your diary went for two days and stopped.
The entries looked like this:
"Played ball this morning. Had lunch at 12:30. Didn't do much the
rest of the day." (Macrorie 1970, 122)

Later in the chapter, Macrorie summarizes, "The man who dreams of
becoming a writer spends his time dreaming of becoming a writer. The
man who intends to become a writer keeps a journal and works the
mine" (Macrorie 1970, 123).

*[While I want to go back and change the pronouns and masculine generics in
Macrorie's text, something about their use seems appropriate. His having to
defend the use of journals and to exhort students to take them seriously and
learn to self-disclose in them seems an argument directed more at the males
than the females. As if anticipating what I have observed in the journals written by my men and women students, Macrorie, I think, has hit intuitively, both
with his introduction and with his exhortation, on claims similar to those I am
exploring here:*

*1) that women are in a journal-keeping tradition which has flourished for the
   most part outside of the academy;*
*2) that more of the men in my classes try self-sponsored journal keeping only
   sporadically, and prefer to record primarily external activities (or use the
   journal as part of their writer's apprenticeship); and*
*3) that the men's and women's academic journals may prove to be qualitatively
   as well as quantitatively different.]*

In sum, the tension between older journal traditions and current
pedagogical uses of the journal—particularly the friction between
notions of the intellectual and the personal, which the terms *journal* and
diary have come, in part, to represent—became explicit from the point at
which academic journals were reintroduced or reemphasized in con-
junction with the development of the writing-process movement.

Journals and Writing across the Curriculum

Precisely because of its adaptability to any number of writing and
critical thinking tasks, its flexible form, and its proven heuristic value,
the journal is seeing its newest pedagogical incarnation in the Writing
Across the Curriculum (WAC) movement. Based on many of the claims
and research generated by the process movement in the 1960s and 1970s

about writing as a way of discovering meaning, a way of discovering the connections between ideas and between ideas and one's self, and as one of the best ways to learn about anything, the WAC (sometimes referred to as the Reading and Writing Across the Curriculum or the Language Across the Curriculum) movement of the 1980s is attempting to restore writing and reading (or more broadly, rhetoric) to the center of the college curriculum.

Randall Freisinger gives a succinct overview and rationale for writing-across-the-curriculum programs based on the experience of the program at Michigan Technological University:

> Our program assumes that *language for learning is different from language for informing*. Britton acknowledges these different kinds of language use by distinguishing the expressive, transactional, and poetic functions of language use. Expressive language, he says, is close to the self; it reveals as much about the speaker as it does about the topic. It is the language the writer uses first to draft important ideas. Transactional language, on the other hand, is language for an audience. Its primary aim is to convey information clearly to other people; it is the language of newspapers, law courts, and technical reports. It is also the language of schools. . . .
> This exploratory, close-to-the-self language is important because it is the primary means we have of personalizing knowledge. As philosopher/scientist Michael Polanyi claims, all knowledge, if it is to be genuine, must somehow be made personal. The Russian psychologist Lev Vygotsky tells us in *Thought and Language* that the connection between language and thinking is vital and organic. "The relation between thought and word," he maintains, "is a living process; thought is born through words. A word devoid of thought is a dead thing, and a thought unembodied in word remains a shadow." When students are not allowed to work out their ideas *before* they report them to others, they are dealing in "dead things." . . . We believe that language must be employed in classrooms as a tool for discovery, an aid to learning, and not merely as an instrument for reporting. (Freisinger 1982, 4-5. See also Freisinger 1980; Freisinger and Petersen 1981; and Fulwiler 1987)

Given this view of writing and the current interest in expressive, close-to-the-self, heuristic writing as a primary vehicle for learning in general, it is easy to see how the journal would be a remarkably appropriate and useful writing tool which could be expanded, refined, and varied to meet the demands of writing-to-learn across the disciplines. One scholar in particular, Toby Fulwiler, is recognized as being instrumental in popularizing the journal as a critical—if not the critical—writing tool for WAC. He has published several articles on the uses of journals in writing across the disciplines, in addition to conducting numerous workshops across the country on using the journal for writing throughout the curriculum. In one of his best known articles, "The Personal Connection: Journal Writing across the Curriculum," Fulwiler provides a good sense of the predominant view of academic journals, including a description of their characteristics and range of potential uses. He asserts that "journal writing, in the broadest sense, is an interdisciplinary learning tool with a place in every academic classroom; it is not the sole province of the English teacher any more than numbers belong to the math teacher or speaking belongs to the speech teacher" (Fulwiler 1982, 15). He also suggests several uses for the journal in the classroom: to allow students to compose their thoughts or make connections, to summarize or synthesize material, to ask questions, do problem solving, or complete homework, and to assess or monitor class or individual progress (Fulwiler 1982, 18-24).

Interestingly, Fulwiler feels it necessary to attempt to distinguish "personal journals," which he sees primarily as writing for emotional growth and understanding, and which he associates with the term *diary*, from the academic journals he promotes. In his 1982 article, for example, he provides a schematic figure with the term *Diary* representing what he labels the purely *Subjective* end of the continuum, and the term *Class Notebook* representing the purely *Objective* end of the continuum. Unsurprisingly, he locates the "Journal" right in the middle of the spectrum, appropriately balanced between subjectivity and objectivity (Fulwiler 1982, 17). Having sufficiently separated the two kinds of writing to his own satisfaction, he does accord the more personal kinds of journaling some value. He writes, "We cannot and should not monitor these personal trips, but we should, perhaps, acknowledge them and encourage students to chronicle them wherever and whenever they can" (Fulwiler 1982, 26). Yet, somewhat paradoxically, in his summary statement he returns to the value of "coupling," that is, connecting, not separating, personal and academic learning, because "*all* knowledge is related," as we see in the following quote:

I believe that journals belong at the heart of any writing-across-the-curriculum program. Journals promote introspection on the one hand and vigorous speculation on the other; as such, they are as valuable to teachers in the hard sciences as those in the more cushioned humanities. To be effective, however, journal use in one class ought to be reinforced by similar use in another class. Of course, for teachers in some disciplines, where the primary focus is the student's grasp of specialized knowledge, the personal nature of journals may be of secondary importance. However, the value of coupling personal with academic learning should not be overlooked; self-knowledge provides the motivation for whatever knowledge an individual seeks. Without an understanding of who we are, we are not likely to understand why we study biology rather than forestry, literature rather than philosophy. In the end, all knowledge is related; the journal helps clarify the relationship. (Fulwiler 1982, 30)

In 1987, interest in the academic journal culminated in a collection of articles titled simply *The Journal Book*, also edited by Toby Fulwiler. This latest distillation of more than forty articles covering both theoretical and pedagogical perspectives on the journal offers an interesting opportunity to assess the most current views on journals. The book is divided into four sections, but only the first section, "The Language of Speculation," explores a set of theoretical "ideas that support the practice of journal keeping" (Fulwiler 1987, 9). The other three sections, which comprise the bulk of the book, offer representative applications of journal keeping across diverse disciplines: English studies, arts and humanities, and the quantitative disciplines. While the three pedagogical sections offer relatively straightforward advice and suggestions, some of the articles in the first section bear further discussion because they treat some of the larger issues surrounding the nature of the journal and its uses and show an increasing theoretical and historical sophistication in the discussion of the journal.

In the introduction to the work, for instance, Toby Fulwiler provides a brief history of the recent research which led to the dramatic increase in the use of journals in the curriculum which began in the 1960s. In addition, he tries to identify some of the formal stylistic features which distinguish the journal from other academic genres—features such as colloquial diction, first person pronouns, informal punctuation, rhythms of everyday speech, and experimentation (Fulwiler 1987, 2-3). More importantly, he lists the varied intellectual "habits of mind" which the journal is intended to cultivate, including observation, questioning, speculation, self-awareness, digression, synthesis, revision, and the sharing of information (Fulwiler 1987, 3).

Some of the articles in this first section signal an important shift in the thinking about journals because they incorporate social constructionist views of language and discourse, and thus, allow us to begin to see the journal simultaneously as a personal and a social discourse. Working from the assumption that "all knowledge is mediated," Ann Berthoff, in her, "Dialectical Notebooks and the Audit of Meaning," reminds us that journal keeping is a valuable literacy practice outside of the academy. She asserts that, "Keeping a journal is probably the best habit any writer can have; indeed, most real writers probably couldn't function without them" (Berthoff 1987, 11). Berthoff is most interested in what she identifies as a "dialectical notebook." In this kind of journal, she claims, students can carry on the kind of dialogue with themselves that is the essence of thinking, in a kind of dialectic movement which allows for the "audit of meaning—a continuing effort to continue to review the meanings we are making in order to see further what they mean" (Berthoff 1987, 12). She is particularly interested in the double entry or dialectical journal as a way of harnessing the constitutive power of language to construct—rather than just reflect—reality.

All acts of symbolization take place in a social world framed by language; hence the importance of dialogue, pedagogically. We can't get under the net to reach "reality" directly. All knowledge is mediated: all knowledge is therefore partial. Making meaning is not very much like learning to ride a bicycle; nor is it "instinctual." Human beings are language animals: we are not controlled, limited, by a repertory of instincts. Language gives us the power of memory and envisagement, thus freeing us from the momentary, the eternal present of the beasts, and recreating us as historical creatures. (Berthoff 1987, 12)

While Berthoff is interested in the ways journals can tap into the social construction of meaning, Geoffrey Summerfield, in "Not in Utopia: Reflections on Journal Writing," takes as his thesis the notion that journals are themselves socially constructed forms of discourse. Challenging the prevalent notion that writing a journal is necessarily a private act, purely self-expressive and without a sense of audience, he writes, "What, if any, are the social dimensions of the journal? Is it a deviant form, a regression into 'talking to oneself'? A manifestation of solipcism?" (Summerfield 1987, 33).

Of course not, he responds, because writing is always "a social act, albeit displaced" (Summerfield 1987, 34). Summerfield also draws an explicit connection between older journal traditions and the current focus on journal pedagogy when he points out that in the "great journals," such as Francis Kilvert's nineteenth-century country diary, journal keepers:

withdraw for the long term purpose of reentering. The ideational work, the reflecting, the speculation, is done so that at some later moment its fruits will be available for the interpersonal work that we inevitably return to, unless we are irreversible hermits. Put it in a nutshell: journals start life as intrapersonal but are directed to long term interpersonal desires. (Summerfield 1987, 35)

Although he recognizes that journals written in school settings are not exactly the same as the self-sponsored and self-monitored journals that have historically been produced in the larger culture, he does see them as both similar and valuable in that they share the quality of a "displaced serial conversation" (Summerfield 1987, 34).

What we see in these essays in the first section of *The Journal Book* clearly demonstrates a shift in perspective on the journal, and begins the process of enlarging and reorienting our previous notions of the journal as personal writing or prewriting heuristic. These essays ask us to consider some of the means by which journals are constructed from within—and also construct—the social matrix of language. They also cast some tentative filamentary connections to the journal as a self-sponsored, rather than academic, writing practice, as well as a literary and historical writing practice (see also Lowenstein 1987, whose work on the history of journals I will treat in a later chapter). Interestingly enough, these important new ideas do not tend to percolate through to the overwhelming majority of the pedagogical articles in the rest of the book. Although there are some interesting exceptions, many of the pieces take the form of "Staffroom Interchange," with titles such as "Six Ways to List" or "How I Use Journals in Comparative Linguistics" or "Look at Deirdre's Journal—What She Learned in Physiology."

Summary, Conclusions, and Vexing Problems

Journals in composition courses and across the curriculum are usually seen as being introduced in the 1960s as powerful prewriting and heuristic "tools." But journals were not invented in the 1960s. They were not invented by the writing-process movement; nor have they always been used primarily for prewriting or drafting.

In the first place, many types of journals and diaries have long been associated with school writing practices, including daily composition books, journals kept by or for a whole class or school, writer's notebooks, commonplace books, and periodic life writing not kept specifically to improve writing. Trudelle Thomas, who has surveyed more than thirty articles and books on journals and journal pedagogy published by the National Council of Teachers of English between 1900 and 1975, has found that teachers have repeatedly "discovered" the journal as a valuable agent of learning (1989). Although she notes that the articles appear sporadically, and often without much sense of a tradition or theoretical base, she has found several enthusiastic and innovative discussions of school journals, from a reference in 1915 to students using "scribbler books to make good use of their leisure," to Elinor Tilford's "Nothing Ever Happens as Interesting as a Story," a thorough account of the use of journals with junior high school students (Tilford 1940), to class journals written in 1947 "to promote world peace and international understanding" (Thomas 1989).[2]

Also, while many researchers and teachers have asserted the importance of connecting expressive writing (writing to or for the self) and transactional writing (writing to share information and ideas with others or to demonstrate knowledge), it's clear that journal writing is generally identified only as expressive prewriting and, as such, is seen solely as a preliminary to more important, more formal writing. While journals certainly can be employed usefully in the service of prewriting, our current predisposition to view journals merely as a form of prewriting is clearly problematic. As Sharyn Lowenstein points out in her dissertation on the relationship between the personal journal and the journal keeper:

> The writing process researchers generally place journal-keeping within the Pre-writing stage, which then emphasizes the journal as a subservient activity for the essay and more formal writing. This view is deceptive because it discourages thinking of the journal-keeping process with its own stages and considering the journal as a separate genre. The entries in journal-keeping are apt to be seen as tentative steps toward the draft. Conceptualizing the journal as Pre-writing leads to the assumption that the main or only purpose of journal-keeping is to facilitate more formal writing. (Lowenstein 1982, 150-51)

This partial view of the journal, Lowenstein suggests, may have unintended negative instructional consequences. For example, "instructors may fail to distinguish among the complexities and subtleties of journal-keeping behavior" (Lowenstein 1982, 151). By conceiving of the journal as some relatively simple, even unconscious task (like list making or furniture arranging), teachers are more likely to use the journal in overly simplistic ways, she argues. One possible consequence is that students "may fail to appreciate and learn how to use the journal" (Lowenstein 1982, 151). Lowenstein's insights in this regard may begin to account for the difficulties many students have with the journal.

A corollary difficulty to which Lowenstein alludes is that the term journal does not always refer to *prewriting*. Sometimes journals are *writing*. That is, both teachers and students know that the terms *journal* and *diary* relate to particular kinds or genres of writing, of which there are many published examples readily available in popular and literary culture. The current focus on journals as prewriting not only reduces or restricts the meaning of the term to a "strategy" or "tool," it also disconnects the concept of the journal from the long and rich set of traditions associated with its use and thus disconnects literacy from literature. Hence, what students know about journals in the popular sense of the word—as writing about oneself and/or one's daily events—becomes a potential source of confusion for them when they enter the classroom and are asked to "keep a journal."

The current literature on journals available to teachers with few exceptions (Lowenstein 1982; Lowenstein 1987; and Thomas 1989), as we have discussed, offers only minimal support for resolving these issues because it rarely attempts to place the notion of the "journal as prewriting" in its larger social and historical contexts. Otherwise, there are only occasional references to older journal forms, such as Murray's comment that his notebooks are like the eighteenth-century commonplace books.

Yet, the palpable—if often implicit—historical, political, and ideological tension between what is perceived to be a set of dichotomous writing experiences—academic/nonacademic, literacy/literature, public/private, intellectual/personal, and as we'll see, male/female—continues to erupt through the benign surficial notion of the journal as a prewriting tool. These tensions continue to render the journal a problematic panacea.

Indeed, much of the forward and introduction of *The Journal Book* is devoted to allaying concern about the personal nature of the journal and defending its academic use. In the forward, for example, Ken Macrorie characterizes the serious controversy surrounding the use of the journal in the following manner:

> Journals are dangerous. Like any other corkscrew, a journal is apt to open bottles containing habit-forming liquids that once swallowed will bring into being Temperance Societies that scream, "Journals read by teachers are an invasion of personal privacy!" "Journals encourage self worship that threatens the authority of

God." I'm not exaggerating. Some of today's teachers are stopped from assigning journal writing to students because of such complaints from concerned parents and organizations. (Macrorie 1987, ii)

One critical question appears to be, How personal is personal? Or, At what point does personal writing (for or about the self) become "too personal" for school? These issues continue to be configured in part by the paradoxically overlapping yet competing term *academic journal* as opposed to *personal journal* or *diary*. Certain groups of parents—particularly those on the political right and those in the Christian right—are upset, and some educators are worried as well.

Don Melichar reports the concern about journal writing as it surfaced in a November 1982 school board meeting in Jamal, California.

[The parents] wanted to know why students had to write secretly and what teachers were using the journals for. The board tried to explain, but the parents left unsatisfied. A few months later, those parents found a source of ready-made arguments when Neil Seagraves, of the Creation Science Research Center in nearby San Diego, introduced them to the "Secular Humanist Conspiracy." Seagraves said that journal writing was one way "change agents" could gather information, for "children spill everything in writing . . . and of course, it is a favorite Communist tactic as well." (Melichar 1983, 55)

Concerns of this ilk are resoundingly expressed in a book called *Child Abuse in the Classroom*, edited by Phyllis Schlafly (1985), which presents selected testimony by parents on the Pupil's Rights Amendment, also known as the Hatch Amendment. The primary contention of the book is that schools are not teaching "traditional basics," but rather are manipulating children through a series of invasive, "psychological head games" that threaten the privacy of the family. Journals are only one of the targets, along with gifted and talented programs, values clarification, gender balancing, critical thinking, and problem-solving activities.

It's certainly possible that schools may occasionally invade a student's or a family's privacy. However, when I read the various testimonies, what I detected was that the family's privacy, rather than the student's, was to be protected at all costs—even if the family was clearly dysfunctional and the child suffering from abuse or neglect. One parent, Sandra Youngblood, for example, said in her testimony:

I find this Values Clarification in any form in the school system is an invasion of our privacy, by trying to get at our children and dig out bits of information about them and other family members to be used against them. I do not believe any parent wants home life brought up for discussion or acted out in class. This is not only humiliating, it is degrading to the student. (Schlafly 1985, 96-97)

[10/28/89 Why I ask? My home life is neither humiliating nor degrading. If parents are living good and decent lives, and raising their children with care and dignity, then the family should be looked up to as a model for social and academic behavior. Indeed, the characteristics of the family are generally seen as the model for all other institutional and political organizations, as in Rousseau.

Also, as any grade school teacher knows, kids have always told teachers whatever comes into their minds, personal or otherwise. My grandmother is 91 now and was a grade school teacher for 57 years. The stories she came home with—the children she was able to help—precisely because they did share with her. Children who didn't have enough to eat or money to buy school supplies because their families were too poor, or whose parents drank and didn't clean or clothe their children, children who were brutally beaten or sexually abused. She didn't work against the family or against the parents; she worked for the children—and often got help for the parents, too. All these diatribes about invading the rights or privacy of the family assume that all families are perfect and healthy and are being ruined by school-inflicted conflict and turmoil. Face it: there are many dysfunctional families, and schools must try to help the children in any way they can. Also, journals are not just used to "tell" on people. Where did these ideas about the journal come from?]

But again and again in these pages of testimony, the journal—especially in its incarnation as the personal journal, or diary—is attacked as a tool of invasion or moral depravity on the part of the schools. The journals themselves are described as containing solely private emotional responses, gossip, and confessional venting. Listen to this sampling of voices from *Child Abuse in the Classroom*:

MARY COLE: The seventh grade requires a private journal to be kept by the student on his feelings. Some subjects written about were on religion and moral ethics. I was embarrassed by some of my son's comments because in his young mind, he had given an unbalanced picture. No efforts were made to correct grammar, punctuation, sentence structure or continuity of thought. What a waste of school time. (Schlafly 1985, 103)

THERESA BAK: Instead of teaching the fundamental basics, schools and teachers are taking the roles of psychologists and psychiatrists and using the classroom for exposing family problems of a personal and private nature. Questions along these lines are asked of students almost daily. Journals are mandated with no motive of having the sentence structure or grammar corrected, but only to invade the sanctuary of the student's mind, heart, or home. (Schlafly 1985, 110)

PATRICIA HARTNAGLE: Violations include family trees, personal timelines, family portraits, "me boxes," *diaries*, Magic Circle, and Sanctuary. (Schlafly 1985, 144. Emphasis added.)

LOIS WOLTHIUS: Educators, psychiatrists, psychologists, and parents agree that these open ended questionaires, surveys, diaries, role playing and other Values Clarification activities are harmful to our children. . . . One of our other children was required to keep a personal diary. Again this is an invasion of a child's privacy and of the parents' privacy. You do not keep a diary of your innermost thoughts at school. At the end of the year they were to give away the diary to a friend or throw it away. They were not to take it home. (Schlafy 1985, 150-51)

ALAN THOMIER: They were encouraged to use diaries and told that what was in the diaries could not be revealed without their own full permission. Can you imagine that a young child might write true or untrue things about his parents, etc., and then reveal this to other children who live in the same neighborhood who could bring tales home to their parents? This could create some dangerous problems. (Schlafly 1985, 302)[3]

Much of the antijournal polemic of many of the testimonies is also explicitly antifeminist and even antifemale, but it doesn't compare in virulence to a comment made by *The Hopkins Bulletin*, a publication of Dartmouth alumni, which came out in November 1989. In a critique of Dartmouth's current curriculum—framed by E. D. Hirsch's claims regarding "cultural literacy"—which condemns the entire women's studies program, the column asserts that students' grades are largely determined on the basis of the personal journals they are required to keep. These journals are characterized as documenting women's "progess in sexual and man-hating development" (*Hopkins Bulletin* 1989, 4). Note the striking concern that women writing about their own ideas and experience in the journal form will necessarily result in writing that is inappropriately sexually explicit or promiscuous, or worse, *man-hating*.

Some teachers are also concerned that the use of the still undefined personal journal will open what has been called a "Pandora's box" of information about children that teachers may not know how to handle or may not want to handle. In 1982, *English Journal*, a publication for secondary school teachers of English, ran its point/counterpoint column, "Bait/ReBait," on "Whether the use of personal journals should be abolished in English classes" (Hollowell 1982). Taking the view that journals should be abolished, John Hollowell asserts that journals promote sloppiness along with their fluency, encourage children to be self-centered, and most importantly:

> The journal can open up a Pandora's box of the child's personal experiences. Do you really want to read entries on child abuse, group sex, alcoholism, or wife beating? Unless we have degrees in guidance and counseling, such personal revelations should be left to the professionals. (Hollowell 1982, 14)

Gail Heath, in her article "Journals in a Classroom: One Teacher's Trials and Errors," does, indeed, find herself in the position of opening Pandora's box:

> Many students, realizing that their journals really were confidential, started writing about personal problems that were terrifying. They bordered on revealing to me events that I was legally required to report to authorities. I had boxed myself in by my own rules. . . . I was compelled to respond carefully, not only as an English teacher but as a counselor and advisor. This soon extended to talking to students during lunch hour, after school, and sometimes in evening phone calls. I worried about the responsibility that had evolved. I had a student who was considering suicide, others who had suffered sexual abuse years before and wanted to work out feelings, and still others who were being physically abused. (Heath 1988, 58)

Certainly, Heath's concerns about her increased responsibility are legitimate, and the decision she reports in the article, which is to set very specific limits on the content of the student journals from then on, is understandable. But it's most interesting that these concerned parents, alumni, and teachers appear to be more concerned that children might be *writing* about sexual or physical abuse, than about the abuse itself. The other interesting implicit assumption that both Hollowell and Heath seem to be making is that somehow these extraordinary events in students' lives either don't or shouldn't affect them in radical ways as learners; that they can be simply shed at the classroom door. If some of the student journal entries were uncomfortable for Heath and Hollowell to read, think how terrifying they must have been to write, and worse, to live. One must ask whose privacy we really protect when we deny students the right to address these topics, and whose interests it serves to maintain the traditional taboo on these subjects.

Yet, questions and challenges to the journal, particularly those raised primarily by fundamentalist Christians and those on the political right, as well as by some teachers, about "the ethics of using journals in classroom settings," "the right to privacy," "the manner in which journals promote self examination," or "the questioning of traditional values" ("Guidelines for Using Journals in School Settings" 1987, 4), were obviously sufficiently controversial to impel the National Council of Teachers of English (NCTE) to make a response, to provide an apologia for the use of school journals.

In fact, Fulwiler's introduction to *The Journal Book* consists primarily of the reprinted guidelines which were formulated to respond to these issues. The document demonstrates a powerful effort to recuperate the school journal by deliberately distancing it from the diary, or personal journal; in essence, to keep the diary at bay. The effort to disconnect the journal from contaminative association with the diary starts in the very first sentence:

> In recent years, teachers in elementary and secondary schools, as well as in college, have been asking students to keep personal notebooks, most commonly known as journals, but also known as logs, daybooks, thinkbooks, *and even diaries*. (Fulwiler 1987, 5. Emphasis added.)

The phrase "and even diaries" indicates immediately the nonprivileged status of the term, and the placement of the phrase at the very end of the list additionally marks the term as the least preferred of the possible namings.

The motivation for the document—which is to clarify the inappropriate and appropriate uses of the journals for academic settings—is taken up in the second and third paragraphs. Notice how the appropriate use is directly linked with the term *school journal* while the inappropriate uses are explicitly linked with the term *personal diary*.

Because journals provide students considerable freedom to express their thoughts and feelings, students often write about private and intimate subjects—subjects that more properly belong in personal diaries than in school journals. The problem for teachers is how to encourage students to write personally and frankly about ideas and issues they care about without at the same time invading their private lives. (Fulwiler 1987, 5)

Also, there is the interesting ambiguity of the trope "invading their private lives." It is situated in the sentence in such a manner that either teachers are invading students' private lives, which hardly seems likely—since students know that teachers will be reading what they write—or that students will somehow be inadvertently invading their own privacy, which is simply incoherent. Also, the agentless "invasion" trope acquiesces to the common polemical metaphor employed by those opposed to using journals in school, a metaphor identified by Ken Macrorie in the quote I offered earlier from the forward of *The Journal Book* and reiterated frequently in the Hatch Amendment testimony cited in the last few pages.

In the final section of the NCTE Guidelines, which offers the actual guidelines for assigning journals, the so-called *privacy issues* raised in the journal debate figure prominently again. In fact, the first two suggestions both deal with this set of issues. According to the first guideline, teachers should always "explain that journals are neither *diaries* nor class notebooks but borrow features from each: like diaries, journals are written in the first person about issues the writer cares about, like class notebooks, journals are concerned with the content of a particular course" (Fulwiler 1987, 7). The second guideline suggests that loose-leaf notebooks be used or that the journal be kept in sections so that intimate entries need not be turned in (Fulwiler 1987, 7).

Again the term *diary* used in these contexts begins to absorb connotations such as "intimate," "too personal," "too private," while the term *journal* is reserved for kinds of cognitive and discursive activity appropriate to school. In polling teachers during workshops on journal keeping, I have found a similar set of tensions, paradoxes, overlaps. Given the request to brainstorm any associations that come to mind, teachers wrote comments like these:

Journal
PERSON 1: enjoyable reading, therapeutic, expressive, stream of consciousness, drawings, poems, the unusual, ideas for papers, opinions, bus schedules

PERSON 2: creativity, personal, free writing, highly emotional responses, structured, opportunity for academic freedom, evocative/provocative

PERSON 3: daily entries, log, keep assignments, writing with self as audience, freedom to write without fear of being corrected, reading responses

PERSON 4: writing you wouldn't mind your mother reading

PERSON 5: thoughts, reactions

Diary
PERSON 1: personal, intimate, not designed for audience

PERSON 2: very personal, intimate, feminine, nonstructured, chance to voice complaints without punishment, peaceful quiet time, vent for rage, Locked!

PERSON 3: what I did today, thoughts I don't want to share with others (confessional), Anne Frank, *locked*, daily entries, Puritans

PERSON 4: writing you would very much object to your mother reading

PERSON 5: day-by-day facts[4]

Clearly, the literature has not yet provided an adequate sociohistorical context from which to understand the complex relationships between journals and diaries and between popular and academic notions of journal keeping. How can we possibly expect our students to know what journals are or should be, if we are not sure ourselves? We need to understand more about the history, traditions, and social conditions in which journal forms have been practiced if we intend to be able to bridge the gap between our perceptions of the journal in the college composition classroom and those of our students or the parents of our students. We need to be able to provide a much more comprehensive context for the notions of the journal and diary if we want to come to terms with them.

In sum, if diaries and journals are clearly such different kinds of writing, why should so many people be at such pains to distinguish between the two? And how did the term diary come to be a marginalized and marked form, derogated as trivial, confessional, and somehow the source of antipatriotic, antifamily, and antireligious values? Why is it that a diary by any other name would smell sweeter?

To take up that question we need to look more carefully at issues of naming and language. In the next chapter, I will review some of the important work on the "gaps" between men's and women's access to, and experience of, language and discourse as a possible frame for understanding how journals, and particularly, diaries, have come to be both marginalized and yet empowering forms, and how they are perceived and practiced by our students both inside and outside the composition classroom.

3

Gender, Language, and Discourse: Critical Issues

Lying is done with words, and also with silence.

Men have been expected to tell the truth about facts, not about feelings. They have not been expected to talk about feelings at all.

Yet even about the facts they have continually lied.

In speaking of lies, we come inevitably to the subject of truth. There is nothing simple or easy about this idea. There is no "the truth," or "a truth"—truth is not one thing, or even a system. It is an increasing complexity. The pattern of the carpet is a surface. When we look closely, or when we become weavers, we learn of the tiny multiple threads unseen in the overall pattern, the knots on the underside of the carpet.
—Adrienne Rich, *On Lies, Secrets, and Silence*

In order to understand the ways in which gender might inform the naming or the writing of journals and diaries, we need to look first at the larger set of relations between gender and language or discourse, because language shapes the construction of the self, and is the *sine qua non* of the book of the self, the journal or diary. But the possible truths about men's and women's relation to language and about the ways in which language itself engenders (and en-genders) us are like that carpet of increasing complexity Rich evokes in the passages I have used as epigraph for this chapter.

The diverse constellation of writers, scholars, and educators who consider themselves to be feminists has generated several perspectives on the relations among gender and language, discursive power, and sexual/textual identity through the lenses of biology, sexuality, psychology, history, and culture. I cannot do justice to the richness and diversity of views that exist on the subject of gender and language because to map the current state of feminist criticism in its entirety is well beyond the scope of this book. Not only are there many full-length works and innumerable articles in this general area of study, there are in fact many book-length bibliographies.[1]

Allow me, however, to extend Rich's metaphor of the carpet to look at just a few of the perspectives I have found useful in examining connections among gender, language, and the journal. While it might seem a rather roundabout way of getting to the discussion of journals and diaries, many scholars agree that "the very terms of debate in feminist literary criticism pivot on the issue of women's relation to language" (Rubenstein 1987, 3). Thus, looking at language itself is a necessary starting point for an examination of texts, as Frank and Treichler suggest:

> Language thus no longer serves as the transparent vehicle of content or as the simple reflection of reality but itself participates in how that content and reality are framed, apprehended, expressed, and transformed. For feminists, who seek to understand the nature, scope, and mechanisms of discriminatory social practices, these issues have become pressing. Thus, the sexist language question, seeming to represent a practical agenda, is a point of entry into the broader study of women and men as speakers, creators, and bearers of meaning within society and culture. Anyone who explores and seeks to change women's place within texts must confront questions of women's place within both linguistic and material reality. (Frank and Treichler 1989, 3)

This encounter is particularly important because "language, like other social institutions and value systems, does not serve all its speakers equally, for not all its speakers contribute equally to its formulation and maintenance" (Frank and Treichler 1989, 15). In particular, I want to explore the claim that men's and women's asymmetrical construction in and through language and discursive practice will account for the gendering and frequent marginalization of the various strands of the journal/diary tradition. Discussions of the gendering of language and the gendering of our relationships to language, speech, and writing take several forms.

For many Anglo-American feminists, considerations of "women's place in material and linguistic reality" have taken the primary form of empirical, analytic, and inductive studies, social and historical critiques of language, literacy, and literature, and recuperative work on women's voices, words and traditions. Elaine Marks and Isabelle de Courtivron, in their introduction to *New French Feminisms*, characterize the Anglo-American feminist literary and linguistic enterprises in the following manner: "They are engaged in filling cultural silences and holes in discourse. The assumption is that women have been present but invisible and, that if they look, they will find themselves" (Marks and de Courtivron 1981, xi).

Indeed, those of us who are working in these traditions tend to hold the view that women's problems with language and texts stem in large part from their difficulty in gaining full access to and participation in the generation of meaning and discursive forms. Elaine Showalter sums up this view thoughtfully in her well-known essay, "Feminist Criticism in the Wilderness," when she writes that "the problem is not that language is insufficient to express women's consciousness, but that women have been denied the full resources of language and have been forced into silence, euphemism, and circumlocution" (Showalter 1985, 255). Needless to say, I count myself among those involved in this kind of critique and recuperation in my efforts to understand why women's journal- and diary-writing traditions have been marginalized and to assist in their recovery as vital and significant discursive practices.

To return to the analogy of the carpet, many Anglo-American feminists have chosen to work on tasks such as analyzing specific sections of the linguistic/discursive carpet and the fibers that compose those sections. We are describing patterns that change across time and culture and trying to order or design new ones. We are also hard at work reweaving the large holes and worn places where women's voices and texts have been cut out, or worn thin from abuse, and doing some necessary stain removal.

Alternate approaches come from continental writers and thinkers, such as Hélène Cixous, Luce Irigaray, Julia Kristeva, and many others associated with what is/are often called "French Feminism/s." These writers and thinkers have used deconstruction, Hegelian and Marxist dialectic, and Lacanian psychoanalysis as some of the main entry points for their fascinating, variable, sometimes nearly inaccessible theoretical and speculative discussions of gender and discourse.

Eschewing conventional language and academic, scholarly traditions, these writers often employ the linguistic medium as the message itself in an effort to create new linguistic realities and fantasies. Catharine Stimpson describes their work as embodying the "lavish, eruptive, unpaginated, both invaginated and polymorphic lexicography of female sexuality" (Stimpson 1987, 3). Marks and de Courtivron characterize the sometimes playful, always polysemous styles of some of these writers in a variety of ways: They speak of Kristeva's "intricate semiotic analyses" and of Hélène Cixous's "Joycean and Lacanian punning" (Marks and de Courtivron 1981, xii).

[25 November 1989: When I read these works I find them both exciting and disturbing. Which may be the point. There is clearly method in the madness. On the other hand, while I am stimulated by the intricacy and power of the texts, I am ironically, frequently silenced by them. Which I doubt is their intention—because their primary intention seems to be to bring women to voice. Still working on this one. I worry about my own ability and patience to follow the mazelike theoretical density of many feminist critics (not just the readily identifiable "French" voices). Like Carolyn Heilbrun, I sometimes think "we are in danger of refining the theory and scholarship at the expense of the women [I would add men, too] who need to experience the fruits of research" (Heilbrun 1988, 19). Then again, maybe I have done too much reading and not enough thinking—or too much citing and not enough synthesizing? Must keep at it—must go on.]

To the extent that these diverse writers can be viewed as a group, they tend to share a much deeper concern than most Anglo-Americans about whether the carpet called language can be saved at all, as it is dyed so completely, so permanently, in androcentrism (or "phallocentrisms") that it saturates the very fibers of the self with notions of gender during the process of language acquisition itself.

Feminism exists because women are, and have been, everywhere oppressed at every level of exchange from the simplest social intercourse to the most elaborate discourse. Whatever the origins of this oppression—biological, economic, psychological, linguistic, ontological, political, or some combination of these—a polarity of opposites based on sexual analogy organizes our language and through it directs our manner of perceiving the world. Whether or not we can escape from the structuring imposed by language is one of the major questions facing feminist and nonfeminist thinkers today. (Marks and de Courtivron 1981, 4)

The feminists authors and thinkers writing from this set of assumptions have stamped their own conceptual and terminological imprint on the discussion of gender and language.[2] One primary and provocative notion uses Jacques Lacan's readings of Freud to argue that the phallus has come to be construed as the transcendental signifier, the meaning maker, endowing the masculine with a unique linguistic privilege. The female, meanwhile, who is anatomically sans phallus/signifier, inevitably represents "absence" or "lack" in the male-constructed symbolic order. One critical consequence of the phallocentricity of language for these thinkers is that in the very process of acquiring language, women learn to see themselves as what Simone de Beauvoir first called the "other." As objects of study rather than knowing subjects, as blank pages rather than as writers, women may thus be denied access to the representation or knowledge of their bodies, their lived experience, and other domains of knowledge or experience. In other words, women are denied voice.

Carolyn Heilbrun presents women's paradoxical relation to language and the symbolic order this way: "Women's access to discourse involves submission to phallocentricity, to the masculine and the symbolic; refusal, on the other hand, risks reinscribing the feminine as a yet more marginal madness or nonsense" (Heilbrun 1988, 40-41). As Julia Kristeva herself writes:

Sexual difference—which is at once biological, physiological, and relative to reproduction—is translated by and translates a difference in the relation of subjects to the symbolic contract which *is* the social contract; a difference, then, in the relationship to power, language, and meaning." (qtd. in Gilbert and Gubar 1988, 228)

Thus, those working in the French or continental traditions find themselves employed in a somewhat different fashion, simultaneously describing and deconstructing the whole pattern of the metaphorical carpet in its dizzying array, primarily by untying the individual knots that bind each of us, male and female, to our sense of self and psychosexual gender as we learn the language and, thus, enter into a linguistic contract with a symbolic order governed by "The Law of the Father." "Like her male counterpart, the female subject is at once positioned and structured by language, but the difference lies in that a women's relationship to language remains paradoxical, as the word is simultaneously foreign and familiar" (Rodenas 1989, 30. See also Homans 1986).

Thus, in order to speak or write, women must both/either accommodate to this alienation, and/or find alternative modes of expression—ways to subvert the dominant discourse or move outside it. Women have learned to speak through "fissures" and "gaps" in the discourse, writing or speaking from the most direct experience of their bodies in order to reconnect language, life, and text. They are trying to valorize the multiplicitous female experiences of intimacy, sexuality, and maternity, and the natural cycles of women's lives from the time before menarche to the years that follow menopause. One common strategy is to invoke some kind of language or linguistic space that exists outside of or prior to the intrusion or saturation of the male symbolic order. This primordial or prelinguistic stage or space, sometimes called the "semiotic" or the realm of the imaginary, is seen to act as a source of meanings that can be used to create what is called an *écriture féminine* or *le parler femme* (feminine writing or feminine speech). Most importantly, these exotic-sounding textual strategies are also consonant with, and helpful in understanding, certain of women's uses of the diary or journal form, which can operate as a kind of linguistic free space and has historically allowed women some access to the uncensored expression of their lived biological, psychological, and historical experiences as women.

The Law of the Father/The Voice of The Mother

Public, patriarchal language, the language of the Father, does indeed position the male as generically human and as the generator of meaning, while alienating and suppressing the female in her efforts to make meaning, a subject that we will explore more specifically in the next section of this chapter. However, other researchers, who are also interested in the relation between language and the psychosexual construction of self, have not only looked at the "Law of the Father," but also at what might be called the "Voice of the Mother"—that is, the active role of the mother, the mother's voice, and the mother tongue in children's construction of self and language. Building their theories of gendered personality development on the consequences of the nearly universal cultural requirement that mothers provide for the care and nurturance of children, thinkers and writers such as Nancy Chodorow (1978), Dorothy Dinnerstein (1976), and Carol Gilligan (1982, 1986) have argued that males grow up with strongly defined boundaries of the self. These scholars claim that males learn very early that they are *not* like their mothers and thus develop their primary sense of self as autonomous, as separate from their central affiliative object, the mother. Males also learn very early that females are less powerful in the culture than males are, which also encourages active dissociation from the mother. According to this view, autonomy and separation, hierarchically-inscribed power relations, and a focus on rights, rules, and boundaries characterize the pattern of the developing male/masculine identity. These features inflect not only the primary sense of self, but also condition one's relation to knowledge, language, authorship, textuality, and genre.

Females, on the other hand, this school of thought asserts, are more likely to identify with their mothers because of their obvious anatomical and physiological similarities to them and to see themselves as connected or coexistent with the maternal figure and the mother's voice. Therefore, females tend to develop more fluid or flexible ego boundaries, defining themselves more by connection than by separation. Again, these critical differences affect not only the emotional or social development of females, but may also significantly affect their development as knowers and their relations to language, textuality, and genre, including women's preference for "coming to voice" as a primary metaphor for intellectual development (Belenky et al. 1986).

Indeed, Sandra Gilbert and Susan Gubar in their chapter, "Sexual Linguistics," argue that, while literary and linguistic misogyny are ubiquitous, they may be, at least in part, responses to what they call the "linguistic primacy" of the mother (Gilbert and Gubar 1988, 262-66). It is the mother, they point out, who first nourishes both male and female children with food *and* words. Thus, children learn the mother tongue quite literally from their mothers. Gilbert and Gubar ask if the deliberate patriarchal bias of language "may be a reaction-formation against the linguistic (as well as the biological) primacy of the mother" (Gilbert and Gubar 1988, 264).

Thus, it seems that the relation between the acquisition of language and the development of the self is a complicated one. While it may be that males confront with some degree of pain their separateness and alienation from the potentially nurturing and nourishing "voice of the Mother," they will inherit the full discursive power of the Father. Females may enjoy a special linguistic intimacy with their mothers, but ultimately their legacy is a public language that often degrades them or renders them invisible and a series of discursive practices that do not allow them full participation as speakers and knowers.

Clearly, each of these orientations or enterprises focuses only on certain features of the carpet or the method of its making; none pretends to be comprehensive or without limitation. As in the parable of the seven blind people who each touch the elephant in a different place and therefore come up with a radically different view of the poor beast, so too must we all continue to grapple and grope to understand the complex features of the relationships among gender, self, and language.

Many feminists—Anglo or continental, deconstructionist or materialist Marxist alike—agree that language has been constructed by men for men over the last several millennia, and that they have divided the linguistic and symbolic worlds according to their own perceptions of gender difference. Therefore, I will draw on these various, disparate, but overlapping theoretical claims, making connections as I go. However, it is important to remember that gender identity and gender difference are not a function of simple conceptual, empirical, or physical dichotomies, but rather of dynamic and shifting sets of relations between the personal and the social. Identity then "can be understood as a dynamic interplay among the fluid layerings of experience: materiality and the body; intrapsychic and interpersonal processes; and the substructure of ethnic, national, or political processes acting upon the individual" (Rubenstein 1987, 7).

This dynamic view allows us, both women and men, to understand how the social constructions of language and discourse can act simultaneously to create commonality and difference, and to be viewed as ongoing sources of oppression, suppression, empowerment, or even liberation. Further, this acknowledgment of the value of both commonality and difference reminds us that we need to explore other kinds of differences between and within women and men: the often hidden differences of race, class, and sexuality that still divide us.[3]

I have come to know, as Virginia Woolf knew, that "When a subject is highly controversial—and any question about sex is that—one cannot hope to tell the truth. One can only show how one came to hold whatever opinion one does hold" (Woolf 1929, 4). I would thus like to take the time to review some specific claims that pertain to the gendering of language and the language of gendering. These claims and studies provided the foundation for the development of my own opinions on the gendering and marginalization of the journal and diary forms, and on the ways in which journals and diaries demonstrate the gendered construction of self and knowledge through language.

Specifically, I am going to look at some of the "linguistic and material realities" of men and women invoked by Frank and Treichler in this chapter's epigraph in an effort to understand:

1. How language (the code, the public language) engenders us;
2. How both the macropolitics of institutions and the micropolitics of conversations, which provide the basis for the public language, additionally work to construct and maintain both gender dominance and

gender difference through socialization and explicit sanction; and
3. How women, as a muted group, have responded to these sanctions: by endorsement, acceptance, accommodation, resistance, subversion, and by creating forms and modes of discourse outside the patriarchal linguistic domain.

Gender and Man-Made Language

Language is our means of classifying and ordering the world: our means of manipulating reality. In its structure and in its use we bring our world into realization, and if it is inherently inaccurate, then we are misled. If the rules which underlie our language system, our symbolic order, are invalid, we are daily deceived.
—Dale Spender, *Man Made Language*

The women say, the language you speak poisons your glottis tongue palate lips. They say, the language you speak is made up of words that are killing you. They say, the language you speak is made up of signs that rightly speaking designate what men have appropriated.
—Monique Wittig, *Les Guérillères*

Nearly four hundred years before Dale Spender and Monique Wittig addressed the treatment of women in language as deceitful, false, or poisoned, Marie de Jars (1565-1645), confidante of Montaigne, the renowned French writer of the Renaissance, uncannily prefigures their concerns. "Since language and speech are the cement of human society, whoever falsifies them should be punished for counterfeit or for poisoning the public water well" (qtd. in Partnow 1985, 129). Why is language so problematic for women? Why do these theorists and writers find language to be "dangerous" or "difficult"? What does it actually mean to say that language is "phallocentric" or sexist in its masculine bias?

Dominance/Mutedness

One key pair of descriptive terms that enables us to begin to understand the difference between women's and men's relation to language—that is, the public language encoded and preserved in dictionaries, handbooks, and other primary texts of the culture, is that of the Dominant (voiced) and the Muted (or Mute). Edwin Ardener (1975) first used these terms to talk about the research bias he perceived in anthropology. He observed that anthropologists would often make "definitive" claims about a culture or tribe, having talked only to the males of the group in question. This anthropological bias, he noticed, excluded women both from the making of meanings within a given culture and from the free expression of those meanings. Ardener's model of the complex voicing relationship between dominant and muted groups, which is a function of such factors as class, race, sexual orientation, and religion as well as of gender, looked something like the graphic that appears in Figure 3.1. I have adapted Ardener's model for this discussion of language and journals.

Elaine Showalter explains the consequences of such a discourse and power relation:

> Both muted and dominant groups generate beliefs or ordering ideas of social reality at the unconscious level, but the dominant groups control the forms or structures in which consciousness can be articulated. Thus, muted groups must mediate their beliefs through the allowable forms of dominant structures. Another way of putting this would be to say that all language is the language of the dominant order, and women, if they speak at all, must speak through it. (Showalter 1985, 262)

Or as Dorothy Smith has stated, simply but powerfully:

> Men attend to and treat as significant only what men say. The circle of men whose writing and talk was significant to each other extends backward in time as far as our records reach. What men were doing was relevant to men, was written by men, about men, for men. (Smith 1978, 281)

This muting takes many forms and encodes itself at many levels in "man-made" language and in the symbolic and knowledge systems that are built with language. For example, the codification of the public language and the rules for its use have been primarily under the control of men since time immemorial. A rare exception was the eighteenth-century Anglo-Saxon grammarian, Elizabeth Elstob, who produced her grammar in 1715. She was "lost" until just recently, the loss of once respected works being another common form of muting (Frank and Treichler 1989, 54; Gilbert and Gubar 1988, 267). Other unacknowledged grammarians include Janet Taylor and Marghanita Laski (Treichler 1989, 54-56.)[5] Men have been the primary lexicographers, dictionary-makers, language scholars, and writers of grammatical handbooks; their work often reflects a masculine rather than a universal perspective

FIGURE 3.1
Dominant/Muted Group

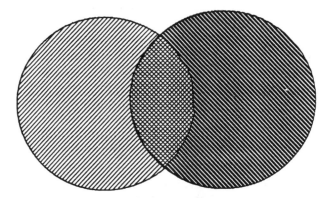

 Dominant Meanings and Expression

 Muted Meanings and Expression

Silence

—Dominant Meanings and Expression: Men as dominant group generate meaning, language styles, and rules for discourse. The Law of the Father. (Many types of public journals, such as ships' logs and accounting journals, will fall into this domain as will some of the secular personal journals, such as the well-known diaries of Pepys and Boswell.)

—Muted Meanings and Expression: Women must use style, topics, and meanings permissible to dominant group. Complex forms of accommodation and resistance. (Journals as forms of social interaction and domestic work. Family chronicling, and Victorian ladies' journals will fit in this category.)

—Silence: Meanings and expression produced outside the dominant discourse. Unheard or invisible to those in dominance, thus considered non-sensical or hysterical. Free zone, or wild zone, for generation of new and "unmuted" meanings and forms of expression. The place of écriture féminine/the Realm of the Imaginary/the semiotic. (The journal can operate like a free zone, a safe place, in which women can write about things that are "unspeakable" in the dominant culture, and therefore, use writing to reconstruct reality and themselves.) (Adapted from Showalter 1985, 262)[5]

(Baron 1986; Bodine 1975; Frank 1989; Gershuny 1989; Martyna 1983; MacKay 1983; Treichler 1989; and Wolfe 1989). Examples of dictionary-making bias include androcentric definitions such as "a failed or vestigial penis" for clitoris, and an abundance of negatively marked words for women. Dictionaries also reflect the valuing of the public male world, preserving hosts of words in an attempt to do justice to the complexity of scientific concepts and inventions, war and all its paraphernalia, or politics and commerce. On the other hand, more privatized and domestic activities linked with women's lives, arguably equally complex, show an impoverished number of entries. Also, dictionaries have traditionally attempted to record "the best published writing," which has usually meant writing by male authors (Treichler 1989, 55). In sum, Treichler reports that "dictionaries have generally excluded any sense of women as speakers, as linguistic innovators, or as definers of words" (Treichler 1989, 60).

As for usage, many of the grammatical rules we have inherited derive from a few self-styled (male) grammarians from the seventeenth and eighteenth centuries, such as Bishop Lowth and James Shirley, who encoded their own bias that males were the "more worthy gender" into such prescriptive usage rules as the "generic masculine" (Baron 1986, 90-97). Their opinions hardened into handbook fiat and reigned triumphant for two hundred years.

Semantic Muting and the Generic Masculine

One important way in which English reflects its man-made bias is by the critical semantic and syntactic rule that a word with the lexicographic feature "+ male" will be the generic, the unmarked, the norm, the universal form. Hence, we have what Wendy Martyna calls the "he/man approach" to language, or "to be human is to be male" (Martyna 1983, 25), which is, in a sense, the semantic equivalent of the French notion of the phallus as transcendental signifier mentioned earlier.

Although the uses of *he* and *man* in all their forms have repeatedly been claimed to be generic (that is, to encompass/embrace both women and men), a host of empirical studies confirms that the masculine generic rarely functions in its generic capacity (see Martyna 1983; McConnell-Ginet 1989; MacKay 1983; Silviera 1980; and Spender 1980, 147-62 for thorough treatment and reviews of many of these studies). As early as 1973, researchers such as Alleen Pace Nilsen were demonstrating that young children understood *man* to mean *male person*, not *human being*, in sentences like "Man needs food." J. Schneider and Sally Hacker's work in the same year found college students responding similarly to the types of titles and headings frequently found in texts, such as "Urban Man" or "Political Man." In all the studies, both men and women understood the supposedly generic masculine forms to refer far more frequently to males. Additionally, masculine pronouns, even when used nongenerically, far outnumber feminine pronouns. In one analysis of one hundred thousand words of children's school texts, pronouns with explicitly male referents outnumbered pronouns with female referents by a four-to-one margin, with ninety-seven percent of the instances of *he* being used exclusively as masculine rather than generic forms (Thorne et al. 1983, 10).

The built-in conceptual ambiguity of these words, which are presumably both masculine and generic at the same time, is demonstrated by the ease with which one can slip from the purely generic to the specifically masculine in the same breath, or to make what appears to all to be a logical faux pas (see Spender 1980, 154-57 and Martyna 1983, 30-31). Muriel Schulz cited one male speaker's slip from the apparently generic to the clearly sex-specific in her 1978 address to the Ninth World Congress of Sociology in Uppsala, Sweden:

"How does Man see himself? As a salesman? A doctor? A dentist?" [So far the speaker could be using Man generically, referring to women as well as men.] "As far as sexuality goes," he continued, "the Kinsey reports on the activities of the American male surely affect his self-image in this regard. . . ." (Qtd. in Spender 1980, 155).

Alma Graham notes a similar slippage:

In practice, the sexist assumption that man is a species of males becomes the fact. Erich Fromm certainly seemed to think so when he wrote that man's "vital interests" were "life, food, access to females, etc." Loren Eisley implied it when he wrote of man that "his back aches, he ruptures easily, his women have difficulties in childbirth. . . ." (Qtd. in Spender 1980, 155)

Indeed, we are variously startled or amused or irritated at constructions like "Menstrual pain accounts for an enormous loss of manpower hours," or "Man, being a mammal, breastfeeds his young," or upon hearing of a gynecologist being given an award for "service to his fellow man" (Thorne, et al. 1983, 31). But men were not at all amused when elementary school teachers were referred to with the generic "she," even though the vast majority of school teachers *were* "shes"

(Spender 1980, 158). Laws, statutes, and court decisions, both in America and in Canada, have been shown to use *he*, *man*, or *mankind* to include females or exclude females at will within the document itself—sometimes within the same paragraph (Martyna 1983, 32; Frank and Treichler 1989, 4).

Frank and Treichler, in their new book, *Language, Gender, and Professional Writing*, which provides a fine review of the current work on language and sexism, offer the fascinating example of the presumably generic term *doctor*. Before World War II, the term was construed by the War Department to refer only to males. During the war, however, when male doctors were in short supply, the usage was declared obsolete and women doctors were welcomed into the ranks—at least temporarily. Indeed, after the war, women found themselves once again excluded from entering the service as doctors, because the term was reinterpreted as having a specifically masculine connotation. Protesting their exclusion in 1946, women made posters with captions such as "Doctors Wanted: Women Need Not Apply" (Frank and Treichler 1989, 4).

This masculine/generic confusion—or more accurately, exclusion—has obvious consequences for men's and women's relation to language and their sense of self. Wendy Martyna (1983) reported striking and pervasive sex differences in the use and understanding of the masculine generic.

> Females use *he* less often than do males, and turn more frequently to alternatives such as *he or she* and *they*. Males have an easier time imagining themselves as members of the category referenced by generic *he*. Seven times as many males as females say they see themselves in response to sex-neutral sentences referring to a "person" or "human being." In general, males appear to be using *he* in its specific more often than general interpretation. To do otherwise would be to encourage self-exclusion. (Martyna 1983, 31)

Clearly, men and women alike perceive both false generics and true generic forms as referring primarily to men or males. Thus, women have to confront continually the paradox of being a part of language and its system by virtue of being human, and yet being essentially excluded from language by virtue of being women.

[7 November 1989: The other night we were watching a NOVA show on the genome project. One of the primary visual symbols in the show was a big, red, ancient-looking tome, engraved in gold letters, representing "the book of life" or the "alphabet of DNA." It was, of course, titled The Book of Man.

Halfway through, Molly, my six-year-old, asked an important question. "Is there a book of woman?" How does one answer that? Man includes women? There is another book?]

The process of semantic muting repeats itself again and again throughout the language, as the patterns of male as norm/female as other, and male as subject/female as object operate ceaselessly in the semantics and syntax of English. Women are defined in relation to men, named by men—Tom's wife, Jack's mother, Harold's widow, Mrs. Timothy Finnegan). Women's family names have not been important; girls in many cultures have, for millennia, started life with their father's names, until they could be married and take a new surname (sirename), that of their husband. In America, for example, for at least one hundred years, many states required that a woman take her husband's name (Stannard 1977). Thus, women have additionally been deprived of a central part of their linguistic and psychological identity—a permanent name of their own (Miller and Swift 1976; Spender 1980, 24-25; and Thorne et al. 1983, 9).

Women also find it hard to use the dominant language because many of the names and labels they have been given derogate or trivialize them. Many of the terms referring to women (titles, address forms, descriptors) define them according to men's interests in or uses for them. Sexual availability, use, and attractiveness appear to be primary criteria for coinages. Thus, women are often named as sexual objects or whores, as body parts, as fruits, foods, or animals (Schulz 1975; Stanley 1977). Words coined without reference to gender, or words first coined with reference to females, have an alarming tendency to take on pejorative meanings, as do the female-marked forms of parallel gendered terms, such as master/mistress, governor/governess, courtier/courtesan, baronet/dame (Lakoff 1975).

And while one might make the case that these problems are simply historical in nature, current language practices demonstrate the fallacy of this logic. An interesting experiment I perform in my linguistics class inevitably yields the same results. When we cover morphology, I ask my students to bring in a list of all the slang words they hear for men and women during the week to show how slang illustrates word-formation processes. They always generate at least twice as many words for women as for men, and the words for women (which are part of the common language stock, regardless of our gender) almost invariably cast women in terms of sexual attractiveness and/or availability—as animals (chick, fox, pig, bitch), fruits or foods (cupcake, tomato, tamale), or body parts (piece of tail, piece of ass, bodacious tatas). The terms for men, while fewer, tend to have more positive sets of association (stud, jock, guy).

The artificial "universal" languages constructed in the nineteenth and twentieth centuries by L. L. Zamenhoff (1859-1917) and others also show that the same set of biases are still being encoded therein. That is, the masculine forms are the base forms or are "unmarked" (the normal cases, occupying the positive semantic space), while the female forms are derived from the masculine forms and are often marked by affixes: "*la knabo*, 'the boy'; *la knabino*, 'the girl'" (Baron 1986, 25. See also Spender 1980).

Also, consider the almost instantaneous pejoration of terms coined by women to rename themselves, their perspectives, and their experiences. "Ms." said in that *certain* manner is most certainly an insult; women's liberation has been clipped to *women's lib*. While it's not necessarily fun to be a "women's libber" or a "feminist" inside the academy, it is the kiss of death to be called one at a party!

[Ironically, just after I wrote this, a young Canadian man went into a university classroom in Montreal, shot fourteen women, and wounded thirteen more. In the three-page letter inside his pocket, he repeatedly blamed "feminists" for all his troubles. Being a feminist, or in this case, just being a woman whom someone thinks is a feminist, is still risky. Indeed, the relation between sexual violence and the silencing of women is an important one that I will continue to explore.]

Semantic Silence

Finally, there is the problem of silences or gaps in the language, which is linked in part to the issue of what words get recorded and preserved, but also has to do with who gets to make up new words and have others acknowledge their meaning, however transitory those words may be. This is a particularly thorny problem to approach because of the difficulty, if not the impossibility, of naming, defining, or discussing that which has no name. While no language contains every possible meaning at every instant, men have always been able to legitimate their meanings far more easily than women. Dale Spender explains it best:

> Because women have not been involved in the production of the legitimated language, they have been unable to give weight to their own symbolic meanings. . . . they have been unable to pass on a tradition of women's meanings of the world.

Both sexes have the capacity to generate meanings, but women have not been in a position to have their meanings taken up and incorporated in the society. They have not been in the public arena, they have not been the "culture"-makers, with the result that any meanings they may wish to encode, but which are different from or at odds with those that have been generated by men, have been tenuous and transitory: they have been cut off from the mainstream of meanings and therefore have frequently been lost. (Spender 1980, 52)

It is easy to see how much of women's experience might be distorted or omitted entirely by the time it gets through the language filter. Many women have reported these "gaps" between their experiences and the language through which they have to render them. In 1963, Betty Friedan was reporting that many housewives were feeling a certain malaise which they could not describe—it had no name. "It" became the women's movement (Spender 1980, 61).

As many feminist critics, and particularly the French, have asserted, the nature and varieties of women's friendships, love, and sexual relationships, the nature of female physiological and cultural maturation, including pregnancy, mothering, nursing, raising children, marriage and domestic life, even the nature of women's spiritual experience, all have little formal linguistic representation. The double burden of *work* that has been the lot of women across most of recorded European history has few names and thus, little value and acknowledgment (Anderson and Zinsser 1988). We still say things like "Do you work?" to women whom we know work very hard. Their answer to that question is often the unconsciously ironic "No, I am at home with the children." The lived experience of women in most cultures and most times includes the ever-present fear—and experience—of sexual violence. From female infanticide, footbinding, and incest, to rape, genital mutilation, and forced sterilization; from wife battering to the burning of brides without sufficient dowry or to *suttee*, the burning of widows with their husbands—the innumerable forms of sexual violence are represented in the public language primarily through words coined by those who perpetrate the violence, not by those who must endure it (Barringer 1992). In essence, large chunks of women's lives are rendered nearly invisible in the common discourse that feeds at the linguistic trough of public language.

Feminists are working hard to create or reconstruct a language that will represent, record, and validate the experience of women. For example, Adrienne Rich has shown an enormous discrepancy between men's perceptions and namings of motherhood and the much more complex associations and namings that only women can bring to the idea of motherhood (Rich 1977).[6]

Historically, however, men and women have had a different relation to the public language as it has been recorded and preserved. Men have been the namers, women have been the named. Men, by virtue of their gender, learn that they are universal, the semantic norm, the standard and the standard setters. They belong to language and it belongs to them. Women learn that they are objects (usually of men's semantic or physical desire) rather than subjects, and learn to define themselves in relation to others, who themselves are usually men. Women can never assume they belong to *mankind*; they cannot assume with surety that they will be part of the anonymous *he* or *him*. We often try to tell our truths in "an alien tongue," as Adrienne Rich describes the process, or tell them "slant," as Emily Dickinson claims. We have to use the language that Monique Wittig and others say "poisons our lips, tongues, palate." Simply put by Thomas Hardy's heroine in *Far from the Madding Crowd*, "it is difficult for a woman to define her feelings in language chiefly made by men to express theirs" (qtd. in McConnell-Ginet et al. 1980, 58). As Shirley Ardener (1975) and Berger and Luckmann (1972) point out, it's difficult to know exactly what you are thinking or feeling if you have no way to name it—or worse, if the language you know and think in runs counter to your perceptions. How do you hold onto the "unnameable"; how do you test an idea's authenticity if you can't articulate it, or if it always seems to get lost in translation? And even if you manage to break into speech or writing, will you be listened to? And under what conditions?

There have been very few places women could go to be "alone" with language, beyond the scrutiny of the "namers." Already, however, we can see that certain forms of the journal might be suited to this purpose, especially when we begin to realize that the muting or silencing of women has not been restricted to the internal workings of language alone. For, "just as they have more rights to the formulation of meaning in the language as a system, so it seems that men have more rights when it comes to using that system" (Spender 1980, 44). Or, as Sally McConnell-Ginet writes, "sexist language has its roots in sexist discourse" (McConnell-Ginet 1989, 36).

Gender and Oral Discourse: Public and Private Voices

Silence gives the proper grace to women.
—Sophocles (Trans. Cora Kaplan)

The true representation of power is not of a big
man beating a smaller man or a woman. Power
is the ability to take one's place in whatever discourse is essential to action and the right to have
one's part matter. This is true in the Pentagon,
in marriage, in friendship, and in politics.
—Carolyn Heilbrun, *Writing a Woman's Life*

While women and men both supposedly use the same language,
then, it's clear that they do not stand in the same relation to that language. Women have been more like borrowers, or even thieves, than
like proprietors of language, as many women poets and writers have
suggested, for men have controlled the manufacture of public semantic
resources and the terms of their commerce in public discourse. As the
primary purveyors of public language, men have controlled the market
value of types of discourse and specified the conditions of their use by
others. More precisely, men have controlled the actual practice of discourse, not only by explicit, institutional sanctions but also by subtle
and implicit stereotyping and socialization. Male discursive control can
be demonstrated at many levels, from the macropolitical, or institutional, level to the micropolitical level of individual conversational
dynamics.

One primary strategy for the political/linguistic control of women
has been the construction of the very powerful—albeit constantly shifting—dichotomy of the public/private spheres, both as conceptual categories and as a set of norms for every variety of behavior. Severely
restricting women's access to what Carolyn Heilbrun has called the
"discourses essential to action" and relegating women's discourse
styles, strategies, topics, and audiences to the supposedly secondary,
private sphere have helped to ensure men's political and linguistic hege-
mony (Heilbrun 1988, 18).

Macropolitical and Institutional Sanctions on Women's Speech

The explicit and public regulation of women's voices has been
linked with the forcible regulation of women's bodies since at least as
long ago as the earliest recorded laws. It appears, for example, that the
establishment of male secular authority during the protohistoric period
from approximately 3500 to 2800 B.C. in Mesopotamia is linked directly
with male seizure of linguistic rule as well. Tracing what she calls *The
Creation of Patriarchy*, Gerda Lerner charts the complex set of shifts in
cultural organization by which male secular and military rulers over-
took the communities built around temples and temple life, reorganiz-
ing them first into city states and, ultimately, into kingdoms (Lerner

1986, 54-57). Cultural changes included the development of militarism, the "eventual institutionalization of slavery, and with it of structured classes" built on the taking and exchange of women (Lerner 1986, 57). All of these "mutually reinforcing processes" strengthened "male dominance in public life and in external relations, while weakening the power of communal and kin-based structures" (Lerner 1986, 58).

One critical example that Lerner discusses at length is the seizing of Lugash, somewhere around 2350 BC, by a ruler named Lugalanda. His successor, Urukagina, greatly increases his authority as king, claiming for himself the important title of "lugal" and issuing important edicts that may be "the earliest documented effort to establish legal rights for citizens" (Lerner 1986, 62). Yet, two of these edicts also demonstrate the critical linkage between the silencing of women, the forcible regulation of their bodies and activity, and the "creation of patriarchy":

> One of Urukagina's edicts reads: "Women of former times each married two men, but women of today have been made to give up that practice." The edict continues to state that women committing this crime in Urukagina's time were stoned with stones inscribing their evil intent. Elsewhere, the edict states that "if a woman speaks . . . disrespect-fully (?) to a man, that woman's mouth is crushed with a fired brick." (Lerner 1986, 63)

Lerner suggests that the first edict probably refers to an injunction against widows remarrying. She comments that the second is somewhat harder to decipher, particularly the word *disrespectfully*, because of the condition of the inscription. Yet, she notes that the very early appearance of these two edicts is an important key to understanding the development of patriarchy:

> We should also notice that in the very first effort by a king to establish law and order by proclaiming an edict, one of the aspects of regulation concerns the gender role of women: that is, their right to remarriage and their speech toward men. That fact, while inconclusive in isolation, will assume greater significance as we later analyze the various law codes. In this respect, Urukagina's "edict" stands near the beginning of a slow and wavering process of transition in the status of women and the definition of gender, which took almost 2500 years. (Lerner 1986, 66)

Urukagina of Lugash's primitive, but powerful, pronouncements on the requisite public silence of women would serve as a pattern that would be elaborated on in the centuries and civilizations to come. Indeed, similar sanctions were well established in ancient Greece, the site of the first "universities." Several researchers have mapped the host of sanctions against women as users of the public, primarily agonistic and polemical, discourse of the academy and in public life generally, and the gradual relaxation of these sanctions in the nineteenth and twentieth centuries (Connors 1986. See also Gearhart 1979 and Kramarae 1981).

Jean Bethke Elshtain, in her book *Public Man, Private Woman: Women in Social and Political Thought* (1981), has provided some of the most exhaustive documentation on the varying forms that the public silencing of women has taken, starting with ancient Greece, the "foundation of Western civilization":

Man's public speech took place in that public realm par excellence, the *polis*. His private, albeit social speech was carried on within the household, though that speech, tied to images of necessity, carried no public weight. . . . This led to, indeed it involved, levels of partially autonomous but interconnected spheres of human discourse. The question of what was appropriate to say, to utter, depending on context—where one was and with whom and why—emerged not so much as a rule of etiquette (etiquette takes over when social forms begin to fray around the edges), but as a public-political, social, individual, even religious or mythopoetic imperative, broken only by gods, fools, madmen, the very bold, or old, or young. . . .

Speech too, had its public and private moments. Some categories of human subjects—in Greek society slaves and women were the most important—were confined to private realms of discourse. Truly public political speech was the exclusive preserve of free, male citizens. Neither women nor slaves were public beings. Their tongues were silent on the public issues of the day. Their speech was severed from the name of action: it filled the air, echoed for a time, and faded from official memory with none to record it or to embody it in public forms. (Elshtain 1981, 14)

During the early Christian era, when most public life *was* religious life, or was controlled by religious power, the apostle Paul's famous dictum that women should keep silent in church, because women, like Eve, were inherently sexually and morally depraved, was widely used for silencing women in the church and throughout the public realm.

Indeed, this injunction, which bears a suspicious resemblance to the earlier edict of Lugash, was used with varying degrees of success right up through the nineteenth century. Strong prohibitions against women speaking or using the powerful religious discourses of the church were established over the course of the first few hundred years of the history of the Christian church. At first, there was considerable conflict among the diverse sects of early Christians about the roles and rights of women to participate in the language and life of the church. Groups like the Gnostics allowed considerable female symbolism and expression. Even their conception of God was dyadic, including the Primal Father—referred to as Ineffable or Source—and the Mother of All Things, which, interestingly enough, they called Silence.

Most importantly, women in Gnostic sects participated fully in the linguistic life of the early church: teaching, prophesying, serving the eucharist, even baptizing. But many of the mainstream church "fathers" objected violently. Tertullian severely rebuked women who used the types of language essential to church life in his writings. "These heretical women—how audacious they are! They have no modesty; they are bold enough to teach, to engage in argument, to enact exorcisms, to undertake cures, and, it may be, even to baptize" (Pagels 1976, 300). These groups and others like them were forcibly suppressed, and by approximately AD 200:

> Roman Christians endorsed as "canonical" the pseudo-Pauline letter to Timothy, which interpreted Paul's views: "Let a woman learn in silence with full submissiveness. I do not allow any woman to teach or to exercise authority over a man; she is to remain silent for . . . Adam was formed first, then Eve, and furthermore, Adam was not deceived, but the woman was utterly seduced and came into sin." (Pagels 1976, 303. See also Lerner 1986 and Stone 1976)

It is important to note that, throughout the ages, Christianity has paradoxically offered both important opportunities for the public expression of women's spiritual ideas and words (we will see this, for example, in the development of the spiritual diary, open equally to men and to women) and yet has often simultaneously worked to suppress women's voices with a vengeance.

Cheryl Glenn Seitz, in a paper called "Muted Voices: Women in the History of Rhetoric from Antiquity through the Renaissance," attempts to recover the experience of several women rhetoricians and public speakers throughout history. For example, she describes the dreadful fate of Hypatia of Alexandria, who became so popular as a public speaker on philosophy and mathematics that she angered the Archbishop of Alexandria.

> Followers of the Archbishop pulled her from her carriage and dragged her into a church, stripped her of her garments, killed her with pieces of broken pots, dismembered her, and burned the pieces of her body. As a public speaker, Hypatia set an unforgettable example for all Medieval women. (Seitz 1987, 11)

Indeed, through the late Medieval period and during the early Renaissance, church and civil authorities actively continued to officially suppress the voices and knowledge of women. They prohibited the *puellarum cantica* or "girls' songs," and Charlemagne himself banned the composition of vernacular love songs by nuns, which were called *winnileodas*, or "songs for a friend" (Kolb 1989, 28). Perhaps the most vigorous and violent suppression of women's knowledge and speech came in the form of the inquisition and witch trials that raged across Europe during the Middle Ages (Christ 1983, 90-92). On the issue of women's silencing by the church, Elaine Showalter writes:

> There is some ethnographic evidence that in certain cultures women have evolved a private communication out of their need to resist the silence imposed upon them in public life. In ecstatic religions, for example, women, more frequently than men, speak in tongues, a phenomenon attributed by anthropologists to their relative inarticulateness in formal religious discourse. But such ritualized and unintelligible female "languages" are scarcely cause for rejoicing; indeed, it was because witches were suspected of esoteric knowledge and possessed speech that they were burned. (Showalter 1985, 254)

Even now, in many cultures, actual silence is quite literally imposed on women during various rituals, in synagogues or during wedding ceremonies (Ardener 1978, 21), and the public muting of women is not limited to religious life. To this day, Greek women who speak in public are considered threatening and are enjoined to be silent (Ardener 1978, 23). In many cultures, women must observe very specific linguistic taboos for public discourse. For example, it has been reported that Mongolian women (specifically daughters-in-law) must always transpose certain words into other words before saying them because of a supernatural taboo (Ardener 1978, 21).

[6 August 1989: I am watching a show on Australian aboriginal culture in a series on Democracy for PBS. A woman translator is being asked about a sacred place used for male initiation. She tells the commission that, as a female translator, if she tells its significance she could be killed. She refuses to speak any further. She's no fool.]

It would be comforting to think of gender-linked taboos on specific words or topics as cultural phenomena that occur only in cultures very different from ours, but alas, such is not the case. As we will see, there is a link between sexual violence and silence, even now in mainstream Western culture. That link is critical to understanding certain aspects of the diary/journal tradition and the current educational controversy over the value and appropriateness of private, personal diaries, which are set in opposition to public, academic journals. We will consider why writing about institutionalized violence against girls and women is seen as private, confessional, and emotional—and is, therefore, a prohibited topic, a "forbidden story" in a journal—while reflections on other forms of publicly sanctioned institutionalized violence, such as military history, are academically revered.

Socialization, Muting, and Silence

The more complete the despotism, the more
smoothly all things run on the surface.
            —Elizabeth Cady Stanton

We have come a considerable distance from the common nineteenth-century experience of Beatrix Potter who, having had a paper on the symbiotic nature of lichens accepted for presentation at the Linnean Society of London, was required to have her uncle read the paper at the conference, and was not allowed to be present (Fausto-Sterling 1985). We are probably more comfortable engaging in public discourse than Charlotte Brontë, who was warm and enthusiastic in private conversation but often could not bring herself to speak in public. Writing to her friend Ellen Nussey on 18 December 1849, she comments, "my occasional silence was only a failure of the power to talk, never of will" (Ardener 1978, 28).

Yet, there is still considerable prejudice against women as public speakers, and many women feel quite uncomfortable in that role or with using the male registers of public speech, which are often authoritarian, even polemical (Kaplan 1986 and Kramarae 1981). As Sally McConnell-Ginet asserts, "women speaking from pulpits and podiums are still rare" (McConnell-Ginet 1989, 35). Dale Spender records one woman's typical angst as follows:

When you grow up female in this society, then you learn not to have confidence in yourself as a person. You have to overcome that, and men don't, or at least not in the same way. But even . . . and if . . . you catch up on that, there is still a problem. I find it easier to talk to women informally. That's the way I want to do it. That's how you can listen and exchange, which is what I want to do when I talk . . . not just speak at, to deliver a convincing monologue from a platform. Public speaking is a pretty one-way process. It gives a lot of rights to the few who do the speaking and none to the many who have to listen.

So it's still a problem for me. Some people tell me I'm good at it, and I get a bit confused. (Spender 1980, 81)

[I was talking with one of my women students from last semester just a few days ago. Marie, an older returning student, had passionately thrown herself into the reading and writing from the Expository Prose course and would often produce reading responses up to twenty pages long. As she put it, she developed a love-hate relationship with writing. She was excited by the acquisition of academic language and by the world of ideas, and at the end of the course, she clearly felt that she had acquired the rights to this world and its discourse, as well she had. During her conversation with me, however, it became apparent that her new discursive abilities had gotten her into trouble.

She explained that she was thinking of leaving school. I was shocked because she was an excellent student, and a committed one. She explained that she was afraid of losing many of her long-term friends because her going to school was coming between them. I asked why. The problem turned out to be discourse. When they would all get together for an evening and talk, she had begun to talk, too. "I just can't stay silent anymore and go 'uh-huh, uh-huh.' I hear these things and I know about them, and I have opinions and I can finally back them up. But when I do, they tell me I'm overbearing. Maybe I am overbearing—maybe I should give it up now. School is so risky. I don't want to lose my friends. But I want school, too."

Marie is not an overbearing person, but she is breaking out of her "normal" discourse, into the world of ideas and public discourse, and those around her are clearly not accepting her expanded discourse roles (Personal Communication, 3 Mar. 87)]

While Beatrix Potter was literally not allowed to speak in public, the discomfort of contemporary female students like Marie with public and academic discourse is more subtly enforced. Indeed, most Western women have been muted because their confinement to the private sphere has made the topics of their discourse unsuitable for any public forum. In addition, because most women have not been educated to use the specific rhetorical forms considered appropriate for public discourse, their speech has not been considered proper to be heard in public (Elshtain 1982, 14).

This kind of linguistic inequality is built into the soft fibers of the brain, to borrow an image from Michel Foucault, as children are socialized to use gendered speech styles, vocabularies, and topics. Not only does our culture teach children to prefer different styles and registers on the basis of their gender, it also labels women's ways of speaking—whether actual or stereotypical—as restricted, inferior, and inappropriate for public use.

Women's Talk as Gossip

One form of control surfaces in the form of stereotypes about the ways in which men and women talk. For example, when women talk, it is often derogated by terms such as *chatter* or *gossip*. Indeed, in most southern European cultures—as shown by studies from Portugal, Spain, Malta, France, Italy, and Greece—women's topics and women's speech are restricted in multiple and varying ways to the private verbal sphere, according to Ruth Borker's fascinating review article on the relation between women's talk and women's social positions in diverse cultures around the world (Borker 1980, 26-44).

Also, the way women talk is often characterized as "wishy washy mommy talk": "weak, trivial, ineffectual, tentative, hesitant, hyperpolite, euphemistic, talkative, gossipy, gibberish" (Kramer 1977, 151). Think of the connotations of "dumb blond" or the vacuity of "valley girl" talk. On the other hand, men's ways of talking are often described positively as "forceful, efficient, blunt, authoritative, serious, effective, sparing, and masterful" (Kramer 1977, 151). Little wonder, then, that Chinese women are often said to attribute their own thoughts to their sons or husbands or other male relatives to order to have them heard (Ardener 1978, 21).

As Oscar Wilde so viciously (and perfectly) put the dominant view: "Women are a decorative sex—they have nothing to say, but they say it charmingly" (Key 1975, 14). Current cartoons, as Figure 3.2 shows, continue to portray the image of women who speak in public as ineffectual babblers.

The Supposed Garrulity of Woman: Silence as Virtue

Not only has the quality of women's speech been denigrated and controlled by male stereotyping, but the quantity of women's speech has been a target as well. From antiquity, women have been depicted as endless chatterers. Slogans, folk wisdom, and cartoons repeat the stereo-

FIGURE 3.2
Stereotype of Woman as Public Speaker

DOONESBURY   by Garry Trudeau

Boston Globe, 29 September 1989

type in endless profusion (Baron 1986; Key 1975; Kramer 1977; Miller and Swift 1976). In the Middle Ages, what Sandra Gilbert and Susan Gubar call the "alleged loquacity" of women was considered a biological disorder; conduct books from the Renaissance cautioned women against "babbling out" (Gilbert and Gubar 1988, 231). The ideal Medieval or Renaissance woman was chaste, modest, and silent, and women who spoke or wrote in the public domain were often considered immodest or unchaste. Dennis Baron, in *Grammar and Gender*, provides a thorough summary of views on the myth of the loquacious woman and the ideal of the silent, virtuous woman. Among the many examples he provides, one of the most interesting and provocative comes from a tract by the Spanish humanist Juan Luis Vives, *De Institutione Christianae Feminae* (1523), translated by Richard Hyrd as *A very frutefull and pleasant boke called the instruction of a Christen Woman* (1531).

> Vives asserts that silence is a woman's noblest ornament, and he warns his female readers not to speak when men are present, for verbal intercourse leads inevitably to sexual intercourse. Vives explains that a woman can defend her chastity "stronger with silence than with speche" . . . and he counsels that children of opposite sexes, including brothers and sisters, should not play and talk together, even in the presence of a chaperone, in order to preserve their purity. (Baron 1986, 57)

Etiquette books right up through the nineteenth and twentieth centuries inevitably admonish girls to be quiet and listen attentively to boys so that boys will like them. Here is a sampling of views on the desirability of controlling women's speech:

Scottish proverb: Nothing is so unnatural as a talkative man or a quiet woman. (Qtd. in Spender 1980, 40)

From *"The Good Wife Taught Her Daughter"*: Laugh not to scornee nodir [neither] olde ne yonge, Be of good bering and have a good tongue. (Qtd. in Partnow 1985, 226)

From *Thomas Wilson's* Arte of Rhetorique (1553): What becometh a woman best, and first of al: Silence. What seconde: Silence. What third: Silence. What fourth: Silence. Yea if a man should ask me til' dowmes day, I would stil crie silence, silence, without the whiche no woman hath any good gifte, but hauing the same, no doubt, she must haue many other notable giftes, as the whiche of necessitie do euer folow suche a vertue. (Qtd. in Baron 1986, 56-57)

Elizabeth Joceline . . . advised her unborn child that, if she should be a daughter, "remember thou art a Maid, and such ought thy modesty to bee, that thou shouldst scarce speak, but when thou answerest." (Crawford 1985, 214)

A woman's air of freedom might disgrace her whole family: "a daughter that is bold dishonoureth both hir father and hir husband." (Crawford 1985, 216)

An eloquent woman is never chaste; and the behavior of many learned women confirms this truth. (Wiesner 1986, 12)

From *Ellin Devis's early nineteenth-century* English Grammar for Young Ladies: A forwardness to talk, and a multitude of words, is no advantage to the character of any person, especially women; whose greatest reproach, in the apostle's censure of them, was, to be tatlers and busy-bodies. (Qtd. in Baron 1986, 58)

[3 January 1990: Reading the ever-popular Anne of Green Gables to my six year old, Molly, when it hit me. Anne is always in trouble because of her mouth. Imaginative, articulate, her words pour out in a lovely luscious stream—which is her critical flaw to almost all those around her. Even the author, Lucy Maud Montgomery, appears ambivalent about Anne's fluency. What a model for Molly.]

The force of linguistic sanction and socialization has had undeniable and immeasurable consequences for women as public speakers. Countless women have been muted by force, rule, or accommodation to culturally generated ideas about femininity. But it is important to remember that some women have always defended their right to participate in public discourse and public life, particularly from the thirteenth through the seventeenth centuries, during which period European women's public roles were substantially curtailed.

While working-class women defended their right to work, aristocratic women defended their right to learning and public discourse. They often invoked divine authority for their speech or writing, as did Marie de France (ca. 1160-1215), who wrote: "Whoever has received knowledge and eloquence in speech from God/should not be silent or secretive/but demonstrate it willingly" (Partnow 1985, 184). In 1524, Katherine Zell (ca. 1497-1562) wrote defiantly to the churchmen who would silence her: "You remind me that the Apostle Paul told women to be silent in church. I would remind you of the word of this same apostle that in Christ there is no longer male nor female" (Partnow 1985, 98). Madeleine des Roches (1542-1587), the sixteenth-century French poet, makes me understand, once again, why I am writing this book, in her defense of women's rights and responsibility for public discourse. "Silence, ornament of women, may cover mistakes of language and of judgment: I'll answer to that, that silence may well prevent shame, but cannot enlarge honor, and that speaking separates us from the beasts" (Sankovitch 1985, 227).

Micropolitics of Conversation: Competition and Cooperation

As for the presumed garrulity of women, studies in formal discourse situations confirm the fact that when women and men talk together it is generally the *men* who do the majority of the talking, not women (Argyle et al. 1968; Bernard 1972; Chesler 1972; Strodbeck et al. 1957; and Swacker 1975). As Dale Spender points out: "The talkativeness of women has been gauged not in comparison with men but with silence. Women have not been judged on the grounds of whether they talk more than men, but of whether they talk more than *silent* women" (Spender 1980, 41).

In fact, recent empirical research shows that many of these stereotypes about the loquacity, triviality, and irrationality of women's speech have little basis in fact, while other differences in speech style have been "named" in ways that clearly distort the actual dynamics of speech. In addition to controlling the semantic resources of the language, and imposing a host of institutional sanctions on women's speech, then, men also have muted and silenced women by controlling the micropolitics of talk itself, both outside and inside the academy.

In fact, new work on gender differences in style and strategy suggests women and men may be working from different conceptions of discourse. Men may use discourse patterns that secure boundaries and maintain "authority," while women are more likely to prefer models of discourse based on cooperation and connection—differences which are consonant with the claims on gendered identity and language we have been discussing. It is important to note that these features do not necessarily approximate the specific speech patterns of specific men and women. They are, however, important historically and culturally conditioned speech norms. It is also important to keep in mind that gender differences in discourse often signal asymmetrical power relations, but also that "women's talk" is not necessarily weak, or trivial, and may have its own forms and value. This discussion of gender and speech style will focus on discourse features that bear directly on the educational experience of female and male students and the forms and functions of the journals and diaries they write.

Male Styles/Male Models: Control and Interruption as Interaction

The dominant model of verbal interaction is one that works on a hierarchical structure for speaking rights and involves competitive strategies for the management of conversation. Many public-discourse forms, including academic discourses, are based on such a model. In chapter 5, we will look at the manner in which teachers' and students' notions of the academic journal will depend, in critical respects, on the discourse models to which they subscribe. In chapter 6, we'll look specifically at the primary discourse forms of the university, such as argumentation, lecture-recitation, debate, and so on, which are based on this model.

According to the rules of this public-discourse game, the person with the most status controls the discourse, by taking up the majority of verbal space, and by choosing whether or not to respond to the topics that others (females or males with less status) raise. Because men tend to:

> construe conversation as a competition where the aim is to be the speaker, . . . their conversational strategies involve trying to seize a turn whenever possible, and then trying to hold onto it. This results in the typical pattern in all-men groups of a few men dominating the conversation while the rest say little. (Coates 1986, 154)

Several studies have documented the competitive, "one-upsman," antiphonal style of single-sex male discourse routines, such as verbal dueling, rapping, and "doing the dozens" (Aries 1976; Baird 1976; Mitchell-Kernan 1973; Spender 1980; and Whitehead 1976). Jennifer Coates explains the centrality of verbal aggressiveness in all-male groups. "Loud and aggressive argument is a common feature of speech in all-male groups: such arguments often focus on trivial issues and are enjoyed for their own sake. Shouting, name-calling, threats and insults are all part of male verbal aggressiveness" (Coates 1986, 153).

The accuracy of Coates's assessment was vividly confirmed for me one April night right outside my own home. My husband and I live right across the street from several fraternity houses so we are constantly privy to "slice-of-life samples" of male single-sex discourse, especially on the weekends and late at night. The sample I offer is certainly extreme, but it is by no means uncommon. It also displays some principal characteristics of one form of male single-sex discourse: it is aggressive, competitive, and antiphonal in structure, as well as rather pure in content.

Two young men and a young woman were walking by our home late one evening. Our bedroom windows, which faced the street, were open. The young woman whose voice was barely audible had obviously reproved one of the young men, presumably her boyfriend, for not being honest with her. He responds:

"What? I'm not a goddamned liar. You think I'm a goddamned liar, don't you?"

Her voice starts up again, the words indistinct, the tone assuaging.

He responds in a louder voice, "Well, Fuck you! I mean it—FUCK YOU!"

The second male intercedes at this point, on the young woman's behalf, and attempts to calm the angry young man down . . . to no avail, as the first man turns now on his companion.

"Well then, fuck you, too!" At this point, the antiphonal structure of the rest of the discourse is assured as we hear two male voices, moving away from each other, volleying successively louder "fuck you's" back and forth at one another, echoing into the night.

The competitive and hierarchical nature of the majority of male speech styles, both in mixed-sex and single-sex discourse situations, is also confirmed by a pronounced male interest in maintaining clear boundaries in turn-taking situations and by frequent boundary disputes, or interruptions. Males are less likely than females, for example, to make a link with a previous speaker's contribution as they take their turn, and are also more likely to shift abruptly from one topic to another (Coates 1986, 152-53).

Interruptions have considerable micropolitical significance because they are, by definition, violations of another's speaking rights. Interruptions, as distinguished from overlapping speech that supports conversation, "establish and maintain status differentials" (West and Zimmerman 1983, 103). Candace West and Don Zimmerman sampled cross-sex exchanges in a variety of discourse situations (homes, drug stores, coffee shops, university campuses). In every conversation, males interrupted females more frequently than the converse and male interruptions counted for ninety-six percent of all interruptions (Zimmerman and West 1975). Additional studies on interruption showed parents, particularly male parents, interrupted female children more than male children, which may promote verbal deference in female children (Berko-Gleason and Greif 1983; Greif 1980; and West and Zimmerman 1977).

Recently, West and Zimmerman have expanded their findings on male interruptions in conversation, by examining unacquainted people in a laboratory setting on a college campus. Although the conditions of this study were quite different from those of the 1975 study, the results were amazingly similar: seventy-five percent of the interruptions were male-initiated, and again, in each of the specific interactions, males interrupted more than females.

Consonant with the gendered distinction between public and private discourse, men's speech has often been identified as more likely to focus on the public domain—politics, sports, business, entertainment, news, and activities—and less likely to treat personal or private-sphere topics at length. Several studies cited in the annotated bibliography of *Language, Gender and Society*, edited by Barrie Thorne, Cheris Kramarae, and Nancy Henley (1983), corroborate this general set of features in male-male and male-female interactions. Elizabeth Aries reports that male groups "established a stable dominance order" and talked "about sports, competition, aggression, and things they had seen, read, or heard" (Aries 1977, 265). Marjorie Goodwin (1980), taping naturalistic conversation during the play of urban black children, found an emphasis on action and achievement in the males' talk. In Mirra Komarovsky's *Blue Collar Marriage*, a series of interviews with fifty-eight couples, "the husbands, who felt their wives talked about gossip and 'silly' matters, talked to one another about cars, sports, work, motorcycles, carpentry and local politics" (Komarovsky 1962, 273. See also Ayres 1980 and Mulchahy 1973).[7]

Robert Lewis, in "Emotional Intimacy Among Men," writes that while men report more same-sex friendships than women, most of those relationships aren't disclosing or intimate because of the pressure to

Zimmerman interpret the role of interruption: "It is, in other words, a way of 'doing' power in face-to-face interaction, and to the extent that power is implicated in what it means to be a man vis-à-vis a woman, it is a way of 'doing' gender as well" (West and Zimmerman 1983, 111).

Certainly, this model of discourse is, as it has been described, "blunt, forceful, masterful." But it is not the only model upon which to pattern the forms and functions of discourse.

Female Styles/Female Models: Collaboration and Consensus as Interaction

As a muted group, women partake of the dominant verbal traditions and have little choice but to use them; rarely, however, do they participate in the generation of those traditions, and they have only limited rights to their use. Therefore, women have developed a set of discourse strategies and a model of language use that may be partly accommodative but that also seems to have developed beyond the bounds of the dominant discourse tradition. Thus, women's relation to language is more complex than that of men in the sense that they are simultaneously part of at least two discourse traditions that are in certain respects contradictory.

As Sally McConnell-Ginet has asserted in "Linguistics and the Feminist Challenge":

> The predominant theory of conversation in social life tends to stress competition for turns. In this framework, conversation is seen as a game of conflict, with women as perennial losers. An alternative might be to view it as a game of coordination, of which women are highly skilled players. (McConnell-Ginet 1980, 19)

Conversation is a critical part of all social relationships, so omnipresent as to be invisible. And in our most important relationships, regular verbal communication is simply fundamental. "In these relationships, in these mundane interactions, much of the essential work of sustaining the reality of the world goes on" (Fishman 1983, 90).

Though they may appear to, conversations/verbal interactions don't just happen; they are initiated and maintained by various kinds of "work," which Pamela Fishman has described as "conversational housework" or, more colloquially, "conversational shitwork" (1983). Taping fifty-two hours of talk between intimates, three white, middle-class, heterosexual couples (1983), she found an "unequal distribution of work in conversation" as the women were "much more actively compete and a fear of vulnerability, among other things (Lewis 1978). What seems to be the most useful commentary on the issue of "inexpressiveness," however, is offered by Jack Sattel in his article "Men, Inexpressiveness, and Power" (1983). He first outlines, then rebuts the common explanation that little boys are prevented from learning to express themselves and, thus, learn to devalue expressive behavior in others, entailing tragic consequences for many men's personal relationships. While he agrees that such conditioning does occur, and that the consequences can be quite destructive, he feels it is an insufficient explanation:

> My argument is that one reason little boys become inexpressive is not simply because our culture expects boys to be that way—but because our culture expects little boys to grow up to hold positions of power and prestige. What better way to exercise power than *to make it appear* that *all* one's behavior seems to be the result of unemotional rationality. . . . This is a style we quickly recognize in the recent history of American politics: Nixon guarded the assault to his position by "stonewalling" it; Gerald Ford asked us to "hang tough and bite the bullet"; while Edmund Muskie was perceived as unfit for the Presidency because he cried in public.
>
> Keeping cool, keeping distant as others challenge you or make demands upon you, is a strategy for keeping the upper hand. This same norm of political office—an image of strength and fitness to rule conveyed through inexpressiveness—is not limited to the public sphere; all men in this culture have recourse to this style by virtue of their gender. The structural link usually overlooked in discussions of male inexpressiveness is between gender and power, rather than gender and inexpressiveness. (Sattel 1983, 120)

Sattel is making an obvious but important point. As speakers, we know that real self-disclosure renders us vulnerable, not simply because of the content of our discourse, but also because we are speaking only for *ourselves*, and therefore cannot invoke the power, the authority, of "the polis" or "received wisdom."

Based on a model of discourse that focuses on territoriality and specific speaking rights, the speech styles and strategies I have been discussing are consonant with the research on masculine personality development, which stresses firm boundaries between the self and the other. These speech styles have specific consequences for the sociolinguistic construction of both power and gender. As Candace West and Don engaged in ensuring interaction than the men" (98). Women asked two and a half times as many questions to initiate and maintain conversations. They used many conversational openings like "do you know X" (which children and others with restricted speaking rights often use to get into conversations), and variants of "this is interesting" or "here's a nice idea" in order to enlist the males' attention. Women also initiated almost twice as many topics as men, but met with much less success at having the topics become conversation. Men raised twenty-nine topics, only one of which met with uncertain success. Women raised forty-seven topics, seventeen of which were incorporated into the general conversation and twenty-eight of which failed, which is to say that they were not responded to by the males. On the other hand, men made twice as many statements just to "fill a turn," but they didn't do much other interactional work.

The following is an example of a "normal" conversation of this type. It was recorded by Dale Spender and shows the woman hard at work at "the art of conversation," drawing the male out until he finally interrupts and takes over.

> *Female:* Did he have the papers ready for you?
> *Male:* Mmmmm.
> *Female:* And were they all right . . . was anything missing?
> *Male:* Not that I could see.
> *Female:* Well that must have been a relief, anyway . . .
> *Female:* I suppose everything went well after that?
> *Male:* Almost.
> *Female:* Oh. Was there something else?
> *Male:* Yes, actually.
> *Female:* It wasn't X . . . was it? . . . He didn't let you down again? . . .
> *Male:* I'd say he did.
> *Female:* He really is responsible, you know, you should get . . .
> *Male:* I'm going to do something about it. It was just about the last straw today. How many times do you think that makes this week . . . (Spender 1980, 48-49)

As Fishman points out, the verbal "domestic engineering" skills women often need to practice take many forms and are complex, even though they are generally invisible:

> While women have difficulty generating interactions, they are almost always available to do the conversational work required by

men and which is necessary for interactions. Appearances may differ by case: sometimes women are required to sit and "be a good listener" because they are not otherwise needed. At other times women are required to fill silences and keep conversation moving, to talk a lot. Sometimes they are expected to develop others' topics, and at other times they are required to present and develop topics of their own. (Fishman 1983, 99)

It should come as no surprise that the same features of women's speech that Fishman describes, features like politeness forms, the frequent use of tag and other question types, conversational fillers such as "uh-huh," "mmmmmmm," and "yes," and pauses or hesitations in delivery are often described as demonstrating weakness, deficiency, powerlessness, and hesitancy on the part of women. Yet they can also be shown to have value in the construction and maintenance of conversational speech. And while it seems apparent that these cooperative or sustaining speech strategies are at least in part accommodative responses to greater male power (Brown and Levinson 1978; Lakoff 1975), there is considerable (and mounting) evidence to suggest that women prefer a somewhat different model of language interaction from the dominant mode even when they are not in the immediate presence of greater male linguistic power. As Shirley Ardener reminds us:

Members of a muted group may thus come to an accommodation with the social structure in which they are placed, and find their own satisfactions in its interstices and outside its dominant structure. Their alternative systems of value, which may be rich and complex, should be respected and should receive greater attention than they sometimes do. (Ardener 1978, 28)

What is women's discourse like when it is at its greatest remove from the conventions, restrictions, and monitorings of the dominant discourse and dominant discoursers? Several studies of talk in all-female groups suggest that women's discourse often operates on a collaborative basis, with personal life, lived experience, and relationships as the primary texts of conversation (Aries 1976; Chesler 1972; Goodwin 1980; Jenkins 1982; and Kalčik 1975). Barrie Thorne, Cheris Kramarae, and Nancy Henley summarize these studies as highlighting features such as the "mutuality of 'interaction work' (active listening, building on the utterances of others), collaboration rather than competition, and flexible leadership rather than the strong dominance patterns found in all-male groups" (Thorne et al. 1983, 18). When women talk together, they often use overlapping speech strategies, telling parallel anecdotes simultaneously that center on a "kernel" narrative, for example. Boundaries between listener and speaker are eroded or conflated, with those present often being in both roles at the same time, or moving fluidly between them (Edelsky 1981; Kalčik 1975). Just as the men's discourse patterns were suited to their psychosexual development, so, too, are the patterns of talk that women prefer in single-sex groups consonant with work on female psychosexual development suggesting that women develop more fluid ego boundaries, at least in part because of their early connection to and nurturance by other women.

Education and the Micropolitics of Talk

Few would question that the process of learning requires both active listening and active speaking (questioning, answering, speculating) on the part of all students. But gendered micro-inequities, often invisible, create what has been called "a chilly climate" for learning for women students (Coates 1986; Gabriel and Smithson 1990; Hall and Sandler 1982, 1986; and Spender 1989), because "the valued patterns of speech in college and university settings are more often found among men than among women speakers" (Thorne 1979, 5). The voluminous research summarized in a series of publications on the chilly climate for women students in American colleges and universities suggests that abstract, impersonal styles are indeed favored, which causes several serious problems for women when it comes to classroom talk (Hall and Sandler 1982, 1986. See also Treichler and Kramarae 1983).

For example, people are more attentive when men speak and are more likely to recognize male speakers by nodding and gesturing and responding more extensively to males' remarks than they do to those of females. Dale Spender's research finds that teachers inadvertently allocate up to two-thirds of the verbal attention in the classroom to males (Spender 1989). (She even finds this two-thirds rule true of informal exchanges between male and female academics! (Spender 1989, 9-10).) This may be due in large part to males' aggressive and competitive speech styles. As Jennifer Coates reports, boys are much "noisier" in school, demanding attention, bragging about their performance, calling out answers, and making guesses, while girls tend to listen or to facilitate turn-taking. A young girl in one study commented, "They all make a lot of noise, all those boys. That's why I think they're more intelligent than us" (Coates 1986, 165).

Women are also more likely to be interrupted in class than men are. They are more likely to be interrupted by male students than other female students, and by male teachers rather than female teachers. Also, their comments are more likely to be ignored, passed over, or attributed to someone else. These patterns of interaction effectively mute women's voices in the classroom. Girls learn that their questions and comments are not important, and they are prevented from engaging in the serious exchanges necessary for learning.

One compelling illustration (at least for me) of the relations between gender, interruption, and power in the academy is reported by Barbara W. Eakins and R. Gene Eakins (1978). Analyzing interruptions in faculty meetings, Eakins and Eakins not only found that males interrupted more than females, but also that the least interrupted person was the male chairman, while the most interrupted person was a female without a Ph.D.

In fact, these same dynamics were noted even at a conference on sexism in education. Dale Spender writes:

> Protests were registered on the grounds that the women did not get as many opportunities to speak, that when they did speak they were frequently interrupted (by men), that they were not listened to with equal attention (or that they were not listened to at all). The general level of noise seemed to increase when a woman was talking and the talk of women was treated as an opportunity/excuse for men and women to exchange information; this did not happen to the same degree when it was a man who held the floor. (Spender 1980, 87)

Women's talk has historically been denigrated in the academy and in the culture at large. Nonetheless, it is still of unquestionable value. Perhaps women understand that, just as we have been bound, elided, effaced, and muted in language and discourse, so too is it through language and discourse that we can be restored. "Seize the word!" as Elaine Marks urges us. The enormous surge of interest and participation in informal learning groups, called Consciousness Raising groups, that accompanied the women's movement during the late 1960s and the 1970s is a superlative example of the liberatory opportunities women seek in language.[8] Journals, as we will see, have been used as another.

Dale Spender sees the exciting possibilities that can arise when women start to talk (or write) freely:

> Women-centered meanings will multiply as the pattern of women's existence begins to emerge in both formal and informal contexts. There will be numerous spheres of female existence that

will begin to come into focus, which will begin to become real. (Spender 1980, 74-75)

Adrienne Rich sums up this view of woman's relation to language in the excerpt from "Thinking of Caroline Herschel, 1750-1848, Astronomer, Sister of William; and Others":

> I am an instrument in the shape
> of a woman trying to translate pulsations
> into images for the relief of the body
> and the reconstruction of the mind. (Rich 1979, 48)

Women's Silences and Violence:
For the Relief of the Body and the Reconstruction of the Mind

What would happen if one woman told the
truth about her life?
The world would split open.
—Muriel Rukeyser, "Kathe Köllwitz"

Could I write all, the world would turn to stone.
—Caterina Sforza (1462-1509)

[21 March 1991: I have tried locating this section of my book at several different points in my large and unwieldy third chapter. No place seems exactly right, but I think I've finally found a spot that won't be too distracting. I have decided that the material in this section is so important that I am willing to sacrifice some symmetry of logic in order to include it. I know it's a thumb, and a sore one at that, but thumbs are important if you want to grasp things . . . even ideas.]

Having sketched out the layers of silencing and muting of women at both the macropolitical and micropolitical levels, I want to take a moment now to show how these discursive strategies work together, and how they act reciprocally to construct and maintain profound differences in the behavior and linguistic experience of men and women. Specifically I want to look at the relationship between violence—especially sexual violence—and the muting of women's voices, which is as old as the early codes of law of Urukagina and as current as the controversy over whether topics such as sexual abuse can or should be written about in student journals.

Rape and wife battering are the most commonly committed violent crimes in America, yet they are radically underreported. This is perhaps because, of the cases reported, only a very small percentage result in actual convictions, which has a powerful muting effect on the victims of these crimes (Boston Women's Health Book Collective 1984, 99-120; Griffin 1983). Incest, the violation of the strongest and most universal of cultural laws, a crime that destroys the sense of self so profoundly that it has been called "soul murder," is terrifyingly common (Rodiman 1989, 89). Yet, it has been wrapped in layers of what Adrienne Rich calls "lies, secrets, and silence" (Rich 1979).

Now the layers of secrecy and lies are finally beginning to be unwrapped by feminist scholars and researchers (Barringer 1992; Butler 1983; Herman 1981; Herman and Hirschman 1977; and Russell 1986). But the task is not easy, as many point out, because the violation of incest is always tied to secrecy; tied to the silencing of the victim by threat, physical force, or verbal coercion. Therefore, in addition to the physical damage of the abuse itself, and the shattering betrayal of trust, many survivors never "tell." They hold the secret inside, to fester for years; they cope by radically suppressing the memory of the abuse, or of entire periods of their childhood. Both of these coping mechanisms have damaging, long-term emotional and intellectual consequences. Incest survivors, confronting a fragmented, dissociated set of external and internal realities, often learn not to "know," or not to speak about what they might know, because the gap between their lived experience and the cultural proprieties they are supposed to mouth is too great to bridge (Belenky et al. 1986; Gelinas 1983; and Rodiman 1989).

Also, because many survivors don't report incest—with good reason—it's hard to know precisely how common it is. Recent studies, however, such as Diana Russell's, suggest that as many as fifty-four percent of all women are sexually abused in one way or another by age eighteen, and, for almost half of the women surveyed (forty-eight percent) the abuse happened by age fourteen (Russell 1986). Some studies suggest even higher figures (Kelley 1988). What is also clear is that the vast majority of incest victims are female (at least ninety-two percent), while the vast majority of perpetrators are male (at least ninety-seven percent) (Herman and Hirschman 1977), although scholars often use sex-neutral language that obscures these shocking numbers (Frank and Treichler 1989, 15). What Herman calls the "conspiracy of silence" around incest can be seen additionally in the misnamings that accompany discussions of its causes and consequences. Parents, friends, judges, therapists, social workers, and researchers have all unwittingly participated in the conspiracy by asserting that the girls themselves might have been acting seductively or lying, or that incest is very rare, the result of rare pathology (Herman 1981, 7-49). When these explanations are proven to be false, they often suggest that incest has no ill effects. Psychologists who have stumbled across it—particularly Freud in his work with female hysterics and, later, Kinsey in his surveys of human sexuality—have explained it away or denied their own data, thus silencing women rather than acknowledging the profundity of the problem (Herman 1981. See also Butler 1983 and Froula 1989).

Carol Barringer, in her important work on the silencing and coming to voice of incest survivors (1992), suggests that the silencing of incest victims is paradigmatic of the multilayered silencing of women in general. In addition to direct silencing, "the nonavailability of words to talk about it with, and the disparaging and discrediting [of] any who dare defy the taboo" act as additional muting devices (Barringer 1992, 1).[9] Even as adults, the women whose writings she has studied, or whom she has interviewed, often panic, "shut down" when speaking:

> You just get silenced about so many other things. So many other parts of your life become silenced because of this first—(pause)—you know, horrendous experience. . . . You learn "Don't tell anybody. Oh God, what if somebody finds out." And to this day I still carry with me that fear, "You know they're gonna find out what you said, and then you're gonna be in big trouble, and oh my God what's gonna happen—" and it's not something you think about once or twice. It's this pervasive thing that you think about lots and lots and lots. You have this thing in the pit of your stomach, you have this breathing problem. (Barringer 1992, 2-3. See also Belenky et al. 1986, 23-30)

Like Carol Barringer, I think that the massive silence surrounding incest and other forms of sexual violence against women—and the shattering of self, knowing, and voice that is its legacy—is paradigmatic of the silencing and muting of women's and other marginalized voices in many cultures throughout the millennia. Nonetheless, the relation between sexual violence (including the abuse of both male and female children) and the silencing or muting of women's voices has yet to be factored into the current theories about gender and linguistic development that we considered earlier in this chapter.

It seems to me that, as scholars and educators, those of us who deal with students on a regular basis must start to acknowledge the ways in which insidious forms of muting and silencing affect our students' and our own sense of self as speakers, writers, and as knowers. We must learn to understand, as Adrienne Rich reminds us in her poem "Cartographies of Silence," that silence "is a presence/it has a history a

form/Do not confuse it with any kind of absence" (Rich 1978, 17). We
need to accept that faltering or fragmented speech or writing is not
inevitably the result of stupidity or indifference, indecision or intellectual confusion. Rather, gaps, silences, and contradictions may testify to
the profound contradictions in reality that survivors, even the most
articulate, confront daily.

    We must also acknowledge that black women and lesbian women
also know in multiple ways the danger of telling the truth about their
lives, as well as the dangers of silence. Audre Lorde, a poet who is both
black and lesbian, delivered a paper at the Modern Language Association in 1977 in which she addressed the issue of multiple silence.

> My silences had not protected me. Your silence will not protect
> you. . . . What words do you not yet have? What do you need to
> say? What are the tyrannies you swallow day by day and attempt
> to make yours, until you will sicken and die of them, still in
> silence? Perhaps for some of you here today, I am the face of one
> of your fears. For I am woman, because I am Black, because I am
> lesbian, because I am myself. . . . And of course I am afraid
> because the transformation of silence into language and action is
> an act of self revelation, and always seems fraught with danger.
> (Lorde 1977, 41-42)

Barbara Smith, another black feminist critic, writes, "Even at this
moment, I am not convinced that one can write explicitly as a black lesbian and live to tell about it (Newton and Rosenfeldt 1985, 15. See also
Culley 1985).

    Susan Griffin treats the significance of these silences in her essay
"Thoughts on Writing: A Diary":

> Silences. Not the silences between notes of music, or the silences
> of a sleeping animal, or the calm of a glassy surfaced river wit-
> nessing the outstretched wings of a heron. Not the silence of an
> emptied mind. But this other silence. That silence which can feel
> like a scream, in which there is no peace. The grim silence
> between two lovers who are quarrelling. The painful silence of
> the one with tears in her eyes who will not cry. The silence of
> the child who knows she will not be heard. The silence of a
> whole people who have been massacred. Of a whole sex made
> mute, or not educated to speech. The silence of a mind afraid to
> admit truth to itself. This is the silence that the poet dreads.
> (Griffin 1980, 117)

These silences are the silences the teacher dreads as well. Behind them are the "forbidden stories" that sometimes surface in student/teacher conferences, in the hallways, or in the diaries and journals of women writers, women students, and members of other oppressed groups, stories that are in part responsible for the controversy over the legitimacy of the so-called (and male-defined) private/personal diary in the public/academic discursive domain.

[24 August 1989. No accident: Public-fascinating and frenetic namedropping diaries of Andy Warhol appear on the bestseller list, while a woman named Elizabeth Morgan is being held in jail on contempt charges for not handing her daughter over to her ex-husband, whom she is sure has been sexually abusing her. She waits and keeps a journal for her absent daughter to explain why they must be apart, to explain that she loves her and wants to protect her. I suspect she also keeps it to keep herself alive.]

Gender and Written Discourse: Public and Private Voices

Every woman who writes is a survivor.
        —Tillie Olsen, *Silences*

Because women writers have had to fit moments of writing between household tasks, or have been considered freaks who denied their primary female creative function, or have been viewed by critics as unworthy of serious attention, they often reflect a self consciousness of themselves as artists.
        —Joan Goulianos, *By a Woman Writt*

Because women are a muted group discursively, their writing has been muted in the same multileveled way as their speech, with similar consequences for the quantity and quality of their written productions, for their sense of themselves as writers, and for their concern with writing as both constraint and release. What women have tended to write about, the forms and styles with which they are comfortable, their complex relation to writing and to language itself, are all an important part of the development of their journal and diary traditions. These factors still inform the perception and practice of both academic and nonacademic student journals.

Several books and countless articles have already been written on the subject of the muting and silence of women writers: Virginia Woolf's *A Room of One's Own*; Tillie Olsen's *Silences*; Joanna Russ's *How to Suppress Women's Writing*; Dale Spender's "Women and Writing," in

Man Made Language, and her newer work, *The Writing or the Sex?*; and Lynn Spender's *Intruders on the Rights of Men: Women's Unpublished Heritage* among them. So I need not treat all the issues raised by these works in depth. I do, however, want to list some of the ways women have encountered the dominant/public, muted/private sanctions and traditions because the proscriptions or the heritage that these opposi-tions represent are an important legacy for both my male and female students of writing. Lynn Spender succinctly addresses several of the various levels of sanction or socialization that affect women's relation to the word:

> Women writers, from the time they dared to circulate their work publicly, have been subjected to harassment from men for entering male territory and for allegedly denying their male-defined femi-ninity. They have had to contend with the imposition of limita-tions to their education, to their opportunities to write and their chances to publish and circulate their work. Even after their words have been printed, women have had to face male literary criticism in order to determine the fate of their work. In each case and at each stage, women have been pressed to conform to men's requirements to meet with male approval. (Spender 1983, 43)

As Dale Spender points out, the public world of writing—including the academy, literature, publishing, reviewing, and literary criticism—has been almost solely the province of men, who were able to maintain their discursive territoriality for a very long period of time simply by exclud-ing or by strictly controlling women's access to literacy and formal edu-cation (Spender 1989). Traditionally, in order to write for the public sphere in the Western world one had to be schooled in written Latin and Greek, and in the classical rhetorical forms. The separation between the written word and colloquial speech was profound. Elene Kolb in her wonderful piece, "When Women Got the Word," explains:

> Spoken language had little to do with writing in an artificial clas-sical style composed according to strict rules of poetics and rhetoric, and based upon literary precedent. The classical author, without regard for his talent or imagination, was the result of a rigorous literary education designed not to form a creative writer, but a civic leader, orator, or official bureaucrat. As women had no place in the political sphere, seldom did they receive this advanced training; and even when a woman did learn enough to write, rarely was her work preserved. (Kolb 1989, 1, 28)

Josephine Donovan, in her insightful study, "The Silence is Broken" (1980), on the entrance of women into the world of letters, offers a similar view: "Latin had become a male public language, which existed only within the male academic institutions. Women could only learn vernaculars and for centuries were denied access to the world of formal, public communication" (Donovan 1980, 206. See also Gilbert and Gubar 1988).

Thus, schoolboys of Shakespeare's day, like those of previous centuries and centuries to come, were trained in the rhetorical patterns of Cato, Terence, Ovid, Virgil, Horace, and Seneca and versed in the rhetorical works of Cicero and Quintilian. Girls, however, generally, were neither so trained nor so versed. Most "schooling" for girls happened at home, rather than in any formal academic setting, and centered on the development of domestic and social skills, not intellectual or professional proficencies. As the sixteenth-century French poet Madeleine des Roches lamented, her parents had the habit of "handing us the spindle instead of the pen" (Sankovitch 1986, 231). "Good women" as we remember, were to be modest, chaste, and silent. Women were often considered "uneducable" and too much book learning, it was feared, might ruin a woman.

Even with the advent of mass literacy in the eighteenth century, far fewer women than men became literate. Even now, United Nations statistics from 1980 reveal that, worldwide, "each year the gap grows between women's illiteracy rates and those of men" (Spender 1983, 16). And even when formal schooling has been made available to women as well as men, it has continued to take somewhat different forms and to serve, at least in part, the purpose of preparing women for their "secondary sphere."

In fact, although a few women were recorded as attending and even teaching at universities on the European continent during the fourteenth century (Mahl and Koon 1977, 5), "when universities in the West took over the church's teaching role and ushered in a Renaissance of classical learning," they once again "barred their doors to women" (Kolb 1989, 29). Women were not granted access to a university education in substantial numbers until the middle of the nineteenth century—and in some cases, not until the twentieth. Oxford did not open its doors to women until 1920; Cambridge did not do so until 1948 (Mahl and Koon 1977, 6). The University of New Hampshire, my own institution, graduated its first four women in 1897.

Clearly, then, the most basic and effective form of muting has been to deny women, in far greater numbers than men, the basic tools of literacy and schooling that would allow women to write, to create permanent records of their thoughts and verbal compositions, and pass them on to the public culture and on to future generations. Tillie Olsen invokes these gaps and silences:

> [Then there are] the silences where the lives never came to writing. Among these the mute inglorious Miltons: those whose waking hours are all struggle for existence; the barely educated; the illiterate; women. Their silence the silence of centuries as to how life was, is, for most of humanity. Traces of their making, of course in folk song, lullaby, tales, language itself, jokes, maxims, superstitions—but we know nothing of the creators, or how it was with them. (Olsen 1979, 10)

A Room of One's Own and Five Hundred Pounds

Like men, women need time, space, financial
security, education, support, and validations
from others, and stamina in order to write well.
—Catherine Stimpson,
Feminist Issues in Literary Scholarship

Discouraged or prevented from learning to write, women, for the most part, were in no position to attempt writing as a career. As for women who were literate, John Stuart Mill pointed out as late as 1859 that "women who read, much more, women who write, are, in the existing constitution of things, a contradiction and a disturbing element" (qtd. in Spender 1980, 192). In fact, Barbara Miller Solomon, in her history of women in higher education, reports that some literate women, such as Jane Grey Swisshelm, gave up reading after marriage because it was a potential source of conflict (Solomon 1985, 38).

Women writers were considered aberrations because their role was to service the domestic sphere, not use it to their own advantage. Women were to be mothers and wives (or provide some other set of domestic services) first. They were supposed to be doing things for others, not sitting and writing for themselves![10] Traditionally, male writers have had only one job, while females have had at least two (Glastonbury 1978). "This makes a significant difference: it has facilitated access to written discourse for males, it has reduced it for females" (Spender 1980, 218). Indeed, Glastonbury's study suggests that it was considered natural by many that women should help produce time for men's writing, while men rarely, if ever, performed the same service for their female counterparts. Dale Spender explains how many talented women, such as Jane Carlyle, Sonya Tolstoy, and Dorothy Wordsworth, served as literary "handmaids" to their famous male counterparts (Spender

1989, 135-94). They sacrificed their own considerable intellectual ener-
gies to the task of transcribing and polishing the writing of their men.
Sometimes they even offered their own writing, which came frequently
from journals or diaries, as grist for the male writing mill; or perhaps
they would have their work taken, as in the cases of Colette and Zelda
Fitzgerald.

For many women who were mothers, the constant fragmentation
that domestic responsibilities entail made it nearly impossible to write:
"It is distraction, not meditation, that becomes habitual; interruption,
not continuity; spasmodic, not constant toil. . . . Work interrupted,
deferred, relinquished, makes blockage—at best lesser accomplishment.
Unused capacities atrophy, cease to be" (Olsen 1979, 19). Very few
mothers have become writers of stature, as Tillie Olsen, with exhaustive
lists, has shown—as Tillie Olsen, herself a mother, can attest (Olsen
1979, 19-21).[11]

*[14 Jan. 1989. Finding a mitten, milk money and the library book. Laundry,
beds, dishes, food shopping, haircut for Molly and the innumerable unname-
ables: finishing the edging on Molly's potholder, helping trace the snowflake
patterns for her "nonfiction story" for first grade, ensuring Ben has found his
30 facts on Honduras, and finished the collage on Robinson Crusoe. Chapter
three nearly done. Far too long. Will probably have to cut it in half. Finished
chapter two in October. Finished grading for the semester the Wednesday after
Christmas. Got through Christmas, New Year's, five birthdays, an anniversary,
Brownies and acting, Molly's asthma and two weeks of flu, Ben's two weeks of
flu (still pending), car trouble, and putting the house back on the market. The
Christmas cards are still waiting along with the monthly bills and tax work
and syllabi for next semester. At least two more chapters to rewrite by the end
of February. School starts in ten days. Thankful for this mottled clump of
time—some days send six, eight, ten hours.]*

Women as Writers: Bearing the Word

But regardless of the obstacles, women have written.[12] Literate,
and even literary (that is, classically trained) women appear in every
age. "For women, if choked, have still spoken. For women, if on the borders of culture have still smuggled messages past border sentries"
(Stimpson 1987, 2).

Indeed, during the Middle Ages, some women, mostly upper-class
or aristocratic women who had taken religious vows, were given nearly
comparable educations to those of the learned monks. Sometimes profi-
cient in Latin, capable of producing learned manuscripts, these women

both wrote and taught (Mahl and Koon 1977, 5. See also Wiesner 1986). However, the price for this learning was great, as they were required to give up any semblance of being a "woman." "They chose celibacy because their desire for learning required it; their male admirers—and there were many—applauded that decision as they felt no woman could be both learned and sexually active" (Wiesner 1986, 13). Hrotswith (ca. 935-1005), a German nun with the distinction of being the first known Christian playwright, composed in classical hexameter; Héloïse, Abélard's famous student, also produced beautiful writing, as did Hildegard of Bingen, whose brilliance was widely acknowledged by her peers (Kolb 1989, 28).

But outside the convents and the homes of the very wealthy or noble, the literacy rate for women was extremely low (See, e.g., Mahl and Koon 1977). At least until the eighteenth century, almost all the women who wrote were of the upper class. These women often tried to write in the privileged modes and styles of men. Mary Sidney Herbert (1561-1621), Countess of Pembroke, sister of the famous English writer, Sir Philip Sidney, used the "Spenserian" sonnet form before Spenser did, producing sonnets of comparable quality (Mahl and Koon 1977, 6; Spender 1983, 48). And Katharine Phillips's seventeenth-century poetry earned her the title of "Orinda, English Sappho" (Spender 1983, 49).

Yet these women and their noble efforts were essentially lost for hundreds of years, until feminist scholars recovered and published them, along with many other women's writings.[13] The fact of their elision signals that a very powerful form of muting is at work: even when women do write and do get circulated or published, they have a mysterious tendency to get lost. They are ignored by literary critics, excised from literary traditions, and excluded from the literary canon. Many have documented, with Deborah Rosenfeldt, the "filtering out of women writers disproportionately to their numbers and significance" (RosenFeldt 1982, 15), a trend that also marks the journal tradition. The suppression of the history of women's writing has left large gaps in the development of certain traditions (Showalter 1977, 1985). Equally importantly, it has left women who want to write in any era feeling orphaned, bereft of women's writing traditions, feeling that women did not write before the eighteenth century, and that the few famous women writers that we are familiar with (the Eliots, the Austens, and the Brontës) have been exceptions or flukes.

This excision of women from our literary heritage helps to reinforce the confines of our muteness. As women we look at the past and find few other women and our suspicions, inculcated, are fed, and we question our own abilities. As writers we have our doubts multiplied. We have been denied the full knowledge of the contribution made by other women writers and this hinders our own efforts. It is a situation in which every woman writer has found herself. (Spender 1980, 205)

Aiding and abetting the process of excision has been the frequently negative treatment both of women-authored works that have dared to circulate and of the women who had the nerve to write them. Aphra Behn (ca. 1640-1689), the first Englishwoman to earn her living as a professional playwright, was extraordinarily innovative, and quite popular, but was often made fun of and insulted, called a "lewd harlot" for using the same language that in male writers was considered fine wit, and then conveniently lost for almost two centuries (Goulianos 1973, 87; Mahl and Koon 1977, 165-67). Margaret Cavendish, an early Englishwoman of letters, was dubbed "Mad Madge" and alternately applauded and treated as a freak. Horace Walpole labelled Mary Wollstonecraft "a hyena in petticoats" without ever having read "A Vindication of the Rights of Women" (Goulianos 1973, xv). Harriet Martineau, writing treatises on political economy in the early nineteenth century, received the following advice in a review of her work: "the less women usually meddle with anything which can be called public life outside of their village, we are sure the better for all parties" (Walters 1976, 332). Elizabeth Barrett Browning's epic poem *Aurora Leigh*, which explicitly addressed the contradictions women faced as writers and as poets, although enormously popular when published, was surgically excised from the body of her work, as it was from the literary canon within a generation (Kaplan 1986, 81-83). Women who wrote novels were termed "dancing dogs" by Dr. Samuel Johnson, and damned as "scribbling women" by Nathaniel Hawthorne.

Again and again came the advice to young women not to write. Robert Southey said to Charlotte Brontë on this score: "Literature cannot be the business of a woman's life and it ought not to be. The more she is engaged in her proper duties, the less leisure she will have for it, even as an accomplishment and a recreation. . . ." (qtd. in Spender 1980, 194).

One might think that as women wrote more and more, the reception of their work would simply ameliorate over time. But just as the development of women's writing has not been one of simple linear progression, so too has the reception accorded to women who write and to women's writing followed a pattern filled with sudden leaps, gaps, and turns. To use a phrase coined by biologist Stephen Jay Gould for evolutionary theory, the course of women's traditions and their attendant criticism has been one of "punctuated equilibrium."

In fact, Sandra Gilbert and Susan Gubar persuasively argue, in *No Man's Land*, that during the early twentieth century, as ever larger numbers of women, including more and more middle-class women, began writing in the public domain, the "war of the words," already a dangerous one in earlier times, intensified, with the "masters" like Henry James, James Joyce, Ezra Pound, T. S. Eliot, Ernest Hemingway, and William Faulkner all venting their linguistic misogyny (Gilbert and Gubar 1988, 231-36). Dale Spender offers an extensive review of current sexist practices in publishing, reviewing, and literary criticism also (Spender 1989, 24-92).

But in my mind, it was Anne Finch, the Countess of Winchilsea, an early Englishwoman of letters, who made the definitive pronouncement on the subject of the woman who attempts to write for the public world. As a young woman at court, she would hide her writing—as Fanny Burney would later (Spender 1983, 54-55), and as the Brontë sisters did even in the nineteenth century (Ardener 1978, 25)—fearing her work would meet with "prejudice, if not contempt" (Goulianos 1973, 71). Years after leaving the court, Anne Finch would write in the introduction to a manuscript of her poetry these classic lines:

> Did I, my lines intend for publick view,
> How many censures, wou'd their faults persue,
> Some wou'd, because such words they do affect,
> Cry they're insipid, empty, uncorrect.
> And many, have attain'd, dull and untaught
> The name of Witt, only by finding fault.
> True judges, might condemn their want of witt,
> And all might say, they're by a Woman writt.
> Alas! a woman that attempts the pen,
> Such an intruder on the rights of men,
> Such a presumptuous Creature, is esteem'd,
> The fault, can by no vertue be redeem'd.
> (Qtd. in Goulianos 1973, 71)

While many women confronted the sanctions that would thwart them head-on, often braving and enduring severe punishment, many more women accommodated themselves to the sanctions in a variety of ways, just as we saw to be the case in our discussion of oral discourse. Sometimes they apologized for works that had been circulated without their knowledge. Such was the case for Anne Bradstreet, whose poems had been carried to England and published by her brother-in-law (Rich 1979, 28), and Katharine Phillips, who demurred that she had never written for publication and was taken quite ill on finding out her poems had been published (Spender 1983, 48).

Another strategy women used to get a hearing was to publish anonymously: in fact the *British Museum Catalog* has twenty-five pages of listings headed cryptically "A Lady." A certain Ralph James issued a pamphlet in 1880, entitled "Aggravating Ladies," that detailed his frustration at trying to identify 150 anonymous works by nineteenth-century English writers, presumably women (Rosenfeldt 1982, 25). Male pseudonyms were also, understandably, quite popular, for women quickly realized that their works received a much better hearing if their authors were thought to be male. And so Marian Evans became George Eliot, Charlotte and Emily Brontë became Currer and Ellis Bell, Elizabeth Gaskell became Cotton Mather Mills, and so on (Spender 1980, 195-211; Rosenfeldt 1982, 25).

When Women Got the Word

But women's writing hasn't always been limited to the strict imitation of more public male styles, models, topics, and voices. As Elene Kolb has argued, women got their first real access to writing during the Medieval period, when vernacular languages became a vehicle for more effective proselytizing on the part of the Church.[14] One inadvertent consequence of this ecclesiastical strategy, however, was that women, who had been excluded from almost all classical learning, could start to write in their native languages. Dame Julian of Norwich (1342-1417?), for example, a contemporary of Chaucer, wrote *Sixteen Revelations of Divine Love*, "the earliest literary work in English known to have been written by a woman" (Mahl and Koon 1977, 12). And an illiterate religious mystic, Margery Kempe (ca. 1373-?), had scribes set down her life in what was to become the first known extant autobiography in English (Goulianos 1973, 3).

Hundreds of songs and lyric poems written from the perspective of a first-person female persona start to appear in almost every Medieval language in the twelfth and thirteenth centuries. The forms are fresh and fluid, not bound by the strictures of classical rhetoric; the language is concrete and sensuous and young, as the languages themselves were at that time; these representations of female experience are candid, passionate, and strong (see Kolb 1989, 29). Consider this section of a thirteenth-century motet, translated by Elene Kolb:

God damn him
Who put me here!
What a villain,
What a sin—
To give a girl like me
To a convent.
And wicked I swear:
This religious life is such a bore—
God I'm too young for this!
Beneath my sash I feel sweet sins:
God damn him who made me a nun.
(Kolb 1989, 29)

Or this Spanish Arabic piece written by a certain Wallada during the eleventh century. It, too, appears in Elene Kolb's translation:

If you weren't such a run-around
you'd leave my slave alone—
but you go ahead and choose her!
You pass up an orchard
for a peeled twig;
you pass up the moon
for a sparkler.
(Kolb 1989, 29)

An important strategy that women have always used has been to write, just as they have spoken, around the margins and in the interstices and seams between the public sphere and the private sphere. In fact, women have always been involved in various types of writing that were considered either acceptable or proper, even necessary to the private sphere. As Elaine Showalter reminds us, "Women's writing is a double voiced discourse that always embodies the social, literary and cultural heritage of both the dominant and the muted" (Showalter 1985, 263).

These public/private writings served primarily domestic and social purposes, such as dispensing advice, sharing recipes and cures with others, conveying spiritual comfort to those in need, maintaining contact with faraway relatives or friends, and chronicling family histories (Wiesner 1986; Crawford 1985). They were often written by women for female readers. Writing became, in fact, another mandated "domestic" task for most literate women from the eighteenth century on (Ardener 1978, 25). And the journal traditions of women have often served these purposes, as we shall see in the next chapter. These "private" or "domestic" women's writings have served the purposes of men, and those of women as well.

The dichotomy of male/female, public/private is maintained by permitting women to write for a private audience (which can be extended to encompass other women) but discouraging them from writing for a public audience, that is, men. In the "private" sphere women have been permitted to write for themselves (for example, diaries) and for each other in the form of letters, "accomplished" pieces, moral treatises, articles of interest for other women, and even novels for women (during the nineteenth century, women were the mainstay of the novel-reading public). (Spender 1980, 92)

And now that scholars have started to reexamine the artificial, male-constructed boundaries between literacy and literature, as Lillian Robinson notes:

[a] wide range of forms and styles in which women's writing—especially that of women who did not perceive themselves as writers—appears. In this way, women's letters, diaries, journals, autobiographies, oral histories, and private poetry have come under critical scrutiny as evidence of women's consciousness and expression. (Robinson 1985, 116-17)

And indeed, just as in speech, women have found value and complexity in the forms of writing they themselves have used, some of which, adapted for women's use and purposes, may parallel those of the dominant traditions. Often, as Joan Goulianos points out, "unusual" or "nontraditional" forms have provided the opportunity for women "to validate [their] own experience" (Goulianos 1973, xiii). All of these alternate kinds of writing, then, precisely because they were less scrutinized or entirely ignored by men, gave women of the past the opportunity to write without having to be "Writers" on men's terms, which they clearly were not allowed to be. They allowed women not only to write, but to start to write about themselves, and to write, if only in a muted way, the truth of their experience.

There exists a rich and complex literature by women that goes back to the Middle Ages, a literature that consists of diaries, of autobiographies, of letters, of protests, of novels, of poems, of stories, of plays—a literature in which women wrote about their lives and from which women and men today can draw insights about theirs. . . . When women wrote, they touched upon experiences rarely touched upon by men, they spoke in different ways about these experiences, they often wrote in different forms. Women wrote about childbirth, about housework, about relationships with men, about friendships with other women, as wives, mothers, widows, courtesans, workers, thinkers and rebels—about the discrimination against them as writers and the pain and courage with which they faced it. (Goulianos 1973, xi)

In summary, we can see that women's relation to writing, as to discourse generally, has been historically quite different from that of their male counterparts. Men have been the creators of public written forms and have controlled access to writing and publishing, as well as the evaluation of published writing. They have been, in essence, "gatekeepers," as Dale Spender calls them. More males than females have been granted access to the education a writer requires and granted access to public written discourse. Males, in other words, could be Writers. That legacy of access (the right to write), comfort with public written-discourse forms, and comfort in judging and evaluating written discourse will be features of the men's journals we will look at in the next two chapters.

Women have not had the same access to public written discourse. They have been denied the necessary education; they have been restricted by their domestic roles in their opportunities to write; they have been repeatedly told that women should not and cannot write in the public sphere. When they have written publicly, they have been ridiculed, rebuked, or ignored. These sanctions have conditioned women to think that they cannot be writers. Even today women are often uncomfortable with writing for the public sphere (see Wandor 1983 and Sternberg 1980). Consider the following comments by women who are trying to be writers. They are just as aware now, as Anne Finch was in 1713, that they are "intruders on the rights of men." One woman laments:

It's useless trying to say I'm a writer . . . and a good one. I nearly said "good as a male." And that's what I'm talking about. By definition you can't be a good female writer, it's a contradiction of terms. (Qtd. in Spender 1980, 21)

Another questions:

Every time I sit down to write, I get an almost overwhelming

sense of inadequacy. Who am I to be so presumptuous? What possible evidence do I have that this is something I can expect to do?
(Qtd. in Spender 1980, 230)

A recent cartoon that I saw in the *Boston Globe* shows the double bind of
the woman writer explicitly (see Figure 3.3).

FIGURE 3.3
Woman as Writer

Boston Sunday Globe, 1 February 1987

Yet finally these restrictions on women writing for the public
sphere have not prevented women from writing for it, and women also
have a rich tradition of more private kinds of writing that they have
engaged in for centuries. As Shari Benstock notes in her introduction to
The Private Self, a collection of essays on women's autobiographical writings, "The 'private' suggests a scene of writing that invites the female, a
separate space at the very limits of the generic divide between the autobiographical and other kinds of writings and the gender divide between
the masculine and the feminine" (Benstock 1988, 1). These genres, nontraditional only by men's standards, have suited many of women's
expressive needs quite well. Letters and other kinds of collaborative
writing, autobiography, memoirs, protest letters and essays, novels and
short stories, and centrally, *journals and diaries*, are all associated,
although not exclusively, with the legacy of "women's writing." The
forms in question tend to be fluid, not rigidly defined; the styles are
plain, vernacular, personal; the subjects and techniques are garnered

from daily life, family events, relationships; the functions are generally those of personal or social (not necessarily public) utility. Women have tended to write texts close to life, to use those texts in immediate and practical ways in their lives, and to use them, paradoxically, to challenge the dichotomy of public sphere and private, the mutings their discourse and ideas were subject to. And from the point at which women began to write in their own tongues and voices, however muted, the journal/diary was a principal form for the representation of their physical and discursive experience.

Let's turn now to the history of the journal/diary itself to explore the ways in which the various socially constructed dichotomies (dominant/muted, public/private, personal/social, literature/literacy, masculine/feminine) have informed the development of journal/diary traditions and our perspectives regarding those traditions.

4

Gender and Journal-Keeping Traditions

> No form of expression more emphatically
> embodies the expresser: diaries are the word
> made flesh.
> —Thomas Mallon, *A Book of One's Own*

When we first examined current views of the forms and functions of journals used in composition courses and across the curriculum, we saw considerable confusion and controversy about their uses. Many people see the journal as a kind of literacy practice that has little intellectual merit. Some see it as too personal or emotional, while others view it as the trivial recounting of daily events rather than the site of heuristic, speculative, or reflective activity. These views consign journals and diaries to popular culture rather than to academic or literary culture and view pedagogy that draws on the journal as ineffective or inappropriate at best—and as dangerous, at worst. Others, like Murray, Elbow, Berthoff, Emig, and Fulwiler, view journals as powerful vehicles of the intellect, as engines that warm and drive the mind, capable of doubling back or going great distances, carrying with them the maps and memories of all previous trips, along with plans for the next. Thus they view journals as not only appropriate to academic culture, but well-suited to a wide variety of intellectual and pedagogical purposes.

We also saw that these tensions are represented in the proliferation of overlapping names we use to describe different journal-writing practices, with criticisms of the journal clustering around the seemingly synonymous, but vaguely feminine, or "feminized," term *diary*, which has somehow become a magnet for nebulous, negative perceptions. As we saw Kagle point out earlier, everyone knows what a diary (or journal) is, until it becomes necessary to define it. The various paradoxical perspectives on the journal, and the implicit tension between the terms *journal* and *diary*, can be better understood by grounding journals and journal pedagogy more fully in their historical and social contexts.

Critical to that understanding is the role that gender plays in positioning us and our sense of self in relation to language, to knowledge, and to all discursive practice. Of particular importance is the imposed but shifting demarcation between public and private, dominant and muted domains of experience and discourse and its consequence: the marginalization of women in both speech and writing.

Indeed, if we take a moment and use our "intuitive sense of the obvious," we see that there is indeed a pervasive, but often invisible, popular-culture tradition of journal or diary keeping, primarily among women, as well as a more public and elite tradition of journal keeping that is primarily male-affiliated. These popular traditions may be informing our own and our students' implicit assumptions about journal keeping generally, and about its academic uses specifically.

Signs of women's journal keeping are simply everywhere. When my daughter goes to the fifth birthday party of her best friend, Katie Mawson, Katie receives no fewer than three diaries as presents.

When we are out to dinner at the Goldenrod in York, Maine with our neighbor's children, B. J. and Erin (ages five and seven respectively), Erin and Molly draw on their placemats as they wait. Erin writes down what she's having and how good it is. Then at the top, she writes "Dear Diere," which Molly copies onto hers. B. J. is also drawing on his placemat and sees the girls writing. I ask him if he knows what a diary is. "Nope," he responds as he draws.

One day in the summer of 1989 I visit Sabbathday Lake, a Quaker Village in Poland Springs, Maine. As we tour the buildings and hear about Shaker life, the guide mentions that stored in one of the buildings is a rich collection of published and manuscript works both by and about the community. I, of course, ask him if there are any diaries. He thinks for a minute and answers, "Well, yes. I think so. But mostly the women wrote diaries. The men tended to write journals." Fascinated, I ask what the difference is. The guide is not really sure. All he can think of at the time is that men wrote more about the weather and the crops, and the women wrote more about themselves.

As I reread Sharyn Lowenstein's dissertation on the relationships between journals and journal keepers, I realize it is probably no coincidence that five of the six personal journal keepers she has studied are women (Lowenstein 1982).

I open a packet of papers to be graded to resolve a student's incomplete. The final paper, which uses Kübler-Ross's stages of grieving, concerns a childhood friend who has died of cancer. The paper is reconstructed from my student's childhood diaries. The dying girl's last request is that her friend, the author of the piece, not only take care of her stuffed animals but also preserve the diaries she herself had written.

At Bookland in the Six Points Plaza outside Biddeford, Maine, where we often stop for ice cream and a good browse after a ride to the beach, I find there are four different types of "women's journals" or "blank books," each labelled as a woman's book, or a woman's diary, or a woman's engagement diary. According to Thomas Mallon, in his recent *A Book of One's Own: People and Their Diaries* (1984), at least five hundred thousand of these blank books are sold in America annually. (The figure may be closer to five million, according to Jean Schinto (1987).) One look at the calico, brocaded, and unicorned covers these books inevitably have is enough to identify the presumed audience of the majority of these books. Also on the shelves are four anthologies of women's journals and five recently published, full-length diaries. Among them are the log of a sea captain's wife and a facsimile country diary of an Edwardian Lady, with her own handwriting and drawings reproduced. There are simply no equivalent offerings for men in other sections of the bookstore. Clearly, there are a lot of women reading and writing diaries, even in the little town of Biddeford, Maine.

Right across the river from Maine, in the small town of Portsmouth, New Hampshire, a full-day symposium entitled "Women's Diaries: What Can They Tell Us and How Can We Use Them?" was recently held by the Strawbery Banke Museum (7 March 1987). Over two hundred people attended, mostly women, including many older women from neighboring communities. During the course of the introductory remarks, the speaker informally polled the audience regarding their interest in diaries. "How many of you in the audience have kept a diary?" she asked. Immediately, over half the people raised their hands. "How many of you read women's diaries?" she asked again. This time nearly everyone's hand went up.

My mother, a social worker, shows me a newspaper clipping about a woman who was recently jailed for hiding her children from her ex-husband, whom she believed was abusing them. Where does her court testimony come from? The personal journal she has kept for years.

Indeed, the stereotype of the female journal keeper is so pervasive that it is culturally enshrined in humor. Thomas Mallon, in the introduction to a section of his book concerning travel journals, uses the following vignette to explain why people would write such a journal—but the implicit gender dynamics are every bit as fascinating as his explanation:

Several years ago the cartoonist Charles Saxon sketched a middle aged couple, both of them heavy with normality. The man is slumped in an armchair, watching television, expressionless. But his wife is aglow, lost in the memory contained in a book she has just discovered in the bedroom. She has come into the living room with it and is reading aloud about charming hotels and waiters and wines on a trip to Paris in 1956. Her husband is paying no attention to her, but the look on her face shows it hardly matters. The diary is doing what she knew—perhaps just dimly, twenty years before—it would someday have to. (Mallon 1984, 42)

What strikes me about this scene is that not only is the woman the probable author of the journal, but she is also the one who finds it more functional, more valuable. She connects with the "life in the text" of the journal. A more recent incarnation of the stereotype (this time of the prototypical adolescent-girl diarist) appeared in the *Boston Globe* during November of 1986 (see Figure 4.1).

On the other hand, a colleague recently sent me another cartoon, which appeared in *The New Yorker* during June of 1989, about a male diary keeper who refuses to disclose anything about himself in his diary because he sees it as a nosey or intrusive, almost hostile presence. The cartoon would not have been effective—indeed, it would not have made sense—if the figure had been a woman. In any event, it clearly demonstrates the common perception of males today, who are seen as nondisclosing (even to themselves) and as having a problematic relationship with the diary (see Figure 4.2).[1]

Yet it is also immediately obvious, though it goes unnoticed more often than not, that when we think about what we may have learned about journals as so-called minor literary traditions in school, we remember mostly the names of famous male diarists or journal keepers: Restoration and Enlightenment figures such as Pepys, Johnson, and Boswell in England; the great Puritan and colonial fathers: William Byrd, Samuel Sewell, Cotton Mather, and John Adams; and later, the well-known transcendentalist diary writers, Emerson and Thoreau; along with a host of other important writers and public figures, all of them male. The few female diarists who are commonly recognized are twentieth-century figures such as the tragic Anne Frank, or the more self-consciously literary diarists such as Anaïs Nin, Anne Morrow Lindbergh, and May Sarton.

In order to explain these gaps and changes, we have to trace the multiple traditions of journaling and diary keeping, as well as how they have evolved and permuted over time. How are the various strands of the tangled skein of journal traditions interwoven both with popular cul-

FIGURE 4.1
Stereotype of Female Journal Keeper

© Chronicle Features, 1982

*"I suppose it's only fair to warn you; I've been keeping
a journal the whole time!"*

Boston Globe, 18 November 1986

William Hamilton's cartoon is reprinted by permission of Chronicle Features,
San Francisco, CA.

ture and women's writing traditions, and with public/academic/literary
culture and men's writing traditions? Finally, how is it that the journal,
or at least the diary, came to be considered as a kind of writing associated with women's discourse? I shall try to answer these questions, at
least in a provisional way, in the next two sections of this chapter.

First, we'll look at the multiple origins of the journal. In the primarily male historical view, the journal has been largely associated with
males, focusing more on public forms, functions, and content than on
private musings, and using the male-generated models of discourse,
textuality, and selfhood that we have discussed, although the
public/private dichotomy as it relates to the journal is not a clear or simple one. Traditional literary scholarship thus provides an important
base of historical and literary information about journal traditions, but
it has not offered a full accounting of women's journal-keeping practice.

FIGURE 4.2
Stereotype of Male Journal Keeper

"Dear Diary: None of your damn business!"

New Yorker, 19 June 1989

Drawing by Mankoff; copyright 1989. The New Yorker Magazine, Inc.

Thus, it offers composition researchers only partial assistance in understanding how women came to be increasingly associated with, and men increasingly dissociated from, the modern, introspective personal journal.[2] So in the final sections of this chapter, we'll look at recent feminist scholarship on women's journals and diary keeping to help us generate a more complete perspective.

Origins of the Journal/Diary

If you were exploring someplace nobody else
had been to, you'd better be able to tell your
sovereign how you got there. A diary would be
the richest supplement to any maps you could
draw along the way; indeed the ship's log—like
the household account, and the commonplace

book—is one of the forms to which the diary
probably owes much of its murky start.
    —Thomas Mallon, *A Book of One's Own*

Two of the things everyone seems to be able to agree on are that
the journal is a protean form and that, particularly as it has been practiced in European culture,[3] it had a very "murky start." We tend to think
of the journal or diary in its currently prevailing form as a secular, personal journal, a "Book of the Self," a book by and about a single, coherent being. But the notion of the self is itself relatively modern. In fact,
Fothergill, in his important work on the development of the diary form,
suggests that the development of the journal or diary as a genre can be
seen "as a manifestation of the history of 'sensibility'" (Fothergill 1974,
11). Lowenstein, for her part, puts it this way: "Investigating the history
of journal keeping is akin to tracing the development of self-consciousness" (Lowenstein 1987, 87). Thus, as we will see, journals written
before the middle of the sixteenth century are primarily public and communal forms of record keeping rather than documents composed by or
for a singular self. The primary incarnation of the journal as we know it,
the personal journal or diary, will be born of the Renaissance and Reformation habit of mind that places value on the singular, knowing self.
Journals will come of age in the eighteenth and nineteenth centuries as
various strands of journal tradition combine and recombine, and as the
social and literary value of journal keeping is exploited.

    In America, the dramatic increase in literacy rates in the nineteenth
century and widesweeping historical events—the exploration of the
continent, the mass westward expansion, and the Civil War—will help
shape the forms and functions of the American diary. Serious scholarly
discussion of the journal, however, did not begin until the twentieth
century, and much work still needs to be done.

    Robert A. Fothergill, in what is probably the first critical study of
the development of diary traditions in England, *Private Chronicles* (1974),
would agree with Mallon in the epigraph opening this section that there
is no single source of diary writing. He contends, rather, that the journal
or diary as we know it today evolved from the "coalescence of a number
of pre-diary habits into a form that exceeds its component elements" (14).
Fothergill proposes four classes of pre- or proto-diary writing that evolve
into different strands of the journal/diary tradition: public journals,
travel journals, journals of conscience or spiritual journals, and journals
of personal memoranda, akin to commonplace books.[4] Some hint of
these diverse functions can be gleaned from considering the origin and
the history of the two primary terms for the genre: *journal* and *diary*.

    Interestingly enough, both *journal* and *diary* come from similar

Latin roots meaning day or daily, and referring to a day's work, a day's travel, or daily entry of information. While both terms have at one time or another been used to refer to most of the traditions Fothergill classifies, there are subtle differences in their respective connotations and ranges of application. To track the evolution of these terms, we shall turn to the *Oxford English Dictionary*, always keeping in mind that this language resource, like many others, has been generated primarily from a masculine perspective and may thus not be comprehensive.

The word *journal* can be traced to the Old French *journal*, meaning daily, as in *papier journal* (a daybook), from the Late Latin *diurnal*, of or belonging to a day. The first uses of the term in English seem to date at least as far back as the middle of the fourteenth century and refer to religious service books containing the day-hours. From 1355-56, one finds "Ad repar, unius Jurnal" under *journal* in the *Oxford English Dictionary*; and from 1454: "Also I wyte to ye said Thomas my jornenall that I bear in my slefe dayly."

Shortly thereafter the word *journal* is used to refer to travel, either to the itinerary itself (in 1552, Huloet noted an "Itinerary booke wherein is wrytten the dystaunce from place to place, or wherin the expenses in iourney be written, or called otherwise a iournall") or to a record of the traveling ("*Leo's Africa* . . . is . . . nothing else but a large Itinerarium or Journal of his African voiages").[5]

In the area of commerce, the term *journal* is in common use by 1540 to refer to bookkeeping and daily ledgers. "The said Cofferer shall yearly within one month after the expirement of every yeare, make a STETT in his booke called the Journall, for entering any Debentures or other Payments into the same." And in public affairs, the term *journal* comes to be used to refer to records of daily events or transactions by public bodies—the records, for example, of the daily proceedings of Parliament are called *Journals*—or institutions, daily newspapers, and other public periodicals, and for personal records kept for official or private use. In 1610, Holland wrote, in *Camden's Britain*, that "Caesar hath in his Iournels or Day-books [in ephemeridibus] written. . . ." This particular use of the word is still prominent in the common practice of naming important public and academic periodicals *journals*, and in newspapers such as *The Wall Street Journal*.

The term *diary*, while allotted only about one third the space the term *journal* receives in the *Oxford English Dictionary*, also has a venerable etymology. Derived from the Latin root *diari-um*, a word closely related to the journal's *diurnal*, meaning daily or daily allowance, *diary* makes its first appearance, at least according to the *Oxford English Dictionary*, during the Renaissance, slightly later than the first recorded uses of *journal*. It is easy to see why the form *journal*, coming as it does from the French, would have been preferred during the Anglo-Norman period. From the moment of its coinage, however, the term *diary* seems to have been nearly an exact synonym for *journal*, representing, as it did, a daily or regular recording of events both public and private. In fact, in a second entry for *diary*, meaning daily or ephemeral from the Latin *diari-us*, one can detect a hint of the future use of the term to signify a written record, in this instance a travel diary: in 1592, Unton records keeping "a diary memoreal of all the places of our marching and incampinge." By 1605, Bacon is using the term comfortably: "It is . . . an use well recieved in enterprises memorable . . . to keep Dyaries of that which passeth continually." In 1642, reference is made to the "diary of the Parliament," and in 1684 the chronicle of a military campaign is titled "A Relation or Diary of the Siege of Vienna." Synonymity seems to be evidenced by the frequent co-occurrence of *journal* and *diary* within a single phrase as in "a Diary or Journal, as the name imports, containing the Actions of each day," from 1674; or "Goffe kept a journal or diary," from 1765. Even into the late nineteenth century, Jessop, in *The Coming of Friars*, uses the term *diary* to refer to the communal records or commonplace books kept by Medieval monks: "In the thirteenth century men never kept journals or diaries but monasteries did."

While the term *diary* has perhaps not been used to cover quite as wide a range of types of public and commercial writing practices as the term *journal*, it is important to note that *diary* was not coined with the negative associations of triviality, excessive sentimentality, or femininity it now carries for many. *Diary* was used synonymously with *journal* for hundreds of years, and referred to a considerable range of both public and private kinds of writing. In fact, when I tried to look for articles on diaries and journals in the *MLA International Bibliography*, I found *Diary* as a subheading under Prose, along with Essays, Letters, Historiography, and Biography; but *Journal* was not even part of the taxonomy. Indeed, the term *diary* is still used from time to time to refer to public documents or to the recording of public events. When attorneys recently requested ex-President Reagan's personal diaries, they were clearly not interested in intimate chatty reflections, but rather in the record of his meetings and their contents. In a similar, more local, vein, the weekly *Boston Globe* column by reporter Laura Kiernan on major events in New Hampshire is called "New Hampshire Political Diary."

The Four Strands of the Proto-Journal

Certainly the oldest source of the journal has been the wide variety of public journals, including a "range of regular-entry books" either

externally or self-imposed, which are done for their public utility
(Fothergill 1974, 16). These types of writing are, in essence, as old as
writing itself. The earliest clay tablets found in Sumeria, dating from
about 3000 BC, for example, function precisely as journals, containing
ration lists, records of tribute and donations, and lists of divine names
(Lerner 1986, 57). In this sense, Roman household accounts called *Commentari*, Chinese historical chronicles dating from AD 56, documents
like the Anglo-Saxon Chronicles, or even the Bayeux Tapestry have
functioned as communal historical journals (Lowenstein 1987). Writings
of this type include record keeping and accounting, transactions of public bodies, historical and political chronicles, military diaries, ships' logs,
and daily records of military campaigns or scientific expeditions
(although the latter may also be classified as travel journals).

The travel journal is clearly another of the earliest proto-diary
forms. In Japan, from the tenth century on, the travel journal was an
important accompaniment to most travel undertaken by priests and
officials. These official journals often included descriptive and narrative
prose as well as poetry and were a highly regarded genre both for their
literary and for their historical value (Lowenstein 1987, 87-89). Diaries of
exploration and travel—such as those of Marquette and Joliet in 1673
(Dunaway and Evans 1957, 57-59), and the later travel/scientific journals of Lewis and Clarke, Zebulon Pike, John Charles Fremont, and John
J. Audobon (Kagle 1982), would be a critical adjunct to the enterprise of
opening up the Americas. These journals not only offered a wealth of
information on the specific geography, terrain, possible routes, and flora
and fauna, but also conveyed the sense of awe inspired by the scale and
grandeur of the wilderness, a curiosity about the native peoples, and the
alternating emotions of courage, despair, fear, and determination that
accompanied these chroniclers on their explorations.

In Europe, in addition to the logs and journals used by explorers
and military travelers, by the middle of the seventeenth century, the
travel journal was considered an important part of every young gentleman's educational *rite de passage*, The Grand Tour. Francis Bacon, in his
essay, "Of Travel," offers advice to such young travelers on how to
employ the journal properly to develop the powers and habits of observation, description, and reflection that are the natural extension of a
"rationally ordered life" (Fothergill 1974, 15). John Evelyn, for example,
one of the first secular diarists who would be discovered and published
in the early nineteenth century, developed his diary form from the writing habits he had practiced during his trips to the continent in the 1640s
(Fothergill 1974, 15). Indeed, by 1782, John Byng, Fifth Viscount of Torrington, would assert that "Tour writing is the very rage of the times"

(Blythe 1989, 307). Byng would take a dozen tours of England during the next twenty years and keep a travel diary to show his estranged wife that there was another England beyond the overly sophisticated court that his wife and her lover devoted themselves to. Travel diaries would remain "the rage" right up through the nineteenth century, and are still enormously popular today.

Another, older form of regular-entry writing that contributed to what we know as the journal or diary is the commonplace book. The earliest extant work, *A Common-Place Book of the Fifteenth Century*, written by the anonymous resident or residents of a manor house in Sussex, England shows how plastic the form is. Among its contents are prayers, sayings, quotes from the poet Lydgate, puzzles, a saint's life, a religious play, all interspersed with recipes, family accounts, and tracts on manorial law (Mallon 1984, 120-21).

The commonplace book is an early ancestor to the journals of readings, quotes, observations, notes, and drafts that educated people, particularly scholars, writers, and artists, have kept for centuries. It seems that the commonplace book served as a sort of self-education program and was a very common, if not essential, adjunct to the work of scholars, possibly because published books were both rare and expensive until recently. Many of the diarists I have read mentioned starting their commonplace books or keeping them either at the request of tutors or while they were away at school. Thomas Wentworth Higginson, for instance, started his journal the day he entered Harvard at age fourteen, and Henry David Thoreau also kept commonplace books while he was in college.

One of Thoreau's journals contained quotes and observations and was called "Miscellaneous Extracts"; the other held extracts from readings, book reviews, and reading lists (Kagle 1988, 132). Years later, of course, at the encouragement of Emerson, Thoreau began the journals of his maturity, which combine many strands of journal keeping and constitute in the eyes of many his major literary work (Kagle 1988). However, Steven Kagle reports that as early as 1835, Thoreau argued in one of his college essays for the value of these kinds of journals to improve writing and thinking—nearly 150 years before the process movement praised their virtues. "As those pieces which the painter sketches for his own amusement in his leisure hours are often superior to his most elaborate productions, so it is that ideas often suggest themselves to us spontaneously, as it were, far surpassing in beauty those which arise in the mind upon applying ourselves to any particular subject" (qtd. in Kagle 1988, 132). No wonder the commonplace book is the strand of the journal that Don Murray, an early leader of the process movement, feels his own journal most closely approximates.

One other "prime source of the genre" is the spiritual journal or spiritual diary (Fothergill 1974, 18), which is probably linked to earlier Medieval forms of spiritual autobiography, but which, like its secular counterparts, takes on specific forms as it is adapted for use by the non-Conformist, or dissenting, religious groups during the seventeenth century.[6] The Puritans, and later the Quakers, Methodists, and other groups who challenged external authority in matters of personal belief, turned to rigorous spiritual self-examination and assessment, for which they found the diary a very useful tool (Fothergill 1974, 17; Dobbs 1974, 16-19). By the middle of the seventeenth century, "how-to" books such as John Beadle's *The Journal or Diary of a Thankful Christian* (1656), were already available to aid potential practitioners in using the diary to examine their behavior, their conscience, their souls, and their relation to God and his works, and to chart or document the hand of God at work in the world (Fothergill 1974, 17; Kagle 1986, 2). As the Reverend James Hervey (1714-1758) tells himself:

> Compile a secret History of your Heart and Conduct. Take notice of the manner in which your Time is spent & of the strain that runs through your Discourse, how often the former is lost in trifles, how often the latter evaporates in vanity. . . . Register those secret Faults to which none but your own Conscience is privy & none but the all-seeing Eye discerns. Often contemplate yourself in this faithful mirror. (Qtd. in Blythe 1989, 2)

Both George Fox, the founder of the Society of Friends, or the Quakers, and John Wesley, the founder of Methodism, were avid spiritual diarists, Wesley sustaining his journal for a full sixty-six years (1725-1791). Both men encouraged their followers to keep spiritual journals as well. This "great Protestant art form," as Mallon calls it, was not only an extraordinarily popular form of diarizing in the seventeenth century, but it continued to "feed a major tributary stream right through the eighteenth century and into the nineteenth" (Fothergill 1974, 17).

In America, settled primarily by dissenters, the spiritual diary is one of the oldest literary traditions, acting as the central strand of American diary traditions, along with travel diaries, up until the nineteenth century. Most of the renowned colonial American diarists, such as John Winthrop, Samuel Sewell, John Woolman, Michael Wigglesworth, Cotton Mather, and John Adams, will use their diaries to share in this heritage (Kagle 1979). The later Transcendentalists will borrow and adapt this heritage of spiritual diary keeping to explore "the transcendent" both in themselves and in nature (Kagle 1988). The diary of conscience paves the way for secular journals that will also focus on the inner reality of the diarist rather than on the recording or interpreting of external reality.

Pepys and the Personal Journal

What makes the secular personal diary possible in its first real crystallization is the major set of epistemological shifts that accompanied the Renaissance and later the Reformation, which spurred several new forms of thinking and writing from and about the self.

Indeed, Brian Dobbs in his work, *Dear Diary*, points out that Irish scribes in the fourteenth century were already making odd little autobiographical entries in Gaelic in the margins of the texts they were copying. A certain Eugene O'Shiell, for example, recorded for posterity his labored breathing and the phlegm upon him "like a mighty river"; William Magfindgaill noted the torment of drinking water on the Friday of the Passion when there was excellent wine in the house (Dobbs 1974, 13). Over the next five hundred years, the self in the margins will become the text itself.

Ultimately, the personal journal or diary, the essay, the epistolary tradition, and new forms of autobiography were all to be generated out of this important new cast of mind:

> It was only with the Renaissance with its revival of classical learning and the Reformation with its concept of freedom of conscience, that religious and intellectual freedoms reach a stage sympathetic to self expression and made it possible for a man to think of keeping a diary.
>
> The landmark of the new consciousness is not actually a diary but a book of essays by a Frenchman. Written in the 1580's, Montaigne's *Essays* are profoundly original. . . . [H]e turned his attention to his own character and attributes and his own preferences and prejudices, so that Montaigne is as much his own subject as anything on which he writes. (Dobbs 1974, 18)

In a comprehensive bibliographical essay on "The Development of the Essay in English," Louis Wann defines the essay as:

> a PROSE COMPOSITION, primarily INTERPRETIVE in nature but permitting CONSIDERABLE FREEDOM OF STYLE and METHOD, treating ANY SUBJECT that author may choose from a

PERSONAL or LIMITED VIEWPOINT, and revealing, in choice of subject, style, method, or general tone, the PERSONALITY or the LIMITED VIEWPOINT of the author. (Wann 1939, 4).

Tracing the genre from classical times, he asserts that the basic impulse that generates the essay is the impulse "to observe life and to contemplate the meaning of one's own observations" (Wann 1939, 4), the same impulse that generates the secular journal. Indeed, Wann frequently identifies specific journals, such as those by John Evelyn and Samuel Pepys, John Woolman's Quaker diary, the diaries of Romantic and Transcendentalist poets, even Darwin's scientific-expedition journals, as instances of the various types and development of the essay itself. To Montaigne (Michel Eyquem, Seigneur de Montaigne), who "named" the genre when he published his first set of *essais* in 1580, he naturally accords the status of the "Father of the Modern Essay." Montaigne's essays are characterized by their frankness, their discursive and freely associative style, and their constant reflection on the author's own sensibility (Wann 1939, 9), habits of mind that accord quite well with the standard diarizing tendency.

But the connection between the birth of the modern essay and the secular personal journal may indeed be even closer than the similarity of intellectual impulse that drives them. Sir Henry Slingsby (1602-1658), one of the earliest known secular diarists, whose diaries were unfortunately cut off by the English Civil War, presumably decided to keep a journal after hearing of Montaigne's father's practice of keeping some kind of commonplace book or family-chronicle journal.

> [Montaigne's father] kept a journal Book, wherein he day by day registr'd the memories of the historys of his house; a thing pleasant to read, when time began to wear out the Remembrance of them. . . . [My intention is] to sett down in this Book such accidents as befall me, not that I make my study of it, but rather a recreation at vacant times, without observing any time, method, or order in my wrighting, or rather scribbling. (Blythe 1989, 2)

Thus, not only may the form and the function of the modern essay and the modern diary be similar, indeed overlapping, but in some sense, they may have been literally sired by the same "father."

The post-Cartesian world, which placed increasing value on individual experience, empirical evidence, introspection, and expression, soon made room for another important, and related, kind of writing: the novel, whose development will also be associated with women writers and readers. Marcia Landy summarizes the major cultural changes and some of their consequences as follows:

> The modern world, formed out of the contradictions inherent in the Protestant views of the self, of marriage, of economic life, produced new forms of social life and of literature. We have noticed how the *gessellschaft* relations characterize arrangements under capitalist society. In literature, the novel, in its portrayal of bourgeois society, its emphasis on romance and sentiment, on psychology, paved the way for a closer examination of social relations, particularly of male-female relationships. The biography and autobiography, the journal and the diary are inevitable counterparts of the novel. (Landy 1977, 20. See also Fothergill 1974, 22-23)

The personal journal or diary, as it was born out of the dramatic changes in culture, intellectual inquiry, and self-consciousness that occurred during the Renaissance, is therefore a sibling of the other important prose genres, such as the essay, autobiography, and, later, the novel, that would come into being during that period. The journal would carry with it the critical habits of mind associated with close observation of and reflection on the physical world, the social world, and the inner world of sense and sensibility.

While favorable epistemological winds made the secular personal journal possible, it has been almost universally acknowledged, at least since the nineteenth century, that Samuel Pepys was the man who "condemned all previous diary keeping to be the pre-history of the genre" (Fothergill 1974, 13). Actually, John Evelyn had started his diaries somewhat earlier (1641-1706), and they would be published a few years before Pepys's, but Evelyn's diaries, exacting and remarkable as they are, a veritable "verbal photograph" both of the age and the events he actually experienced, are not as powerful, or nearly as colorful, as Pepys's, according to most scholars.[7]

It is Samuel Pepys, then, and nearly a hundred years later, James Boswell, who will stamp their imprimatur on the diary or personal journal: the "book of the self," the "imprint of a man's being-in-the-world," as Fothergill critically defines it with a typical bias toward his sex (Fothergill 1974, 43).

Even though histories of the personal journal have been written that show how the journal form has taken on the literary and cultural characteristics of each age, for most twentieth-century literary scholars of the journal (most of them male), it is almost as if the diary form not only began, but also reached its apogee with Pepys and Boswell. The heights will be difficult indeed for other diarists (particularly female ones) to scale. Dobbs writes, for instance, following the lead of the first important scholars and compilers, notably Lord Arthur Ponsonby and William Matthews:

> And it is only those few, like Pepys and Boswell, whose diaries deserve to be published *in toto*. Their diaries, even allowing for the disadvantages of the diffuse nature of the genre, have achieved the status of great literature. Of precious few can that be said. (Dobbs 1974, 6)

Lord Ponsonby himself penned this encomium to Samuel Pepys in his introduction to *English Diaries* (1923): "By general consent the diary of Samuel Pepys may be awarded the first place among English diaries. It fulfills all the conditions of what a diary should be" (qtd. in Fothergill 1974, 42). Here is Thomas Mallon, starting his first chapter, "Chroniclers," in much the same vein:

> The idea of the diary as carrier of the private, the everyday, the intriguing, the sordid, the sublime, the boring—in short, a chronicle of everything—seems to have occurred accidentally, and not before Samuel Pepys began what may be the best-known diary of all. If he cannot be said to have invented the form as we now think of it, he nearly did, just as he more or less perfected it within months of starting his book on January 1, 1660. (Mallon 1984, 1-2)

Just what is so wonderful about Pepys's diary that it should become the paradigm for all personal diaries? To answer this we must consider a bit more history. That is, while Pepys was writing in the seventeenth century, he was not discovered, deciphered, and finally published until the nineteenth century (in 1825). Diary writing was a genre in many respects unaware of itself as such until the early nineteenth century, as most diaries were not published or circulated widely until then.[8] Various diaries were, however, well-read and well-known within certain social circles much earlier.

   With the discovery and publication of John Evelyn's diaries in 1818, however, diaries suddenly became very popular, both to read and to write. "Diary keeping was in the news and people may have felt keen to emulate their distinguished predecessors" (Dobbs 1974, 224). John Letts, a stationer, was producing a single Lett's Diary for business transactions in 1809. By 1836, aided by developments in print technology and the availability of inexpensive paper, he was publishing twenty-eight different diary formats (which would also help shape the form and structure of diaries written in those books) and selling several thousand diaries annually.

It was the Victorians, then, who initially found Pepys so engaging and elevated him to his status as a classic diarist. Several features of Pepys's writing appealed to those mostly male Victorians who savored his work; they continue to appeal to the critics of today. Fothergill argues that the chief pleasure of Pepys's diary is its commodiousness, Pepys's ability to render "all his experiences, from the most public to the most private, in the same key, as it were, treating all the contents of a day impartially" (Fothergill 1974, 13). While such a diary may not have the personal intensity of the more "one-sidedly confessional diaries of the period," Pepys integrates a certain "range and variety of experience" that can't be outdone in Fothergill's mind (Fothergill 1974, 13). Here is a sample of the kind of entry Fothergill might have had in mind. It was written on 13 October 1660:

> . . . I went out to Charing-cross, to see Major-General Harrison hanged, drawn, and quartered—which was done there—he looking as cheerful as any man could do in that condition. He was presently cut down, and his head and heart shown to the people, at which there was great shouts of joy. . . . Thus it was my chance to see the King [Charles I] beheaded at White-hall, and to see the first blood shed in revenge for the blood of the King at Charing-cross. From thence to my Lord's and took Captain Cuttance and Mr. Sheply to the Sun taverne and did give them some oysters. After that I went by water home, where I was angry with my wife for her things lying about, and in my passion kicked the little fine Baskett, which I bought her in Holland, and broke it, which troubled me after I had done it. Within all the afternoon, setting up shelfes in my study. At night to bed. (Pepys 1970, 265)

However, my sense of Pepys's appeal is also consonant with Brian Dobbs's view and Thomas Mallon's: Pepys was enormously attractive to the Victorian mind, as he is to current critics, not only because he was a "Restoration success story" and a self-made, genially successful man (Dobbs 1974, 53-57), but also because he was "a great booby" (Mallon 1984, 5), and most specifically because of his constant, candid, and quite graphic depictions of sexual exploits and pecadillos. Indeed, the fact that his journals are written partly in shorthand, partly in dog Latin, an odd Frenchified code, in order not to be read by his wife and other members of his family, only makes them more attractive. Both Dobbs and Mallon, contemporary critics, devote major parts of their discussions of Pepys to this aspect of his diaries, although they explain their interest in somewhat different ways. Dobbs revels in Pepys's candor, which he insists is *not* tainted by smuttiness:

> In our own post-Freudian times, there is something infinitely refreshing about Pepys' Chaucerian frankness. He treats his continuing sexual appetite, his momentary bodily disorder, his defecatory and urinary functions, his wife's menstrual discomforts, and his erotic dreams of Lady Castlemaine, all with such openness and in such matter-of-fact terms that even if the details would win him no friends in polite drawing-rooms, he is never offensive in the slightest. There is no smut, no snigger behind the hand, no desire to do anything but to set down the truth without self-deception, and this, remember, in an age of almost unparalleled license in the court, and its social adjunct, the theatre. (Dobbs 1974, 60-61)

Mallon unabashedly enjoys the smuttiness that Dobbs denies:

> Goodness knows Elizabeth Pepys has her hands full, mostly, because her husband's always are—of the pliant flesh of servant girls and married ladies about the town. . . . Of course, one needn't be bilingual to figure out what he does with Mrs. Martin on June 3, 1666: "Did what je voudrais avec her, both devante and backwards, which is also muy bon plazer." Or what happens between him and Deb on March 31, 1668: "Yo did take her, the first time in my life, sobra mi genu and di poner mi mano sub her jupes and toca su thigh." . . . When you're twelve and someone offers to show you a dirty postcard, you're interested. But when you're told it's a French dirty postcard, then boy, you're really interested. In matters of the flesh, Pepys was permanently twelve. (Mallon 1984, 4)

Or, as Mallon remarks later on the character of Pepys's diaries, "'Mens cuiusque is est quisque'—that's his motto on the bookplates. It should have been 'Did poner mi mano sub her jupe'!" (Mallon 1984, 292).

Given that Pepys is said to be the paradigm for the personal journal, and Boswell and several other men are said to be its major practitioners, we are almost no closer to understanding the ways in which women might be associated with the personal journal than we were before we started our study of the history of the journal. The reason for this is quite simple. As we have seen repeatedly with regard to men's and women's discourse, not only have men written the majority of public discourses, they also have been the ones to decide which ones to save and why, which ones will become public, or even literary, and why. Much of the work on diaries and journals to date is a product of the same oppositions between dominant and muted, public and private voices, and the same time-worn assumption that the masculine case is generic in all discourse.

The standard diary literature, as we've already begun to see, from compilers and bibliographers such as Ponsonby and Matthews and commentators and critics such as Fothergill, Dobbs, Mallon, and Kagle, tends to be a series of discourses by male critics primarily about male diarists. Female diarists, while not excluded completely, are simply not given much attention in the development of the conceptual frameworks and categories that define diary scholarship or in the establishment of criteria for evaluating the worth or literary value of particular works. Nor are the numbers of women's diaries written or preserved represented in a meaningful way.[9]

For example, when I checked William Matthews's massive annotated bibliography of both British and American published and manuscript diaries from 1442 to 1942 (1980), I found that he includes a few very early women diarists. But, while Matthews lists such figures as Lady Grace Mildmay (1570), Lady Margaret Hoby (1599), Lady (Anne Clifford) Pembroke (1616), and Mrs. Alice Thornton (1625), all of whom were writing considerably before Evelyn and Pepys, almost none of these women are discussed in the major histories of the diary. And the one woman diarist who does receive mention gets very short shrift. All in all, very few women are listed, either as representatives of the British or the American traditions; in his work on unpublished American manuscripts (1945), Matthews lists only six women out the first two hundred diarists. While it is quite possible that there were fewer women diarists at the very beginning of the tradition, it is highly improbable that the numbers listed in the traditional bibliographic works are an accurate reflection of women's participation in a diary tradition, as we'll see shortly.

Interacting with subtle exclusion, the criteria and descriptive frames applied to works by the important men in the field have continued to efface the presence of women's diary traditions. Lord Arthur Ponsonby, the first important compiler of diaries working in the early twentieth century, preferred the diaries that have some inherent comedic appeal, a criterion that is certain to exclude many, if not most women's diaries. Others favor diaries written over a large part of the life span, which would require the constant modicum of leisure that fewer women than men have ever had. Consider, too, for a moment, the effect that Pepys and Boswell, Byrd, Sewell, Mather, Adams, Darwin, and Audobon must have had as the standards for the genre. How many women lived the very public kinds of lives these men lived? How many women could have afforded, in any age, the supposedly perfect impartiality towards public and private subjects, the brash, but genial, display of ego, the autonomous and coherent sense of self and self-confidence with language that these men exemplified? And how many women could or would have risked the comfortable and graphic sexual candor these men engage in?

Fothergill, who has written the most fully developed theoretical work to date, discusses several female diarists in his work on the development of the journal as a form of "serial autobiography," yet five of his six "milestone" diarists are men. And while Boswell's candor is applauded by Fothergill, the personal commentary in the diary of Hester Thrale, Boswell's contemporary and also the author of a work of social and biographical miscellany concerning Samuel Johnson, is treated as too private, sentimental, even "histrionic," by the same commentator (Fothergill 1974, 31). Fanny Burney, the early novelist and noted diarist, appears during what Fothergill calls a "blank period," and he considers her "transitional" (Fothergill 1974, 32). He does think that Katherine Mansfield, Virginia Woolf, and Ivy Jacquier might have been used as the representative figures for the early twentieth-century personal journal—the serious exploration of the psyche coming out of the tradition of the *journal intime*—a journal form developed by yet another woman, George Sand. In comparison to Barbellion, however, Fothergill's choice of a representative figure, he finds that "they lack, in their published state at least, his organic consistency" (Fothergill 1974, 37). That is, they have been, in essence, too edited (as though that were a fault of the diarist rather than the editors). Only Anaïs Nin, whose diary becomes "the crucible of consciousness" itself, is allowed to be the final capstone of the twentieth-century diary tradition.

Dobbs also sprinkles women here and there in his discussion, and at the end of his book, he devotes a chapter to "The Female of the Species," which naturally suggests that female diarists are the exception, an anomalous case to be handled at the end, after the real work on diaries is done. Even Mallon's most recent study treats the whole tradition of girl and adolescent female diarists as a form of "confessional" writing, and his discussion has the effect of trivializing what is actually a rich, elaborate, and poorly understood journal tradition (see Jane Dupree Begos 1987).

Kagle's important series of works on *American Diary Literature*, for example, would be more properly titled "American Men's Diary Literature." They focus mostly on male diarists and, like many other of the texts written by men, while offering critical information about the historical development of diary traditions and the effects of important historical and political events, they still tend to use categories and criteria based primarily on male public (or public-male) experience. In his first book, *American Diary Literature, 1620-1799*, for example, Kagle treats the spiritual diary, three kinds of diaries of occasion or incident (travel diaries, diaries of romance and courtship, and war diaries), and what he calls "life diaries," which "transcend the limitations of function and incident" (Kagle 1979, 142). No women are included at all as major representatives of either the spiritual diary or the life diary. From time to time, however, Kagle will add that someone's wife, daughter, or sister had also kept a diary of this type. Only one woman is included from the travel-diary category (Sarah Kemble Knight), one as a civilian war diarist (Margaret Morris), and two, of course, from the section on courtship and romance (Sally Wister and Anne Home Livingston). Only four women out of thirty principal diarists appear to have written journals worthy of consideration in colonial America. In Kagel's next two volumes on early and late nineteenth-century American diary literature, the numbers of women represented improve somewhat (which suggests a "feminization" of the diary tradition), but the categories still favor the public, more male-dominated types of diaries.

Even the most recent book on diaries I could find, an engaging book of diary excerpts called simply (generically) *The Pleasures of Diaries: Four Centuries of Private Writing* (1989) by Ronald Blythe, treats only British diaries, most of them written by men. In his grouping of diary extracts into thirteen or so categories, women are well represented in categories such as Artist, Love, The Difficult Marriage, Sickness, and Despair and Death; they are poorly represented in most of the other categories and not represented at all in three of them. In part, the larger proportions of women in the categories dealing with emotions and relationships may be an accurate reflection of the muted discursive practices of women, but no discussion is given to those differences, and even the labelling of the categories tends to trivialize them. Also, as we will see shortly, women have written every type of journal, but they are less likely to be acknowledged either in the more public forms or in the muted and privatized traditions.

Thus, two overlapping sets of difficulties prevent us from seeing clearly how women have contributed to, and ultimately come to be a central part of, the diary tradition in the twentieth century. The first is that the discourse about diaries and journals, until recently, has been carried on by males about males, using male criteria for evaluating works, which has marginalized or elided women's diary traditions. The second problem, a related one, is that men's diaries have generally been considered more important and thus have been more frequently preserved.

One recent and important reason for the presence of gaps in the discourse about journals, is that New Criticism, the most important literary criticism of the first half of the twentieth century, placed enormous value on autonomous, self-contained, formal, and deliberately artful forms of writing, while devaluing several other kinds of writing, including diaries and journals:

> Memoirs, diaries, personal essays, letters—forms in which women writers have excelled—were increasingly considered subliterary genres, except for those works that had been acknowledged as literature for so long that their status was secure. Hence Franklin's *Autobiography*, but not that of Linda Brent, Elizabeth Cady Stanton, or Mary Hunter Austin; Emerson's or Thoreau's essays, but not those of Margaret Fuller. (Rosenfeldt 1982, 21)

Since the 1970s, however, critics, including poststructuralists, psychoanalytic critics, feminist critics, and reader-response critics, have begun to expose the implicit ideology of the literary genre and canonicity as elite (upper- or middle-class), European, white, heterosexual, and male. These investigations, both in composition and in literary studies, have reopened the questions of the boundaries between public and private, literature and literacy, and between traditional and nontraditional forms of discourse. These questions are helping us to sort out the status of the journal as a marginalized set of discourses, with women's journal traditions marginal even to those.

Women's Journals and the Problem of Preservation

In addition to the workings of literary canonicity, the conditions under which women's journals have been preserved or published have also worked to blur and trivialize women's journal traditions.

First we must look at the question of whether women writing journals or diaries really were exceptions to the rule until recently. We know, for example, that fewer women were literate than men, which certainly precluded some women from writing a journal; but we also know that there were increasing numbers of literate women, many of whom wanted to give shape to their world and the worlds of their minds in some form of writing. For them, the privatized writing of a journal was certainly going to be better tolerated than more public, more prestigious, more masculine forms of writing.

We also know that much of what has been reconstructed as the history of the journal has had to rely on either published journals or preserved journals. Historically, women's journals have had much dimmer likelihood of undergoing either process. Penelope Franklin, author of a recent book on women's diaries, *Private Pages: Diaries of American Women 1830s-1970s* (1986), recalls her search for women's diaries:

> What I found amazed me. The vast majority of published journals were those of men. The thousands of unpublished women's diaries were in archives across the country—thousands more, I realized, were in attics like mine. I noticed that the men's diaries published were often tales of exploration, war, politics, or adventure; or were those of famous literary or historical figures.
>
> The women's diaries published were sometimes by a famous woman, but very often they were by the wife, mother, or sister of a famous man. Since women weren't for the most part climbing mountains or running for office, no one had considered their personal diaries particularly interesting. (Franklin 1986, xiv)

Archivist and scholar, Elizabeth Meese, like most women working with women's nontraditional materials, has encountered the same phenomenon: "Public libraries, historical societies, attics and basements are frequently better sources of women's manuscripts than are the rare book rooms and archives of larger research libraries" (Meese 1982, 41). And even when women's journals, letters, or papers are preserved in libraries or other public places, they are frequently cataloged under male family names. In essence they are saved because of their relation to some man. Varina Howell Davis's fascinating journals are filed under her husband's name, Jefferson Davis. Worse still, Julia Peterkin, a Pulitzer prize-winning writer, was found to have her letters to a lesser-known male writer filed under *his* name (Meese 1982, 41). As Harriet Blodgett points out, Mary Shelley's early diaries were considered valuable only because they shed light on her husband. And the diaries of Claire Clairmont, Shelley's sister-in-law, were preserved and ultimately published solely for her connection with the Shelley family (Blodgett 1988, 1-2).

Related to the issue of preservation is the problem of literal destruction (severe editing or outright destruction) of women's journals, either by the author herself or by those who had possession of a journal after the death of the author, usually a family member or the executor of the estate. While it's clear that some men have destroyed parts of their journals (often early journals) or have been overly edited, the reading I've done suggests that far more women's journals have met with radical surgery or untimely death. Since women have often committed to journals the very sorts of things that would not have been allowed to become a part of public discourse, it's quite understandable that many women would not want their journals read by others even after their deaths, and that they therefore would be likely to destroy parts or all of them or to request that they be destroyed. Katherine Mansfield, for example, destroyed all her early diaries (Willy 1964, 31. See Blodgett 1988, 44-45 for a longer list). Commonly, however, it appears that women's journals are either edited beyond recognition, or destroyed entirely, by presumably well-intentioned family members, under the guise of protecting the woman. Equally likely, however, these family members and friends are protecting themselves or the dominant world view the diaries may have challenged. While Pepys and Boswell and Scott appear on the pages of their diaries in all their naked splendor, Fanny Burney's, Elizabeth Wynn's (sixty-eight volumes pruned to three), and even Queen Victoria's journals have been heavily edited. They are littered with fig leaves, one might say. Fothergill mentions several other female diaries that might have been excellent, but that were "too edited." After Caroline Fox, a well-known nineteenth-century Quaker diarist, died, her sister Anna Maria allowed a one-volume edition of her diaries to be published, then methodically burned the twelve original volumes, "presumably taking the view that discretion in family affairs was more important than literary or social history" (Dobbs 1974, 204). This process is still happening, according to Eloise Bell, who teaches a course on women's journals in which students do their own archival work in the community. As one student discovered:

> A woman of eighty-five had custody of some thirty six years worth of day-by-day journals written by her mother, an early Iowa pioneer and farmer. The journals were not merely health-and-weather jottings but considered, thoughtful entries. The aging daughter—her mother was dead, of course—was going through volume by volume, copying out important birth and death dates, and then methodically burning the journals, because she believed such books were private. (Bell 1985, 171)

Husbands and brothers have also played a pernicious role in the process. Genial Pepys himself was not as charitable regarding his wife's candor in her journals as history has been regarding his. His wife Elizabeth made the mistake of reading aloud to hubby Samuel a somewhat rancorous account of their marriage and her grievances. He admits in his diary that the account was quite honest, but he grabs it from her and tears it up anyway, along with many of her other papers (Dunaway and Evans 1957, 513). Jane Carlyle, wife of the essayist Thomas Carlyle, remarked at the beginning of her first extant diary: "I remember Charles Buller saying of the Duchess of Praslin's murder, 'What could a poor fellow do with a wife who kept a journal but murder her'" (qtd. in Rainer 1978, 44). While Thomas Carlyle did not murder his wife, he did indeed destroy several of his wife's diaries, and she herself presumably destroyed others (Rainer 1978, 307). Leonard Woolf literally dismembered Virginia Woolf's diaries (though they were later somewhat reconstructed); Ted Hughes burned up "the bits the children should not see" when editing Sylvia Plath's journals; and John Middleton Murray excised significant parts of Katherine Mansfield's journals (Caws 1986, 51-53). Henry James was opposed to the idea of his talented sister Alice's journals being published, even privately, after her death (Caws 1986, 53). Pepys's and Boswell's transgressions, indiscretions, and opinions, even Oscar Wilde's, Evelyn Waugh's, H. L. Mencken's, and Benjamin Haydon's vicious satire and occasional ranting don't seem to be nearly as dangerous as any of these women recounting some semblance, as reticent as it might be, of what they perceived to be the truth about their lives.

As a final comparison, consider the rather different treatment the journals of Boswell and Pepys have received at the hands of posterity. When Boswell died in 1795, he left an enormous number of private papers, including his journals, which were very candid not only in terms of commentary about those around him, but also, like Pepys's, in terms of their sexual frankness. The executors, not wanting to offend the Boswell family, and not wanting to give his arch antagonist, Macauley, any more ammunition, but also wanting to provide for "posterity's claim," made the studied decision to postpone any public release of the journals until Boswell's son was old enough to decide their fate. Unlike women's private writings, Boswell's private, even controversial and indecorous papers, were treated with respect and decorum, and saved for public posterity by the family. Ironically, it was two of Boswell's great-grandaughters in the early twentieth century who rediscovered and saved the papers (Dobbs 1974, 65-67).

It is also difficult to imagine a woman's journal being preserved in the same manner as Pepys's. Pepys left his papers to the library at Magdalene College, Cambridge, his alma mater. For over a hundred years, his six leather-bound volumes sat quietly and safely in that revered location waiting for someone to break the odd little transcription code he had used. Indeed, just as Pepys might have suspected, someone did become interested in those eccentric, seemingly unreadable books, and a poor undergraduate named John Smith was set to work for three straight years, ten hours a day, to break the code and transcribe the entire six volumes (Dobbs 1974, 50). What care. What reverence. No wonder Pepys's journal survived.

While it is possible, then, that somewhat fewer women wrote journals in the 1600s and 1700s because of the different literacy rates for men and women, certainly far more women have kept journals than has been recorded in the public, primarily male, histories. And in spite of the treatment so many women's journals have received, those thousands of extant unpublished women's journals Penelope Franklin refers to speak to other traditions of journal keeping and journal care. Take the case of Martha Moore Ballard's journal. Begun at age fifty in 1785 by a midwife in Hallowell, Maine and spanning twenty-seven years, the journal (several hand-sewn books) passes to her daughter Dolly, who gives it to her daughter, who gives it to her niece, Mary Hobart, in the early twentieth century. Mary Hobart wants to be an obstetrician, and the journal from her great-grandaunt midwife empowers her in her quest. The diary becomes for her such a precious legacy that she has it beautifully bound, and has a mahogany box made especially for its safekeeping (Ulrich 1987, 1990).[10] The fate of Martha Moore Ballard's journal suggests that women's journals were important, not necessarily in the public forum, but rather in the more muted social, domestic, and familial networks in which women's discourse has flourished. While the male journal-keeping tradition has been marked by more public discourses and functions, women's journal traditions have tended to develop, as with most of their discourse, in the privatized social and domestic sphere.

Women and the Personal Journal Tradition

Women's diaries provide invaluable testimonials to individual female lives and reveal patterns of female existence over many centuries. Moreover, they constitute a literary tradition of female serial writing. The serial form women use may parallel that of men's diaries; the topics, attitudes, and self-concepts differ from men's because the interests, status, and lives of the diarists have done so.
   —Harriet Blodgett, *Centuries of Female Days*

Even the male critics I have been discussing will often grant, paradoxically, in a paragraph or sentence somewhere in their work, that the
diary, for example, is a "genre to which women have always felt especially drawn" (Mallon 1984, 19). Thomas Mallon reminds us that
Japanese women were confiding to their "pillow books" centuries
before diary keeping came to the West, and that "the diary was, after all,
available to them for expression in centuries when their attempts to
practice other forms of literature—say, produce a play—were considered presumptuous or silly" (Mallon 1984, 19). Brian Dobbs agrees that
diaries have provided through the ages a "sympathetic ear for women
to confide opinions which have been considered too outrageous for the
society they lived in" and an outlet for the "human qualities of wit, perception, and sensitivity" (Dobbs 1974, 178). He concludes that the "qualities that were shown in the boudoir rather than in the drawing room
and demonstrated only in the privacy of the journal have been society's
loss but unquestionably the diary's gain" (Dobbs 1974, 220). Dobbs
understands, at least tacitly without making them his focus, the domi-
nant/muted, public/private distinctions that have operated in even
some of the most private texts of one's life. The questions remain: What
has been society's loss with regard to the journals of women? What has
been the diary's gain?

It is a common occurrence in research to come upon a problem or
a set of issues and then discover that others are working on it, too. Some
feminist scholars and critics have recently begun to sketch out the con-
tours of women's journal-keeping traditions, and I have had the good
luck to discover two excellent books on American and British women's
personal diaries. First, I came across Margo Culley's *A Day at a Time: The
Diary Literature of American Women from 1764 to the Present* (1985), an
anthology of diary excerpts that includes an important introductory
chapter on the development of American women's journal traditions.
Just recently, I located Harriet Blodgett's wonderful book, *Centuries of
Female Days: English Women's Private Diaries* (1989), the first full-length
critical work on English women's diary traditions.[11]

Women's Journal Traditions: Dominance and Muteness

Not surprisingly, women's journal traditions manifest the same
complex, overlapping, muted, yet distinctive, set of relations with male
journal traditions that we have seen in discourse generally and in the
discourse about journals specifically. As Blodgett puts it: "Englishwomen's diaries may be part of a larger historical tradition, but they
also constitute a tradition of their own" (Blodgett 1988, 22). Thus, while

women have kept journals of the same general types that men have kept—including public journals of commerce and politics, travel journals, commonplace books, scientific and naturalist's journals, spiritual journals, and journals of personal memorabilia—they have used, combined, and adapted these genres somewhat differently as a consequence of their different discursive and social positions and needs (Blodgett 1988, 21-24).

For example, while the standard diary literature points to Evelyn and Pepys as the "fathers of the secular diary," Lady Margaret Hoby (1571-1633), writing a full sixty years before Pepys, might prove a more representative parent for a central strand of women's diary traditions (Blodgett 1988, 26-27), as she intuitively creates the domestic diary. A Puritan, Lady Hoby, starts her formulaic diary of conscience to record her moral and spiritual activity, failings, and progress. Yet it expands to incorporate more and more of her personal and domestic life and soon becomes more of a record of her stewardship here on earth, or of her "domestic" relationship to Providence, than a spiritual examination (Fothergill 1974, 19). In the following entry, written 5 October 1603, Lady Hoby describes a walk with her husband and mother and the wonder of red and white roses in bloom:

> Mr. Hoby, my Mother, and my selfe, went to the dalls this day; we had in our Gardens a second sommer, for Hartechokes bare twisse, whitt Rosses, read Roses; and we hauing sett a musk Rose the winter before, it bare flowers now. I thinke the like hath seldom binn seene: it is a great frute yeare all ouer. (Blodgett 1988, 29)

Blodgett suggests that Hoby "anticipates much of what is to come in women's diaries" (Blodgett 1988, 30). Hoby's diary entries convey well the nature of daily life for many women of her time, and indeed women for centuries to come: "praying, attending church, performing chores—and hers were endless, spanning house and estate, doctoring, entertaining visitors, and taking conjugal walks" (Blodgett 1988, 30). She and other early female diarists—such as Lady Grace Mildmay (1551-1620), whose diaries span the years from 1570 to 1617, and Lady Anne Clifford (1590-1676), who kept a diary from 1616 to 1619—were initiating a central diary tradition for women, often adapted from the combination of the spiritual journal and the journal of personal memorabilia, that would integrate and confirm women's perceptions of domestic, social, and spiritual life, and invoke a sense of self very different from that of the large and lovely ego of Pepys for centuries to come.

Sara Heller Mendelson's study (1985) of twenty-three seventeenth-century women's diaries from the Stuart era is consonant with Blodgett's findings on the early forms and functions of women's diary traditions and their long-term legacy. Looking at the journals of six middle-class, thirteen gentry, and four aristocratic women, she also notes how similar their lives were, being centered on domestic work and activity. Like Blodgett, she asserts that women wrote in all the major journal types, yet she, too, sees the synthesis of the daily-activities log and the spiritual journal as a characteristic type of diary writing for seventeenth-century women.

Unlike most men's diaries, the women's diaries studied by Blodgett and Mendelson, and later Culley and Huff, also suggest that the experience of female life as it is rendered in most journals tends to be constituted in three distinct and critical phases for the vast majority of women, in accordance with the primary cultural roles they are assigned: maidenhood, marriage and motherhood, then often widowhood. Their lives seem to be centered on the cycles of birth, maturation, courtship, marriage, pregnancy, child care, illness, and death. Indeed, women not only wrote about these critical shifts in their status and experience, they often start, stop, or shift the nature of their diary keeping in response to these changes, so that the diaries themselves begin to take on the shape of the women's lives.

Mendelson also suggests that these spiritual/domestic journals would offer women, as they did Lady Margaret Hoby, ways to organize and interpret their lives in a positive manner, providing satisfying explanations for both domestic and more global events, and transforming their rigorous, task-filled days into a kind of "higher drama."

These early diaries already suggest a different orientation to the self from that of male diarists, and to domestic, social, and intellectual life. This difference may be best considered by looking at two primary functions of women's journals, which take into account women's muted relation to discourse. First, I want to consider some of the ways women's journals can be said to be muted or to serve the discursive needs or desires of others, as women's discourse often does. Second, I want to discuss the ways in which the journals and diaries of women have both indirectly and directly allowed for the creation, confirmation, or reconstruction of a sense of a positive and knowing self, with its own voice or voices, in the "wild zone" of the journal. Bear in mind, however, that the motivations and functions of journal keeping for women have often entailed a combination of personal and social utility, and that journals kept by a single person also have the tendency to shift in form and function over time.

Women's Muted Journal Traditions

Given that women have been both implicitly and explicitly discouraged as speakers and writers and have been socialized to focus on
the needs or interests of others, it's not surprising that the diaries many
women have produced over the centuries show the traces of women's
mutedness in their content and/or their functions, which often serve the
dominant discourse community's needs. While women's journals tell us
more about the lives of women in earlier times than most other kinds of
documents, many women's journals, up until the early twentieth century, are still "inclined to be reticent and inhibited, candid neither about
[women's] bodies nor about their minds and feelings, neither self-reflec-
tive nor self-revealing, except minimally and inadvertently" (Blodgett
1988, 41). Many women diarists treat illnesses and pregnancy circum-
spectly and rarely mention other aspects of female physicality, like sex
or menstruation, especially during the Victorian era.[12]

Even so, there clearly are gaps and silences in the women's diaries
due to women's muted discursive status; women were trained not to
talk or to think about their bodies; they were trained to consider other
people's feelings rather than their own, and "the very language they use
may silence them" (Blodgett 1988, 52-54. See also Bunkers 1987 and
Cooper 1987). Finally, as Blodgett and others have pointed out, few
women could be sure that their diaries would not be read, and therefore, they censored themselves. From the very beginning, as with the
Stuart-era women Mendelson studied, many women have tried to keep
their diaries as private or as secret as possible, destroying them themselves when they feared they might die in childbirth or requesting that
their husbands or families destroy them at their death. Remember too,
Jane Carlyle's remark that it was no wonder the Duchess of Praslin had
been murdered by her husband because she had been keeping a diary.

Aware of the cultural pronouncements against them as writers,
many women apologized about their writing, even in their journals
(Blodgett 1988, 21-22); some women used their journals to accommodate, to make some kind of sense of their inferior status and prescibed
cultural roles rather than to challenge those views.

Looking at the seventeenth-century diaries, for example, Mendelson found a whole array of both happy and unhappy marriages, but
noted that a frequent theme in the diaries was the women's use of the
journal to exhort themselves to the religious teaching of "wifely obedi-
ence." They would often reproach themselves for "marital insubordina-
tion," as in the Countess of Warwick's humble admission that she had
talked back to her husband over some minor matter, and would try to

be more restrained from then on (Mendelson 1985, 194). Two hundred years later, in December 1837 and January 1838, Mary Richardson Walker is using her journal to help her to accommodate herself to her marriage, but she is also aware that her difficulties may not be all her fault:

> Should feel so much better if Mr W. would only treat me with some cordiality. It is so hard to please him I almost despair of ever being able to. If I stir, it is forwardness, if I am still it is inactivity.
> I am almost certain that more is expected of me than can be had of one woman.
> . . .
> Last night we were disturbed by the howling of the wolves. Baked some biscuits. The first cooking I have done since I was married. Mr. Walker remarked that I had done very well. May God help me to walk discreetly and please my husband. (Bank 1979, 72)

Women's diary traditions bear other traces of mutedness as well, however, as women's diary keeping has tended to focus on others rather than on the women diarists themselves and to service the social discursive needs of the dominant discourse community. As Culley writes:

> Many eighteenth- and nineteenth-century diaries were semi-public documents intended to be read by an audience. Those kept by men, in particular, record a public life or are imbued with a sense of public purpose or audience. (Culley 1985, 3)

If we grant that, as Culley asserts, the majority of men's diaries have been public by virtue of their author, content, or purpose, and that many women's diaries, while generally not fully public, have not necessarily been fully private either, then what were their functions? And who were their audiences?

Women's Journal Traditions: Public and Private

In fact, the terms *public* and *private* (or *personal*) don't really account very well for the complex possible relations among diarists, their subjects, and their audiences. For example, publication is no guarantee that a journal or diary was intended to be public, since it is common to publish private diaries after the death of the writer. And do the terms *private* and *personal* have to do with the subject matter alone, or with the function of the journal, as "by and for the self," regardless of content? Does it matter whether the journal is ever read or shared?

While these questions are equally valid for both men's and women's journals or diaries, the answers to them differ rather significantly depending on the sex of the diarist. In the area of subject or content, men could choose much more easily whether they wanted to focus on public events, personal events or activities, or the inner life of the mind. So their journals were more likely to be private or personal by choice. Even their personal diaries, however, were more likely than women's to be published or taken up into the public world.

Since men had a much wider range of audiences across the public/private continuum, they could direct their journals to themselves, to intimates and colleagues, to the public, or even to "future generations," their remote and abstract "posterity." Thoreau writes, for example:

> My Journal is that of me which would else spill over and run to waste—gleanings from the field in which action I reap. I must not live for it, but in it for the Gods—They are my correspondent to whom I daily send off this sheet post paid. I am clerk in their counting room & at evening transfer the account from day book to ledger. (Qtd. in Kagle 1988, 133)

In contrast, it might be more useful to say that women's journals tend to be "privatized" rather than simply private by choice. Thus, for example, while both male and female children were encouraged by their parents and tutors to keep journals in centuries past to monitor their behavior, correct moral lapses, and use their time wisely (Huff 1988, xxiv)—or as DuPree Begos puts it in the case of little Marjorie Fleming writing her journal in 1807 in Scotland, "to correct both their spelling and their character" (DuPree Begos 1987, 71)—girls and boys would ultimately be socialized and educated to quite different journal traditions as adults.

For example, formal schooling was often the impetus for some form of academic journal keeping, usually in the form of the journal/commonplace book, but many fewer women were encouraged toward that kind of schooling or literacy experience. Published blank journals with genteel names like "A Ladies Diary" directed women toward journal keeping as an observance of the social graces. Etiquette books in the eighteenth and nineteenth centuries offer specific instruction for females on keeping journals, usually promoting industry, and counting one's daily blessings, while cautioning vigilance against moral and personal flaws (Blodgett 1988, 24-25, 37-38, 63-64. See also Morgan

1987 and Schinto 1987). Since many girls' academies were more like finishing schools than academic institutions, even those girls lucky enough
to attend schools might be encouraged in diary keeping primarily as a
form of etiquette and social grace. Such was the case, for example, for
little Catherine van Schaak, who writes in her journal for the summer of
1809 about her daily activities, which included journaling, quilting,
grammar, and psalm singing:

> Thursday attended school in the Morning—recited a lesson in
> Grammar and painted. In the evening went to Conference. Satur-
> day morning, wrote journal, in the afternoon quilted for Miss
> Anne Baldwin. After tea took a short walk, in the evening sung
> psalms and heard prayers. (Qtd. in Bank 1979, 37)

Having a very restricted set of possible audiences, women tended
to write for other women, often close female friends, or for family, usually their children, if they wrote *to* anybody at all. Otherwise they wrote
to themselves or to the diary, parts of which they may or may not have
shared with others in their immediate domestic or social circles. In contrast to Thoreau's mythic sense of audience for his journal, Ellen Weeton, for example, who is forbidden to see her child after she leaves her
husband, writes her journal for her daughter, Mary, to read when she is
grown (Blodgett 1988, 16). Charlotte Forten (1838-1914), a young middle-class black woman from Philadelphia who goes on to write and
teach freed slaves on the Sea Islands off the Carolina coast during the
Civil War, starts her diary at boarding school in Salem, Massachusetts at
age sixteen in order to store memories of her friends and to monitor the
course of her intellectual development. She does so only for herself,
however, not for the "Gods":

> A wish to record the passing events of my life, which even if quite
> unimportant to others, naturally possesses great interest to myself,
> and of which it will be pleasant to have some remembrance, has
> induced me to commence this journal. I feel that keeping a diary
> will be a pleasant and profitable employment of my leisure hours,
> and will afford me much pleasure in after years, by recalling to my
> mind the memories of other days, thoughts of much-loved friends
> from whom I may then be separated, with whom I now pass
> many happy hours, in taking delightful walks and holding "sweet
> converse"; the interesting books that I read; and the different peo-
> ple, places and things that I am permitted to see.
> Besides this, it will doubtless enable me to judge correctly of

the growth and improvement of my mind from year to year.
Salem, May, 1854 (Forten 1981, 42)

Women's Journals: Serving Others

From the beginning of women's diary traditions, then, most
women have written diaries that tend to fulfill a variety of social and
domestic purposes, rather than being personal in the sense of being just
for one's self. In the late sixteenth and early seventeenth centuries,
women's diary keeping starts with the combination of the spiritual journal and the family commonplace book focusing on the domestic lives of
women in the context of family life.

In the eighteenth century (and well into the nineteenth), an era
much interested in the social world, many women will write "social
diaries." Usually aristocratic or upper-class women, sometimes Ladies
of the Court, like Fanny Burney, Lady Cowper, or Lady Margaret
Cavendish, who reported on the goings-on and life at court, or women
otherwise socially well-placed, like Hester Thrale, the close friend of
Samuel Johnson, they wrote journals filled with anecdotes, conversations they had listened to, *bons mots*, and the current activities of the elite
social groups they moved in. Being taught, as females were and often
are, to be good listeners, they produced diaries that were focused
mostly on what others (usually famous men) said and did, and helped
buttress and enhance the social networks that supported these men's
lives and reputations. One can understand easily enough why these
diaries were more likely to have been preserved or published: they illu-
minated the public world and sustained the public and social images of
famous men. Also, these journals can be seen as the logical extension of
females' muted social-discourse responsibilities, to listen and record, to
encourage others in their speech, and to facilitate communication.

Sometimes, in fact, the journals of women turn out to be written
almost entirely for others. Elizabeth Wynn, a well-known diarist from
the eighteenth century, composed a considerable number of her sixty-
eight-volume journals from the extended correspondence she had with
her sea-captain husband, Captain Freemantle. In many respects, she
became *his* chronicler, and even her descendent many generations later,
editing the volumes, felt Freemantle's material was "news," while poor
Elizabeth's was "only life" (Mallon 1984, 18; Blodgett 1988, 63-64).

As we saw earlier, Mary Shelley's early journals were kept primarily for and about her famous husband, his reading lists, his ideas, his
conversations. Not only do Dorothy Wordsworth's journals record
more about William Wordsworth's activities than her own, but the lyri-

cal descriptions she jots down also become raw material for his professional writing. Frances Stevenson kept a diary from 1914 until 1937 so entirely concerned with Lloyd George, her lover, and later her husband, that it was published as *Lloyd George: A Diary by Frances Stevenson* (Blodgett 1988, 31).

Indeed, an enormous number of journals written by women until the late nineteenth century fulfilled the domestic-discourse function of family and social chronicling. Additional proof of this frequent function of women's diaries is the existence of diary cycles: that is, multiple generations of women keeping diaries in the same family.[13] These diary cycles also speak to the ways in which diaries were preserved and diary writing handed down from one generation of women to the next. And you didn't have to be rich or famous or related to a famous man to keep one, as all families needed someone to record and be able to recall critical events in the life of a family and its members, to keep networks of communication open. Margo Culley writes that throughout the eighteenth and nineteenth centuries:

Women diarists in particular wrote as family and community historians. They recorded in exquisite detail the births, deaths, illnesses, visits, travel, marriages, work, and unusual occurences [sic] that made up the fabric of their lives. (Culley 1985, 4)

The idea of keeping a journal as a part of the social- or domestic-discourse network seems a central and unique aspect of women's journal traditions; and while these journals certainly performed important verbal housekeeping in accordance with women's muted discursive responsibilities, they also appear to have served women's discursive needs and networks and their sense of self as well.

Women's Journals: Serving the Self

Current views see the female self as developing in connection with others rather than in separation from others, as muted with regard to the dominant discourse community, but voiced within the primarily collaborative community of female discoursers. Women's journals have often worked to sustain these fluid, muted networks and affirm this female sense of self as linked to others.

Women's journals were often practiced, indeed, as part of a continuum of domestic discourse that included letter writing. Fanny Burney, many of whose journals are written to her sister, Susan, wrote of her letters as *journals* or *journalising* and often conflated the two forms in practice, seeing them as overlapping rather than distinct. Celia Fiennes, a Restoration diarist born in 1662, wrote some of her vivid travel journals on her trips to the north of England in the form of letters to her sister as well (see Blodgett 1988; Bunkers 1987; Cooper 1987; and Culley 1985). Tristine Rainer reports that the journal functioning both as diary and as letter was a common and important part of women's discourse traditions for hundreds of years:

> Women's diaries in Europe and in the United States had their own independent tradition throughout the seventeenth, eighteenth, and nineteenth centuries. By the eighteenth century literally hundreds of American pioneer women had created a network of correspondence and mutual support that stretched from North Carolina to Massachusetts and was based on a shared interest in journal writing. In fact, so many women relied on the diary to preserve their history and culture that 200 years later, many people had come to think of the diary as primarily a woman's mode of expression. (Rainer 1978, 11)

As Smith-Rosenberg shows in her classic essay, "The Female World of Love and Ritual: Relations between Women in Nineteenth-Century America," based on hundreds of diaries and thousands of letters, most women in eighteenth- and nineteenth-century America lived in:

> a world bounded by home, church, and the institution of visiting—that endless trooping of women to each other's homes for social purposes. It was a world inhabited by children and other women. Women helped each other with domestic chores and in times of sickness, sorrow or trouble. Entire days, even weeks might be spent exclusively in the company of other women. (Smith-Rosenberg 1986, 233)

In this "closed and intimate female world" (Smith-Rosenberg 1986, 235), women's primary affiliations were most likely to be with their mothers, sisters, cousins, or best friends. Smith-Rosenberg notes the importance of diaries and letters in the maintenance of these bonds:

> Quite a few young women kept diaries, and it was a sign of special friendship to show their diaries to each other. The emotional quality of such exchanges emerges from the comments of one young girl who grew up along the Ohio frontier:

"Sisters CW and RT keep diaries and allow me the inestimable pleasure of reading them and in turn they see mine—but O shame covers my face when I think of it; theirs is so much better than mine, that every time, I think well now I *will* burn mine but upon second thought it would deprive me the pleasure of reading theirs, for I esteem it a very great privilege indeed as well as very improving, as we lay our hearts open to each other, it heightens our love & and helps to cherish & and keep alive that sweet soothing friendship and endears us to each other by that soft attraction." (Smith-Rosenberg 1986, 240)

The massive dislocations and disconnections caused by waves of immigrants to American shores and by the westward expansion cut women off from their primary, female-based discursive networks and affiliative bonds. Thus, countless journals and journal letters written by women during this period function as long-distance connections that help maintain these important networks and the self constructed in part through them.

Women for whom that fabric had been torn, who emigrated to this country, traveled as part of the westward migration, joined their husbands on whaling ships, or went to distant lands as missionaries, used journals to maintain kin and community networks. The diaries kept by those women functioned as extended letters often actually sent to those left behind. (Culley 1985, 4)

Such is the case with Margaret Van Horn Dwight (Bell), who left New Haven, Connecticut in 1810 to travel to the "wilderness of Ohio" in the company of a certain "parsimonious Dean Woolcot" and his family and keeps a journal as a promise to her cousin Elizabeth Woolsey back home.

Peach Orchard, P—— Thursday night—
Phelp's Tavern——
I do not feel to night, my dear Elizabeth, as if I should ever see you again—3 mountains & more hundreds of miles part us; & tho' I cannot give up the idea of returning, I cannot think of traversing this road again—If I live to return I will wait till the new turnpike is finished. . . . We found a house at the foot of the steepest part [of the hill]—a woman & her two sons live there and keep cakes and beer. —The woman told us she had no husband at *present*—suppose she has one in expectation —On the first mountain I found

some sweet Williams—We stopt at noon, at a dismal looking log
tavern. . . . It rains most dreadfully & and they say it is the clearing
off shower —Oh if it only proves so— ——"Oh had I the wings of
a dove, how soon would I meet you again." (Culley 1985, 82-83)

In addition to maintaining women's discursive communities and
affirming the sense of self constructed relationally, women's journals
have allowed the kind of recursive intellectual dialogue with the self,
the "audit of meaning," as Ann Berthoff has called it, that has worked to
help women locate or construct a sense of their own self and develop a
voice from which to speak, question, and know (Berthoff 1987).

Journals and Self: Text as Life/Life as Text

I write, therefore I am. . . . They wrote, therefore
I am.
        —Margo Culley, *A Day at a Time*

Everyone knows that a place exists which is not
economically or politically indebted to all the
vileness and compromise. That is not obliged to
reproduce the system. That is writing. If there is
a somewhere else that can escape the infernal
repetition, it lies in that direction, where *it*
writes itself, where *it* dreams, where *it* invents
new worlds.
        —Hélène Cixous, *The Newly Born Woman*

Since women have always had fewer ways to act or to inscribe
themselves on the world at large, and since women's lives have often
"involve[d] an endless series of tasks: cooking, washing, cleaning house,
tasks which are not permanent" (Cooper 1987, 97), they have found
ways to inscribe themselves, to make their own modest, but unique and
lasting imprint, on texts. They have created texts out of their lives and
new lives out of their texts. Texts are marks on the world; they are physical objects, and journals and diaries, while silent, are visible, potentially
permanent markers of a life lived, even if just for the diarist herself. The
diary of Elizabeth Fuller (1776-1856), for example, is simple and sparse,
consisting almost entirely of the amounts of spinning or weaving she
does each day, along with mentions of the occasional visitor and the
theme of each Sunday's sermon; but it is a powerful testimony to a quiet
but productive female life.

May 1 1792—I wove eight Yards.
May 2—I wove eight yards.

May 3—I wove two & a half Yards. Got out the piece, there is thirty one Yards & a half; have finished my weaving for this year I have woven a hundred and forty Yards since the ninth of March. . . .
May 29—Sabbath. I went to church in the A.M. Mr Saunders Preached from Matthew 15th Chap. 28th verse. "Then Jesus answered and said, O Woman great is thy faith: be it even unto thee even as thou wilt."—Exceeding hot to-day.
May 30—Mr. & Mrs. Hobbs & Mr. Saunders here a visiting to-day. Mr Saunders is a very agreeable pretty Man. I wove three yards to-day. (Qtd. in Culley 1985, 73)

As Margo Culley puts it:

Keeping a diary, one could argue, always begins with a sense of self-worth, a conviction that one's individual experience is some-how *remark*able. Even the most self-deprecating of women's diaries are grounded in some sense of the importance of making a record of the life. (Culley 1985, 8)

And Harriet Blodgett agrees that the act of diary keeping itself is an implicit assertion of identity:

I suggest that diary keeping has been practiced so extensively by women because it has been possible for them and gratifying to them. The diary by its nature as a genre of personal record, by the opportunity it offers the diarist to record what is important to her, and by the daily time that it claims for itself, counters the patriarchal attack on female identity and self-worth. A diary is an act of language that, by speaking of one's self, sustains one's sense of being a self, with an autonomous and significant identity. (Blodgett 1988, 5)

Culley asserts that the notion of the journal as a book for the explicit exploration of the self is a very recent idea (dating from the second half of the nineteenth century); and Blodgett has persuasively argued that women's diaries are in certain respects muted or silenced. I, however, found in several of the many social and domestic journals that I studied, even the very earliest ones, fascinating "ruptures of self" suggesting that women found immediate and profound *personal* value even in their journals about others.

Fanny Burney, for example, a contemporary of Boswell and Johnson, writing in her mid-teens, explains her impulse to write as that of confiding her secret thoughts to the sympathetic ear of the diary. She decides to call her diary "Miss Nobody" a century before the convention of "Dear Diary" is ensconced and writes, "To Nobody, then, will I write my Journal! since to Nobody can I be wholly unreserved—to Nobody can I reveal every thought, every wish of my heart, and with the most unremitting sincerity to the end of my life!" (qtd. in Fothergill 1974, 88). Fanny Burney's early diaries, or what is left of them, are indeed personal; they contain precisely the kinds of things she would not say aloud or write for others to see. Fortunately or unfortunately for Fanny, as her literary talents are increasingly perfected and recognized, and she grows into her proper place in society, "her journals soon cease to be private and become family property, they increasingly assume the character of letters designed to entertain an immediate audience with the latest exercise of Fanny's gift for social comedy" (Fothergill 1974, 54). Notice, however, that Fanny's journals become *family* property, not *public* property.

As for her slightly older contemporary, Hester Thrale (Piozzi), nearly the reverse is true. Hester Thrale *tries* to write a series of social diaries, filled with anecdotes of Johnson and Goldsmith and Burney, but in spite of her conscious desire to write an elegant, acceptable, witty diary, her less conscious anger at her limitations and her frustration at trying to be perfect for her husbands and children seethe beneath the surface and occasionally erupt into the journal (Spacks 1975, 206. See also Blodgett 1988). Remember it was this sensitivity and passion that irritated Fothergill, who was clearly looking for a different sort of "imprint of a man" in his conception of the personal journal. Yet as a model of a woman's being in the world, Hester Thrale's diary is an utterly compelling work.

Finally, consider Nancy Woodeforde, who wrote volume after volume about the comings and goings of visitors and the changing of the seasons at a parsonage in rural England, including nothing about herself in any of them. In 1792, however, and only in that year presumably, she kept a second journal, an anonymous brown notebook full of herself and her difficult relationship with her estranged mother (Dobbs 1974, 190-93). Clearly, then, even in the most "other-directed" of women's journal traditions, women have for centuries also discovered in small but powerful ways that the journal was a place they could try to locate, and be, themselves.

Interestingly, Thomas Mallon writes about the notion of "creating a life" as a particular motivation for diarists, but suggests that it is primarily "prisoners and invalids" who would be using the journal for this purpose (Mallon 1984, xvii). Indeed, he provides several striking examples of men (for the most part) who have been physically imprisoned (Alfred Dreyfus, Albert Speer), or imprisoned by sickness (George Orwell, William Soutar, W. N. P. Barbellion) or by society's punishing attitudes toward homosexuality (Arthur Christopher Benson), and who must use their diaries to live in (Mallon 1984, 248-91). These men, who have been temporarily or permanently placed in the position of being outside the normal, dominant spheres of activity, experience, or world view, have written journals in which they could be safe, healthy, alive. Is it any wonder that women, who have always been, in critical respects, in the position of outsider to the dominant world, might write from similar impulses? While I don't want to oversimplify women's relations to the diary, women's need to commit their lives to text and their corollary tendency to bring their diaries to life seem central. As Penelope Franklin writes:

A diary can be a "safe place" where new roles can be tried out, protected from censure; a sounding board for ideas or emotions that may not be acceptable to friends or family; a testing ground where creative experiments of all kinds can be tried, with no one to laugh if they fizzle; a means of regaining balance when caught by conflicting emotions; a valuable record of progress and growth; a place where past, present, and future, live together—and all under one's control.

The diary often evolves into a friend, a confidante, the first place to run with an exciting secret and a last refuge when other people can't or won't listen. This has been especially important to women, who are often isolated physically by the conditions of their lives or psychically by restraints placed on the expression of their feelings. . . . The act of keeping a journal is often a way for the writer to get in touch with and develop hidden parts of herself—often those parts for which little support is given by others—and establish emotional stability and independence. The process can even be a means of keeping the personality intact, even under great stress—as the diaries of prisoners and invalids attest. (Franklin 1986, xix-xx)

For many women the journal will operate as a sort of self-repair kit that is ever at hand. Nancy Shippen Livingstone (1763-1841) will use it to keep herself going when her unfaithful husband refuses to divorce her and takes her child to his wealthy mother's home to be reared (Culley 1985, 56-68); Abigail Abbot Bailey (1746-1815) will use it to write what is unwritable (though common): the frightening story of her husband's continued attempts to sexually abuse their teenaged daughter and her efforts to get support to stop him (Culley 1985, 36-48). In 1890, forty-seven-year-old Emily French, abandoned after thirty-one years of marriage, is forced to work outside her home as a laundress, nurse, and cleaning woman to keep herself and her crippled half sister alive. Her diary for that year maintains her sense of self as she documents her hard work and confides her exhaustion and concerns to her one and only friend—the journal (French 1987). And for Charlotte Forten, made constantly aware of her blackness, her femaleness, and her supposed inferiority, the journal becomes a place to express her anger and resentment at the treatment she receives and to express her inexorable determination to excel for herself and for all black people (Forten 1981).

Countless women will use the journal to deal with sickness and death. Since women have been the primary caretakers, attending the sicknesses and deaths of both the young and the aging, they have always used the journal as a means of preparing themselves for the myriad illnesses they nursed others through, or for death, which frequently accompanied childbirth: their baby's, that of the women they attended in childbirth, or even their own.[14] Often death scenes are described at length, with petitions to God, and reflective entries on the anniversaries of the deaths of infants are a regular feature. The diary of Laura Murray Hamilton (1864-1898?), written when she is twenty years old and pregnant with her first child, gives a good sense of the diary used in this way:

March 20: I am very busy making my dress. I am worried with thoughts, sometime I really think I will go wild. The subject is death and the thought that death must come. Oh Lord let me be submissive to Thy will.
. . .
April 24: I got the blues for a while. Think perhaps our little baby would not live but I must submit to what must come but I do not want it to die even if it is a little girl.
. . .
April 27: Was taken with pains in morning which lasted all day growing more severe but in spite of them I kept up baked pies and so forth. F. [her husband] came home on leave of absence for ten days. Oh me what I have soon to endure Lord help me.
. . .
F. went for the Dr. at 10:30. Mrs. Ross was here. F. staid right by

me. Baby was born 15 min. to One on the morn of the 28th. This is the 13th of May. I am writing from memory.

. . .

April 28: First day of confinement. Feeling very comfortable. No milk for baby. He looks like he is going to die. (Qtd. in Sterling 1984, 475)[15]

Thus, the journal has always functioned in part as a place to mourn and to heal, and as it was primarily women who tended the sick and the dying, this journal function has been central to women's journal traditions.

The "New" Diary

But several shifts in the late eighteenth and nineteenth centuries refocused the journal to allow for a more explicit exploration of the self, while at the same time gendering the journal in obvious ways. In particular, romanticism, as both a cultural and a literary movement, encouraged the fuller expression of emotion and sensibility; and the development of psychology, with its emphasis on understanding the structure of consciousness and the nature of the unconscious, changed cultural notions about the nature of the self as it is manifested in journals and diaries. The nineteenth-century *journal intime*, associated with women writers like George Sand, takes as its subject the intimate description of one's own mental and emotional consciousness.

Later, widely-read diarists will demonstrate these new shifts: Marie Baskirtseff, the young Russian artist; Marie Bonaparte, who is psychoanalyzed by Freud and becomes a psychoanalyst herself; and Mary MacLane, whose self-absorbed diaries become the rage in the late nineteenth century. Jung's diaries of his own dreams, inner images, and speculations help him chart the inner terrain of the "collective unconscious" and also help spawn diaries that are similarly introspective. These new ideas will ultimately generate what Tristine Rainer calls "The New Diary" of the twentieth century, which will be associated with self-exploration, creativity, personal growth (meaning growth of the whole person), and healing or therapy.

Culley summarizes these changes and their consequent "feminization" of the diary. As the diary or personal journal became increasingly affiliated with the rigidly demarcated women's sphere of the nineteenth century, it probably suffered a loss of prestige, which may well have hastened the departure of men from the ranks of its practitioners and contributed to the pejoration of the term *diary*:

In the course of the nineteenth century, as a split between the public and private spheres came increasingly to shape the lives of women and men, those aspects of culture associated with the private became the domain of women. Simultaneously, changing ideas of the self, influenced by romanticism, the industrial revolution, the "discovery" of the unconscious contributed to the changes in the content and function of the diary. As the modern idea of the secular diary as a "secret" record of an inner life evolved, that inner life—the life of personal reflection and emotion—became an important aspect of the "private sphere" and women continued to turn to the diary as one place where they were permitted, indeed, encouraged to indulge full "self-centeredness." American men, unused to probing and expressing this inner life in any but religious terms, found as the secular self emerged as the necessary subject of the diary, the form less and less amenable to them. (Culley 1985, 3-4)

While the cultural shifts Culley mentions certainly played an important, if not decisive, role in turning the journal into a forum for self-encounter, the specific, muted relation of women to discourse and experience has always powered women's use of the journal as a subtle but potent tool for self-exploration, discovery, and reconstruction. One has only to listen to the many women's voices, from different times and places, testifying to the ways that journals and diaries have provided a receptive audience, a momentary wild zone, a "place that is not politically or economically indebted to all the vileness and compromise," as Cixous so felicitously puts it, a life for their texts, a text for their lives. Indeed, the diaries and journals have taken on lives of their own in such guises as "dear diary," "dear friend," "old friend," "my confidante."

TABLE 4.1
Women and Journal Keeping: Text as Life/Life as Text

SEI SHONAGON (963-?): "If writing did not exist, what terrible depressions we should suffer from" (qtd. in Partnow 1985, 39).

FANNY BURNEY, writing on 27 March 1768: "To have some account of my thoughts, manners, acquaintance and actions when the hour arrives in which time is more nimble than memory, is the reason which induces me to keep a journal. . . . I must imagine myself to be talking to one whom I should take delight in confiding and remorse in concealment . . ." (qtd. in Dobbs 1974, 186).

(Continued)

TABLE 4.1 *(Continued)*

CHARLOTTE FORTEN, writing on 31 December 1856: "Once more my beloved Journal, who art become a part of myself,—I say to thee, and to the Old Year, Farewell!" (qtd. in Culley 1985, 11).

HELEN WARD BRANDRETH, writing in 1876: "I have determined to keep a diary. I shall call it Fannie Fern" (qtd. in Culley 1985, 11).

CAROL POTTER, Helen Ward Brandreth's great-grandaughter: "Most people would laugh to think that a personal diary was of such significance to a person, but this one is to me. When Nellie [Brandreth] writes—my dearest darling Fan—over and over, I know how she felt about that little book. It was a friend and so is this dumpy little blue notebook. How I wish I had started in a really nice one. But no one knows what will become of a first meeting or even a few" (qtd. in Culley 1985, 11).

MARY MACLANE, writing in 1882: "I write this book for my own reading. It is my postulate to myself. As I read it it makes me clench my teeth savagely: and coldly tranquilly close my eyelids: It makes me love and loathe Me, Soul and bones.
. . .
I don't know whether I write this because I wear two plain dresses or whether I wear two plain dresses because I write this" (Qtd. in Culley 1985, 13-14).

MARY MACLANE: "I am a true artist, not as a writer but as a writing person. . . . I once thought me destined to be a "writer" in the ordinary sense. And many good people visioned a writing career for me. It has a vapid taste to it, just to recall it. . . . My writing is to me a precious thing—and a rare bird—and a Babylonish jade. It demands gold in exchange for itself. But though it is my talent, it is not my living. It is too myself, like my earlobes and my throat, to commercialize by the day" (qtd. in Spacks 1975, 177-78).

MARIE BONAPARTE: "In writing [the notebooks] I found unspeakable relief, a supreme catharsis. I fled into an imaginary world, far from this world with its torments, its conflicts and its disappointments. . . . This habit of taking refuge in writing whenever I have been hurt by life has remained with me" (qtd. in Spacks 1975, 281).

BEATRICE WEBB: "It would be curious to discover WHO IT IS, to whom one writes in a diary? Possibly to some mysterious personification of one's own identity, to the Unknown, which lies below the constant change in matter and ideas, constituting the individual at any given moment. This unknown was once my only

(Continued)

TABLE 4.1 *(Continued)*

friend: the being to whom I went for advice and consolation in all the small troubles of a child's life" (qtd. in Spacks 1975 284-85).

VIRGINIA WOOLF: "This diary may die of London if I'm not careful."
"[I]n a bound volume, the year has a chance of life. It can be stood on a shelf."
"I think it is true that one gains a certain hold on sausage and haddock by writing them down" (Qtd. in Mallon 1984, 33-34).

VIRGINIA WOOLF, writing on 28 December 1919: "Oh yes, I've enjoyed reading the past year's diary & shall keep it up. I'm amused to find how it's grown a person, with almost a face of its own" (qtd. in Mallon 1984, 1).

LYDIA SMITH, writing in 1805: "I find that my idle habit of scribbling interferes so much with all regularity that I have determined to relinquish it, tho not entirely, yet I must so constrain it as to pursue my duties and studies, etc. I must wean myself by degrees for I have not the strength to quit at once" (qtd. in Culley 1985, 13).

MARION TAYLOR: "How nice a diary is. I could not get along without one. I enjoy writing what has happened as much as I enjoy the happenings themselves almost—thinking about them—living them over again and putting them in words" (qtd. in Franklin 1986, xvii).

ANNIE COOPER, writing on 28 May 1892: "Three years almost of life have passed since I last looked upon this book. They have been years of prosperity, years of comfort, years of OUTWARD free-heartedness and yet to you ALONE, my Diary, I confess—they have been years of mute suffering" (qtd. in Franklin 1986, xix).

ANNIE COOPER: "I may as well put one more line to my history. . . . Then, too, the old longing seems to be to TELL someone—and that I never do—so I resort again as when a child to you my Diary" (qtd. in Franklin 1986, xix).

WINIFRED WILLIS, writing on 9 September 1932: "How did I ever think I could give you up? Though I shall never go back to driveling I shall come back to you at intervals. I shall always need you. I need you now" (qtd. in Franklin 1986, xx).

ANAÏS NIN, writing in November 1945: "The real Anaïs is in the writing" (qtd. in Mallon 1984, 85).

ANAÏS NIN: "I only regret that everyone wants to deprive me of the journal, which is the only steadfast friend I have, the only one which makes my life bear-

(Continued)

TABLE 4.1 *(Continued)*

able; because my happiness with human beings is so precarious, my confiding moods rare, and the least sign of noninterest is enough to silence me. In the journal I am at ease.

Playing so many roles, dutiful daughter, devoted sister, mistress, protector, my father's new found illusion, Henry's needed all purpose friend, I had to find one place of truth, one dialogue without falsity. This is the role of the diary" (qtd. in Moffat and Painter 1975, 14).

MARIE BASKIRTSEFF: "What if seized without warning by a fatal illness, I should happen to die suddenly! I should not know, perhaps, of my danger, my family would hide it from me; and after my death they would rummage among my papers; they would find my journal, and destroy it after having read it, and soon nothing would be left of me—nothing—nothing—nothing! This is the thought that has always terrified me" (qtd. in Moffat and Painter 1975, 14).

Indeed, as some of the passages in Table 4.1 suggest, sometimes the journal and the life become synonymous with one another, even to the degree that authors tried to match or synchronize the end of their journals with the end of their lives. The following three diary entries demonstrate this fascinating symbiotic quality:

Cynthia Carleton, writing just before she died in 1899: "I am not very well. Tried to straighten diary" (qtd. in Culley 1985, 13).

Alice James, written by companion Katherine Loring in 1899: "One of the last things she said to me was to make a correction in the sentence of March 4th 'moral discords and nervous horrors.' This dictation of March 4th was rushing about in her brain all day, and although she was very weak, she could not get her head quiet until she had it written: then she was relieved" (qtd. in Culley 1985, 13).

Elizabeth Ann Cooley, written by her husband on her death: "This journal is done! The author being Elizabeth Ann McClure died March 28, 1848. Tho happy in Christ Jesus being the only consolation left me. She was 22 years, 7 months old" (qtd. in, Culley 1985, 14).

Virginia Woolf: Writing to Heal and Writing to Know

Although it is still common to think of the healing function of writing as unrelated to intellectual growth, it should be obvious by now that writing to heal is a form of intellectual empowerment which allows for the development of a self that is sufficiently integrated to be capable of knowing. Perhaps the clearest case of the use of the journal as a way of writing to repair and construct this kind of knowing self, is that of Virginia Woolf, not only one of the most important diarists of the modern period, but also one of the foremost writers and critics of the twentieth century. While most people know of Woolf's talent as a writer, until recently it was not known that she, like so many other women, was a victim of profound sexual abuse and all of its consequences. As Louise DeSalvo has written:

> Born in 1882 into a Victorian family where incest, sexual violence and abusive behavior were common, Woolf was molested from the time she was six years old well into her adulthood. Woolf not only suffered sexual abuse, but also carried the scars of that abuse until her death; what was previously taken to be her "madness" by nearly everyone, including her husband Leonard, was actually a typical reaction to painful childhood experiences. (DeSalvo 1989, 6)

DeSalvo's brilliant book on Woolf shows not only the significance of incest and the inevitable silencing and epistemological fragmentation that accompanied it in Woolf's life and work, it also shows how Woolf literally wrote herself into existence. It should come as no surprise that what initiated her life-long process of self-reconstruction was the set of diaries she started in her teenage years.

Like other Victorian children, Virginia had been encouraged (or required) to keep a diary because of the discipline it fostered. After her mother's death, her half-brother George Duckworth had begun to assault her. She knew she could not speak of it and would not be protected. Both furious and frightened, she turned to her diary as the one place she could break her silence:

> Her 1897 diary was her first successful attempt to break the silence that she herself believed was an outcome of her sexual abuse. After her mother's death "a dark cloud settled over us; we seemed to sit all together cooped up, sad, solemn, unreal under a haze of heavy emotion. It seemed impossible to break through."
> . . . For a girl like Virginia, keeping a diary was the beginning of a lifelong process of self-actualization, of self-verification, of breaking the silence, even if the diaries themselves sometimes made her feel ashamed. . . . Writing her diary was the first and most defiant

act of her adolescence, but she did it in a socially acceptable way. For in its most radical manifestation, a diary is a potential historical time bomb; it lies in waiting until it explodes misapprehensions about the past, misconceptions about the role of women or other outsider groups in history, misrepresentations about how a particular life was lived. (DeSalvo 1989, 236-37)

These first diaries allowed Woolf to start the process of reconstructing her-self. Soon she would start the diaries in which she would begin her extraordinary apprenticeship in the craft of writing. Her writing would ultimately keep her alive and healthy enough to produce some of the best writing of the twentieth century. As Woolf herself has put it so perfectly: "Melancholy diminishes as I write" (Moffat and Painter 1975, 229).

Certainly other women who wanted to be writers have found the journal of indispensable assistance toward that end as well. Men, quite clearly, have used the writer's journal or commonplace book as a practice ground for more public writing, but for many women writers the journal has been essential, partly because it was a form they were already comfortable with as women, and partly because of its patient receptivity. While public writing by women often drew immediate criticism, "Paper never refused ink," as the saying goes. Plath used the journal to "get life"; Jean Rhys, Adrienne Rich, May Sarton and many others have used it to get unblocked, using the refuge of the journal to regain their confidence before starting to write publicly again, to literally find their voices (Olsen 1978). Others like George Sand and Anaïs Nin used journals to release, to let go, to write through an emotional difficulty in order to clear themselves for other kinds of writing. For women, then, who have wanted to write more seriously, the journal has been more than a practice ground or commonplace book, as important as both of these might be. For women, the journal has been one of the few places in which they could be writers and women, without paradox. In fact, Julia Penelope and Susan J. Wolfe suggest that much of women's writing in the twentieth century has evolved from the writing traditions and characteristics associated with the diary.

The women of the 20th century who write speak out of a tradition of silence, a tradition of the closely guarded revelatory language of diaries and journals. Our style, therefore, does not conform to the traditional patriarchal style we have been taught to regard as "literary" and "correct." Perhaps the autonomy of the written word frees women from the constraints of conversational and situational

contexts, which serve patriarchal social structures; and the relatively informal contexts of the diaries frees them from the limitations of "formal" prose. (Penelope and Wolfe 1983, 125)

It is no wonder, then, that in the nineteenth century, Charlotte
Perkins Gilman wrote "The Yellow Wallpaper" about a woman who is
driven insane because she is denied the right to write in her journal, nor
that Doris Lessing built her classic twentieth-century novel *The Golden
Notebook* around the recursive, fragmented, but cumulative form of the
journal; or that current writers Rachel Blau DuPlessis, Susan Griffin, and
Dale Spender generate "essays" using the form and the language of
journals and diaries. It is no wonder that Adrienne Rich speaks of "that
profoundly female, and feminist genre, the journal" (Rich 1979, 217).

The Gendered Legacy of the Journal

I hope I have shown that understanding the historical and cultural
contexts of journal and diary keeping will help us better understand the
multiple functions and forms of journals and diaries today and our complex associations with the terms *journal* and *diary*. Beginning as public
and communal forms of record keeping for the whole spectrum of religious, commercial, military, and political uses in ancient and medieval
times, the journal/diary is recast (although its public, record-keeping
functions continue) during the epistemological shifts that accompany
the Renaissance and the Reformation. The new emphasis on the individual mind and its ability to observe, reflect, and examine, manifests itself
in the forms of the spiritual journal, the Baconian travel journal, the
commonplace book of self-education, and most importantly, the secular
personal journal made famous by Pepys, Boswell, and a myriad of other
important men or male writers.

But while the supposedly generic histories tell us primarily about
men's journals and journaling traditions that have often been public in
nature, there is also an important, overlapping, but muted set of women's
journal traditions that is similarly centuries old. Although women have
practiced all forms of journal writing, women's journals have historically
often been used to maintain familial and social-discursive networks, to
chronicle domestic life and social relations, sometimes in the form of letters to other family members when speech communities were disrupted
by emigration or westering travel. Journals or diaries were a kind of writing practice that allowed for the expression of a relationally organized
sense of self and were flexible enough to allow for the discontinuity, gaps,
and silences that were an inevitable part of female life.

Both journals and diaries, as used by men or women inside and outside the academy, have been used in intellectually empowering ways. The commonplace book, scientific journals, writer's journals, and other secular personal journals, which we often associate with men's writing traditions, have obvious intellectual and scholarly uses: as an *aide-mémoire*, a way to cultivate close observation and careful reflection, a place to store information for long-term intellectual use, and monitor progress, as well as a place for linguistic and stylistic experimentation.

Women have written these types of journals as well. In addition, even in the nonacademic, nonpublic discursive domains women have often been relegated to, many women have found ways to use the journal to connect personal and intellectual empowerment. In what is sometimes called the "wild zone" of the journal, women have been able to explore their world and *the* world with less interruption or judgment. They could discover themselves as subjects, learn how to work through language to inscribe themselves onto the world textually, and learn to listen to their own voices and experience.

Women and men, including the young women and men in our classes, have inherited several overlapping but distinct journal traditions that, I suggest, will profoundly shape their understanding and use of the diary or journal in the academy, and that I will explore in the final chapters of this book. The terms *journal* and *diary* refer to many types of private, privatized, shared, and public writing, and both forms of writing have been employed, albeit in somewhat different ways, as powerful vehicles for the development of the mind and the body. The increasingly gendered history of these forms, however, leaves both me and my students with overlapping and complex sets of traditions to draw on. These traditions include a legacy of several more public and academic journal types that men can explicitly or implicitly draw on—although since the nineteenth century, they appear to have been increasingly less interested in the diary form. In addition to having somewhat restricted access to more privileged journal types, women belong to a powerful popular-culture tradition of journal/diary keeping that sustains women's discourse networks, although women have been socialized to see their diary keeping as less important, as belonging only to the private sphere and to the realm of emotion rather than that of the intellect.

And, come to think of it, these are the traditions I have inherited as well. My first journal, a green, leatherette "One Year Diary," was a Christmas gift from my best friend, Krissy Lasch, when I was thirteen. She wrote: "Keep in here a record of all the exciting things you'll experience in your 13th year. A year from now you will read this over and

really be glad you kept a record. Good luck and have fun in 1965. Love
ya, Kris."
    The entries in that first green diary are not particularly earthshat-
tering—in fact, they are exactly what one would expect from a thirteen-
year-old girl. Here, for example, is my entry of

> *3 January:* Tomorrow is school and I'll find out what Joe Zauner is
> giving me. I'll wear my blue sweater and try to find a skirt to
> match. I'm trying something new with my hair, just hope it works.
> (Sorry my handwriting's so crumby.) Goodnight. P.S. Hope I feel
> more in the spirit for homework tomorrow.

But that little diary, filled with pep rallies and boy's names and
passed notes, launched me as a journal keeper, albeit a sporadic one.
There are now five more journals, a brown one written during my
poetry phase, a black one (with unlined paper for drawings) used to
write myself through the last years of a failing marriage, the unicorn
book (another gift), one called "Moonflowers: A Book of Affirmations"
(still another gift replete with women's sayings and aphorisms), and the
grey and maroon, paisley-lined book I now find myself writing in. I use
mine as do other women diarists: to value the quotidian, to heal, to
understand the connection between my personal worlds and how all
my roles (wife, mother, daughter, sister, teacher, scholar, student,
friend) fit together, and to understand and give shape to my imaginative and intellectual universe.
    Even though I never associated my personal journal with the jour-
nals I had kept or assigned in school, I realize now how intellectually
empowering it has been for me. I use it because, to paraphrase Molly
Dorsey Sanford, while I'm not sure I'll ever be a writer, I want to be
more than a mere machine, as the following two entries show:

> *[7 September 1986. Two years later it starts up again, the rusty or at least
> dusty, slow sputtering unoiled brain wanting to start up. Especially because of
> the new dissertation on JOURNALS and because I start teaching writing again
> tomorrow and I want to "do it" if they "do it." Also simply because I found it
> again—it had been lost in the accreta of my desk/shelves, interlarded between
> old resumes, unaccepted abstracts, and oddly enough, Sharyn Lowenstein's dis-
> sertation on journal keeping. Synchronicity. I'm thinking of using sections of
> it somehow in the diss—another voice—the journal voice—documenting
> itself—its values, the writing, the gaps, the silences, the shame, all the other
> jobs, the babies, the multiple tries at restarting the diss, the quiet blank page
> biding its time—forgiving—waiting for me.*

31 October 1986 (Brainstorming on the Dissertation). While I am not suggesting that it was a "good" thing that women have been excluded from the creation, maintenance, and practice of public discourse, I am suggesting that most of the forms we have are "agonistic," "competitive," even assaultive forms hierarchy-producing status displaying—which might not have been in most women's inclinations to produce—given any alternative. Which is to say that letters, journals and diaries, memoirs, generally—etc. are valid and viable forms in themselves. They serve critical individual, artistic, familial purposes just as men's do. That while the efforts to silence women have been enormous, women's efforts to give voice, fragmentary and isolated as they have been, a chorus built one at a time, over many years, a set of voices too loud to silence now, too unified to ignore, too lovely and sad not to want to hear. I hear you now—more and more of you. All those women speaking and writing those messages of ardor and arduousness, fear, timidity, pride, hope, and putting them in journals, bottles of language washing across oceans of time, across years of terrain. Only now have I begun to watch for them to wash up. Only now do I comb the beaches.]

5

Gender, Pedagogy, and the Student Journal

It's been eight years since I kept any kind of a journal, since seventh grade English. I can't say that I miss doing it, I used to hate it—five pages a week.

—Ted, a student

3/5/86 Write now. I've taken about forty-five minutes to write in my journal. I feel better.
5/1/86 I love my journal because it helps me put my struggles, my anxiety, my pressures, my feelings, my good times into perspective.

—Cathy, a student

When I first went to graduate school, I had illusions of many kinds. One in particular was that I would be a poet in addition to being a literary scholar and a linguist. I remember sharing my work eagerly with a few of my teachers, whom I considered professional "readers." One, a woman, said that some of the poetry was as good as "anything going" and that I ought to send it out. The other, a man, refusing to comment on the quality, said simply that he couldn't connect with them at all. As I was easily discouraged in those days, I stopped writing poetry. Many years later, as I reconsider that small but personally agonizing set of events, I realize that the sharply contrasting responses my poetry triggered may have had as much to do with the gender of my readers as with the texts themselves. Now I am a teacher of composition and a professional reader for my students, and I know that gender shapes the experience of reading and writing for my students and for myself in many ways. Indeed, it even shapes my reading of the workings of gender in their journals.

But I was certainly not fully aware of the connections between gender and discourse, or of the gendering of the journal, when I started looking at student journals in my classes. In fact, I would probably have ignored the whole matter entirely had it not rather forcibly presented itself to me at the end of one semester.

At the beginning of spring semester in 1985, one of the young men in my expository prose class the previous fall stopped in to say hello and pick up his work.

"You know, about the journals . . ." He hesitated, scuffing his Nike sneaker back and forth in the door jamb.

"Yeah," I said helpfully, but vaguely.

"Well, I was never able to get into that stuff like some of the others . . . Especially the girls." He paused, then started up again. "I mean I just didn't know quite what to put down ever. Whenever they'd read or write they always had so much to say about it, how it related to their lives, and what they thought of it. It was harder for me. It just seemed too personal."

I asked him why he thought that was. He said maybe it was because girls are more used to keeping diaries, so they are used to writing about themselves. I then asked him if he would have felt more comfortable writing about "personal things" for a male professor. "Sure," he said. "Absolutely."

"What do you think you could have written about for a male professor that you couldn't for me?" I asked, really wanting to know.

"Oh you know, a lot more about sports." He waited a moment, and added, "I hope my not writing about myself much and not writing as much as they did, didn't work against me in my grade."

"No, of course not," I declared somewhat hesitantly.

Although I thought at the time that he was a bit confused about the difference between journals and diaries, and a bit overly concerned about his grade, that conversation got me thinking. I went back to reread all the journals from that class and have studied the journal writing of women and men in academic settings ever since. What I have discovered so far is obvious—but what is obvious is often invisible. I found that, just like their professors, students coming to composition and literature courses, indeed to any classes, are not *tabulae rasae* when it comes to journals and diaries. They have inherited, consciously and unconsciously, a complex set of assumptions and practices regarding journal and diary keeping and textuality generally that powerfully inform their notions about school journals, and the writing they do in them.

In short, my student, Tom, was right, and *I* was confused . . . Women do often keep diaries and those popular-culture writing practices shape the writing they do in their composition journals; men rarely keep diaries and their academic journals show the tension they feel about the proximity of the school journal to the traditional notion of the diary. In addition to confirming Tom's insights, I found many other interesting traces of the journal's gendered legacy both in the students' attitudes toward journal keeping and in the journals themselves, differences which are clearly related to the dominant/muted, public/private, academic/nonacademic discursive traditions that are also marked by gender.

A First Look: Retrospective Readings of Six Student Journals

Like many other composition teachers in the mid-1980s, I had been moving more and more toward informal, but intensive, journal writing as a significant component of my writing courses. Borrowing informally, if somewhat haphazardly, from the writings of James Britton, Peter Elbow, Donald Murray, Toby Fulwiler, Janet Emig and others I discussed in chapter 2, I had begun to use journal writing to relieve the pressure of formal mechanical scrutiny, to allow, indeed encourage, experimentation, and to develop fluency. My sense was that journals would allow students to personalize the experience of learning to write, to make sense of the raw material of their intellectual and emotional lives, to respond to other texts and ideas freely, to read themselves as potential texts, and to read and reread themselves as writers.

The students whose journals I first studied were enrolled in Expository Prose 501, an elective, second-year writing course often taken by sophomores, juniors, and seniors for liberal arts credit at the University of New Hampshire. Located in the southeastern corner of the state, the University of New Hampshire is a relatively small state university (undergraduate enrollment approximately 10,000) with comparatively strict entrance requirements. Of the original nineteen students enrolled in Expository Prose 501, one man and one woman eventually dropped the course for financial or work-related reasons. This left seventeen students, eleven women and six men.

As for the journal assignment itself, the students were to write in their journals frequently, daily if possible, and keep reading and writing responses in them as well. We had discussed prewriting techniques such as brainstorming, freewriting, mapping, role playing, and others as being useful activities to try in the journal, which was to be a seedbed for their developing ideas, perceptions, and associations as well as a log of their evolving sense of themselves as readers and writers. We had also discussed what I felt *at the time* to be critical distinctions between the journal each student would keep and a diary, which I had character- ized as the simple listing of events or activities without any attempt to interpret or analyze them. (I, of course, had entirely ignored my own diary keeping, which I did not associate particularly with writing con- nected with school and which never consisted of merely listing my daily activity.)

We also read the views of professional writers like Donald Murray on journal keeping and Joan Didion's essay, "On Keeping a Journal," from our text, *A Writer's Reader* (Hall and Emblen 1982). Later in the course we read excerpts from Sylvia Plath's journal, which were also in the reader. The students knew that I would read portions of their jour- nals regularly in conference, and that they would have to choose entries from time to time to share with their peers. I also read and commented informally on their entries twice during the semester. Outside of these constraints, they were free to write what they wanted, and assured that if they did not want me to read certain sections that were personal or embarrassing they simply needed to mark them as such. The openness of the assignment, therefore, may have encouraged students to draw implicitly on their previous, nonscholastic associations or experience with journals.

After reading all the journals, I chose six representative journals to study more carefully: three men's (Steven's, Tom's, and Ted's) and three women's (Jennifer's, Sarah's, and Carrie's) journals. My intention was to demonstrate the significant gendered patternings that I had discovered and yet allow for the individuality of each student's voice.[1]

Form and Function: Gender Similarities and Differences

As one might expect, all the journals had certain features in com- mon, partly because some entries were assigned, and partly because cer- tain functions of the journal are nearly universal. First off, all students had been required to write reading responses to some of the essays we read in the class from *A Writer's Reader*.[2] Since they also had been asked to comment on a regular basis on their writing, the progress of individ- ual papers, and the changes they saw in themselves as writers, everyone had some entries on their development as writers, some of which had been in-class assignments.

In addition to the reading and writing responses, many of the students used their journals for planning, listing, and monitoring daily activities, that is, as a daybook, and for venting various emotions often relating to school and schoolwork. Tom writes, for instance, on Thursday, 27 September:[3]

> Today was the first class I missed this year. It was an eight o'clock Poli Sci course which is very boring. I was up late last night going through Rush and cuts and decided it would be best getting some sleep and have a good day instead of the other way around. Today was also the first day I've used the UNH computer system. It was only a short use for my Community Development class, but I think it's a little weird not using the computer all the way until your junior year. It really wasn't that bad though. The use is going to gradually increase as the class progresses gradually.
>
> I was just assigned three new books for my CD class also. I'll be reading *Brave New World* by Aldous Huxley, *1984* by George Orwell and *The Little Prince* by Antoine de Saint-Exupery. I've already read all three but I'm going to again because all three were so good.

On Friday, 12 October, Tom enters the following:

> Today was the day of my big quiz. It was on 24 upland game birds yet what we had to know about them wasn't made too clear. On most we had to know I.D., habitat, food, and range. Also the order family and subfamily they fit into. I studied all morning long even though I didn't want to since it was almost 80 degrees outside. All my friends were going to the mountains to play golf and I was studying. I went to my quiz and only had to know five birds and one distinguishing characteristic about them. This was really easy and I should have gotten a 100% but I was careless and wrote down the wrong name on one.

Here is Tom's entry from Tuesday, 23 October:

> What a day! This seems like it's already finals week. I've been up since seven o'clock and it's now 11:00 pm and I haven't stopped to have a spare moment to relax and sit down. The worst part is I'm going to bed right after this because I'm so tired and I haven't even come close to finishing all my work. I have a test Thursday morning on material I haven't read or studied yet and then another test Friday afternoon.

Here are some comparable entries by Sarah. They are clearly similar in that they show her planning for schoolwork and other college activities, and responding to academic pressure, yet her tone already foreshadows an interesting difference. While Tom tends to document what's irritating or frustrating about his academic situation, Sarah focuses less on the negative. When she does she tends to start with her anxiety or frustration but usually works toward some solution or resolution to her worries. Here is an excerpt from Sarah's entry for 12 September:

> 2:45 pm
> Life is great. I'm finally starting to get organized. I want to take a photography course. It really fascinates me lately and has been on my mind alot. What a way to express yourself. I want to take a MUB mini course—Ballroom dancing would be cool!!

On 24 September, she writes:

> I'm so tired. I have so much work to do. I can feel the tension rising. I just have to calm down, take a deep breath, and get my work done. 3 exams and a paper.

Here is a passage from 3 October:

> I'm drained and I'm definitely sore. I went to aerobics last night—what a workout!! I can't believe I stayed up till 5AM. The morning hours are kind of cool . . . so quiet. I had a caffeine fit—so I trudged over to SUB STOP to get two large diet pepsis. I also smoked two cigarettes—YUK. I could really write well at 3AM. My thoughts flowed easily onto the paper. I overslept this morning. I missed 2 classes—bad news. I have to get my act together. I will.

Four days later, she entered the following:

> Wow—this is wild. I'm sitting in class and Cindy's talking about linguistics. The English language is silly. We're going to go listen to a speaker next Monday. Should be interesting.

Men's Journals: Characteristic Topics, Uses, and Functions

Logging and keeping track of school assignments, along with

venting the frustrations associated with them, were central to several of the men's journals. So, too, were questions of social power and responsibility. This was particularly true for two of the three men, Steven and Tom. Steven's journal, for example, had fourteen entries not relating to the reading we had done in class, and of those fourteen, fully ten dealt either with the problems he was having in his advanced Spanish class or with the constant frustrations attendant to being the dorm President for Randall Hall. (About twenty of the twenty-seven pages that constituted Steven's journal that is, almost four-fifths of it, dealt with matters such as these.) Here are some characteristic excerpts from his entries.

Entry 7: What to do. The Randall Semi-Formal is next Friday, we don't have a dj, a bus and the hall isn't paid for yet. I'm president of the dorm so I'm responsible for the whole affair. It's my ass if we can't pull off the social event of the whole semester.

Entry 9: What a stupid place to be: the language lab at Murkland. I listen to tapes of Spanish drills and exercises. The situation reeks of mechanized teaching. When I get to my Spanish phonetics class, we go over the same material with the teacher. The Spanish program is very disappointing to me. It seems the lower levels sucker you in with promises of interesting and beneficial learning. Then the upper level professors act like the Gestapo.

Entry 13: Political science, my major, my official course of studies. What am I doing in a major that I consider to be mostly worthless?

Entry 15: The presidency of Randall Hall is characteristically unfulfilling and frustrating. Presidents rarely serve for a full year. Most last for one semester or less. I ran for President last semester and have encountered only hassles and headaches. Even during the summer, I took the time to design and approve the printing of Randall Hall T-shirts. Did I get any help? No-o-o-.

Tom, another of my representative journalers, uses his journal more to summarize classes and classwork, what's been assigned, or more often what hasn't gotten done. Like Steven, he writes frequently of his social position and responsibilities and the activities of his fraternity. Several other entries detail his interest in professional and intramural sports, evaluating his and other's performances. He expresses considerable emotion, mostly anxiety, frustration, boredom, and sometimes, anger, with his workload and performance, although not quite in the same manner as Steven.

Entry 7: Reading for my Community Development class is very

boring and the bad part is I have a lot to read. The first book is
about a futuristic community taking place in the year 2000. It takes
the perspective of our society as it is today and how much it will
change in the future—if at all. Typical reading though . . . Kind of
boring.

Entry 11: only one class today—work for about ten—at least it
seems. In my Wildlife Ecology class we have to design and carry
out our own biological experiment. Sounds easy huh? Wrong. The
write up that follows is even worse.

Entry 13: Again another bad day. Why do I have to wait to weekends to get into a bad mood. The pressure from school is already
getting to me and we've only been here three weeks, but it already
seems like we've been here for the semester. It seems like we never
left.

Entry 19: Today was short, yet it was bad. I only have one class on
Fridays and it begins at 1:00 but today it was cancelled and that is
bad because it meant I was bound to blow the rest of the day off,
which I did.

Entry 21: Today wasn't one of my better Sundays. I didn't know
why, but it seemed very drab. I guess it's because I'm writing at
night, right after our weekly fraternity meeting. I ran for a position
which is elected every semester. It's called pledge committee and
I ran for it last semester and I really wanted to do it again. There
were eight very potential people and only four were to be elected.
Since I did it last year and did a very good job, I felt that I was
automatically going to be elected, but that wasn't to be the case. . . .
(Later) I found out that two of the guys elected were Seniors, who
had never held an elected position and probably never would
after this semester. So, in essence they were elected out of pity, not
because people felt they could do a good job. To me, I feel that that
really sucks and I don't know right now if there's any other job in
the house that I would really want to do. A bad thought but a
strong feeling.

In addition to the frequent daybook-type entries, planning, and
venting, the journal of the third male student, Ted, also demonstrates
some of the characteristic features of the men's journals quite well. Like
the entries of many of the men in his class, most of Ted's entries are
responses to readings, peer responses to drafts of student papers, occasional commentary on his own drafts, and other in-class journal activities. He starts out, much like Steven and Tom, frustrated with school
and particularly with writing in the journal. On 24 September he writes:

9/24 After an unbelievable start—actually the entire month of
September, I am sitting down to my first homework assignment—my daily journal. It's been nine years since I've kept any
kind of a journal, since 7th grade English. I can't say that I miss
doing it. I hated it—five pages a week. I think that class is what
made me dislike writing. I'm feeling very lost right now in the art
of journal writing. I'm already so far behind in all my classes. Get
so pissed off when I think about [it] because it wasn't my fault.

Ted comments regularly on his problems with writing, especially with
freewriting and *journal writing*. He sees the two as similar, as we will see
in his drafting entries in this section and again in the section on attitudes
toward the journals. But he also does some interesting things in the journal that are characteristic of the men's journals more generally.

To begin with, his entries, whatever their nature, are often focused
on external events and facts: specifically, sports facts. He writes about
books he's reading in his sports literature class; he writes about fans of
various ball clubs; he reports sports statistics; he tries a sort of Bob
Ryanesque sports column; and he repeatedly reconstructs the final
moments of the year's National Basketball Association playoffs, which
ends up being one of his final pieces for the course. Yet, he only occasionally connects his own immediate sports experience with the content
of the sports entries, although it's clear that he has played sports all his
life and has a great deal of experience to connect with the pieces. Maybe
a better way of putting it might be to say that sports is central to his life
and that he does connect with sports in several ways, but that he generally resists writing about *his* immediate experience with sports. He
prefers to write about sports events or sports facts, to demonstrate his
knowledge of sports.

Here is a sampling of his entries on the subject of his sports literature class. Note that he becomes increasingly derisive of the class (he
will call it "another worthless sport lit class" in a later journal entry), but
continues to enjoy the reading. Notice also that he enjoys reading sports
journals and diaries of athletes but, like many of us, he makes no connections between the journals he reads and the journal he's writing. In
the last example I cite, he *does* connect personally with the experience of
the text he's responding to in a powerful and potentially textable way,
but then leaves it and does no more with it.

Page 5: Read three excellent stories today for Sport in Lit class. My
favorite was an excerpt from Jerry Kramer's *Instant Replay*. Great
book. It's a one year diary/journal kept by Jerry Kramer, an offen-

sive lineman for the Green Bay Packers during the Vince Lombardi days. So far I love this class. Everything we do is sports
related. Our assignment this weekend is to watch at least one
sporting event. Ha! What a joke.
Page 9: I have a lot of work to do before Friday because I won't be
doing any studying this weekend. Today is the best day of the
week for me. Only one class, and it's one that I like (Sports in Literature). It could be a great class but it's only a good class because
of the teacher. Not too impressive.
Page 16: . . . It also reminds me of a book I read called *The Basketball Diaries* by Jim Carroll. Despite the title, it's not really a sports
book. It's the actual diary of Jim Carroll from ages 12-15. It is
supposedly all true and it tells about this 5 year period of growing
up and getting into serious trouble (drugs, prostitution, etc) . . . I
wonder sometimes how a guy that intelligent could of had such a
screwed up childhood.
Page 20 [Talking about *Instant Replay* by Jerry Kramer again]: I loved
the book. I read it once in high school and liked it then. I wish I had
been old enough to see Vince Lombardi and the Packer dynasty. . . .
Kramer talks about being in the locker room after the game,
swamped by reporters for hours. Even after the last reporter had left,
he says "I was still in uniform still perched in front of my locker. I
really didn't want to get up. *I wanted to keep my uniform on as long as
possible.*" What a great line. I remember feeling the same way after
basketball games in high school. After a win we would stay out on
the court talking to friends, parents as long as possible. And then
hanging out in the locker room, being the last ones to leave.

Ted often chooses to write about sports (sports facts or sports
moments) when he's trying to develop paper topics. Thus, Ted does
indeed *try* to use the journal as a seedbed for developing essays, but for
whatever reason, he usually gets what looks like a serviceable first-draft
lead to me, then drops it abruptly, as in the following two examples:

Page 11: Sportsfans. Every city has them, from the hateful hecklers
of Philadelphia to the laid back folks of Los Angeles. Each hometown
crowd is unique.
    The most loyal fans are the Boston faithful. Celtics, Bruins,
Patriots, Red Sox—it's usually the same people—just different sta-
diums. When their teams are winning, you can't walk ten yards
without hearing someone talking about Larry Bird or Jim Rice.
                    —to be continued—

This is not working. It was supposed to be a free writing type
piece but I can't do it. I'm constantly editing myself in my head. I
might be able to do a paper on this subject because I like the topic,
but I can't do it in the free writing style.
Page 26: possible paper. Twenty-six point 4 yards every time he
touches the ball. Fifty point 6 points per game. One homerun
every twelve at bats . . . [and so on].
Stats can mean alot. They can also be misleading. . . . [Ted
fills the page with statistics, then stops.]
I'm getting bored with this paper already. I don't I think I
could stay with it for five pages.

But Ted's interest in sporting events also leads him into his
longest, most fluent writing in the journal, a kind of writing filled with
action, which might be classified as an "adventure story" in the vein of
the classic Animal House "road trip." Full of high adventure and personal risk, these entries seem quite reminiscent of the journals of travel
and adventure, exploration and exploit, that draw on venerated traditions of male journal keeping. Interestingly, all three of the men whose
journals I studied contained at least one extended entry of this type,
while none of the women's journals I examined carry equivalent kinds
of discourse.

One such entry by Steven (22-25), for example, reports on several
rowdy events that happen at the Randall Semi-Formal Ball (which he
has planned as dorm president). This four-page entry features vandal-
ism, someone getting his hand cut rather badly, a trip to the hospital,
and "partying" with a pretty nurse after it all. Tom, in his journal, nar-
rates a wild road trip to Dartmouth for a football game. Ted writes two
of these "adventure entries" consecutively, each at least two and a half
pages long. These short excerpts from the beginnings of both of the
entries should give a feeling for this sort of entry:

Page 31: What a weekend. Two trips to Boston and both times I
almost died from fear. Friday night I decided to go down to B.U.
with the boys to see the U.N.H. hockey game. I had a bad feeling
from the start as we packed nine people into a Buick Skylark. Little
did I know the troubles that awaited us. After about 40 minutes of
driving (flying) a few of the boys started cutting up lines of coke
on a mirror. Five minutes later there was a set of blue light(s) right
on our ass. Needless to say we were shitting bricks. Anyway we
pull over, the cop comes up to the car orders everyone out and
started chewing everyone out. For starters, we were doing 85

mph., there was a case of beer on the floor and the car was filled with smoke. . . .

Page 34: Here's another Boston story. Two days later. Same reason—B.U. vs. U.N.H. hockey. This took place after the game. We're trying to find our way out of Boston. Driving down Commonwealth Ave. and this jerk in a Trans Am pulls out of a alley and almost hits us. Naturally we honk the horn and give him the finger. Just as we slip past him the light turns red and we stop, with this guy right on our ass. Before we know it, 2 guys are outside pounding on the window. The light turns green, we take off, and so do they, after pelting the truck with a couple of rocks. Minutes later we come to another red light. We see the assholes a few cars up, so one of the guys jumps out, grabs a rock and whips it at the car. Two guys jump out, chase him back to the car, and just as he jumps in we take off, the guys jump in their car and we start a high speed chase, right out of a Burt Reynolds movie. . . .

For the majority of the men, then, the personal writing journal (outside of the writing and reading responses) seemed to function, at least in part, in a powerful and useful way for focusing, managing, and releasing pressure from academic and social responsibility. The journal was often used by the men as a daybook, a place to track and monitor activities and assignments, and to track and monitor their social positions in dormitory or fraternity hierarchy. All the men also included important and detailed entries about sports, from intramurals to the NBA playoffs, often borrowing on sports writing conventions and usually focusing on statistics, dramatic moments in sports history, winning, and losing. Sometimes, however, the entries on sports triggered more personal connections, such as in Ted's comments on staying in the locker room long after the game. Yet, those writings were not often seen as potential texts for further writing.

The men in the class did, of course, occasionally allude to interpersonal relations, family or friends, or, more rarely, girlfriends, in their journals but tended not to write extended or reflective entries on those topics. Ted, for example, mentions once, in passing, that he is going up to the University of Vermont for the weekend to see his girlfriend. But by the end of the paragraph he has turned his attention to the "Big Raid tonight with Alpha Xi Delta. It's their bids night so the girls should be *fired up!*" (9). While the men frequently refer to "girls," they almost never write at length about their relationships with their women friends (or their men friends for that matter). Although Tom does mention going home to see his family once and remarks on how good it feels to be there, his comment at the very beginning of the chapter, "it just seemed too personal," speaks for most of the men in his class. The men were, for the most part, not very interested in self-disclosure or self-examination on paper, although as we've seen they were quite candid in other ways, documenting their academic and social achievements, lapses, and irritations almost meticulously. However, they often seemed uncomfortable with the possibility that they might lose control over what might come onto the page. Ted, as we have seen, is always "editing" his freewriting and feels it's not a good way to start drafting a paper. And Tom is articulately and acutely aware of his need to control his writing, to keep his "free" ideas and associations at a distance when he writes about his freewriting:

> *Entry 61:* It seems like I'm only touching the surface. I should talk about something that isn't so superficial. I know there is something way down inside just waiting to be revealed. This exercise is designed to clear my senses, but it won't accomplish anything unless I let it. Nothing is really bothering me though. Why am I trying to block it? What's behind the wall?

Similarly, the men did not tend to find their experience textable, that is, capable of becoming more public or formal texts, such as essays for class or letters that might be sent. Ted mentions writing a letter "outside of class" once, then adds simply, "I hate writing letters." Even the long, fluent, powerful, "exploit" entries, which are full of action and adventure, rarely generated other writing. Ted makes the point explicitly in commenting on a draft of a personal narrative he has abandoned:

> *Entry 4:* I finished my first paper tonight. Don't like it at all. Never written a narrative paper like that before. Probably won't do it again. Some stories I guess are better left unwritten. As I wrote I started to recall more and more memories from that weekend, each one could be a whole paper in itself. The more I think of it the more I dislike the paper. I still love the story and thinking about it, but it just doesn't work on paper. It's one of those stories you just tell . . . It was a great fun wild weekend that I won't forget—and that's that.
>
> Enough about the paper. I don't even want to read it again. Much less revise it or do another draft on it.

For these men, the journals served some very important functions then, but they were not as often used in the ways I had originally conceived of them: as seedbeds for ideas for papers, or as spaces wherein to develop ideas for further writing, or as places to write and read the self—to personalize the acquisition of knowledge. The men did use the journals to comment thoughtfully on the problems and progress they noted in their writing and in school generally, although it is hard to tell how often they would have done that on their own, since many of the entries of this type were in-class journal assignments.

On the other hand, it might be useful to consider the possibility that the men did use the journal in some respect to "read and write the self." Perhaps their journals were "impersonal" in the common sense of the word, yet it seems to me that they do evoke or represent a sense of personhood, or of a discursively-positioned self. That self, as is consistent with contemporary theory, seems to be built around autonomy, around the marking, maintenance, and control of clear boundaries between inner and outer, self and other, life and text.

One last important kind of journaling often historically associated with men's journal keeping can be seen quite clearly in the journal kept by David, one of the other men in the class. Although I did not include his journal in the original study because he left the class for financial reasons before the end of the semester, his journal demonstrates another important set of journal traditions that men have participated in extensively: the commonplace/writer's-apprenticeship book.

Interested in becoming a writer, David has read many writers' journals and draws deliberately on these traditions in his own journal keeping. David's journal is a fascinating compendium of descriptions of people and things, including his bedroom wall (which has a pink abstract design and a poem by Mao on it), his opinions on whatever strikes his fancy ("10/2: I'm finding a very strong attraction to odd numbers lately"), fragments of fiction, interlarded with ambitious reading lists, lists of things to do, and lots and lots of quotes. One of his reading lists includes fiction by Joseph Heller, May Sarton, Albert Camus, Jean-Paul Sartre, Thomas Hardy, John Cheever, Upton Sinclair, Primo Levi, Thomas Mann, and Milan Kundera, and expository prose by Montaigne, Emerson, Nietzsche, Chomsky, Foucault, Arendt, and Eco. David finds himself and his mind a compelling subject for his self-conscious literary journal. I detected traces of Thoreau, hints of Pepys and Boswell resonating throughout the entries. Here is a taste of it (6-7):

It had always been like this—He felt most alive in the midst of death, namely, a cemetery.
"Live like a bourgeoisie, and think like a demigod"
—Flaubert

"An artist mediates between the world and minds; a critic merely between minds. An artist, therefore, even at the price of uncouthness and alienation from the contemporary cultural scene maintains allegiance to the world and fervent relation with it."
—Updike
Hemmingway signed letters as:
   Hemmy, Ernest, Ernie, E. H. Hemmingstein, Stein, Hem, Wemedge, Steen, Lovepups, Oin, Yogi, Liveright, Herbert J., Messkit, and of course . . . Papa.
   I met a man with the perfect voice for being a professor—a beautiful timbre, probably the way Jesus spoke—low but not full of vibratory bass, clean and sharp, but blunted as if pastel sounds—his voice is warm rich earthy hues of bronze heather, and duck-blind brown.
   Talk to C. G. about Amnesty International and Greenpeace. Write about Mental blocks.
   What is it about human nature—while traveling aboard a train we long for the natural beauty of the outdoors. Yet when we have a view of such, replete with exotic trees, stone laden streams, and compelling vales, we shy away somewhat—because it is too close. We are creatures who require "space" to define "beauty."
   Research Eastern religion and Martial Arts, also Scandinavian culture (esp. Finnish) Check on Hesse—dichotomy, idea much like own—aesthetics of futility concept.

The men's journals in that expository prose class clearly, albeit implicitly, manifested several important journal traditions historically affiliated with men: the daybook as a place to record daily activity, monitor productivity, and vent frustration with academic and social responsibilities; the exploration/expedition/travel journal updated for twentieth-century American college culture; and the commonplace book, as an essential adjunct to the developing writer/scholar. As we'll see shortly, however, most of the men, unaware of the rich intellectual traditions of the journal, were uncomfortable with the class journal because they were worried about its proximity to the dreaded *diary*.

Women's Journals: Characteristic Topics, Uses, and Functions

While the women did write about school and social life, keeping track of work and responsibilities as the men had done, the journals they produced were generally consonant with the women's journaling traditions sketched out in the previous chapter and with their muted discursive heritage.

For example, though the women did express anxiety about school and their classwork, they did so much less frequently than the men. When the topic came up, it tended to be associated with some kind of problem solving (as we saw in Sarah's entry), with sheer exhaustion, or with self-blame or exhortation rather than irritation and anger.

The extended journal entry by Jennifer that follows is a good example of the women's tendency to use their journal to write through their academic stress. This one is interesting because it also shows us something of Jennifer's attitude toward journal writing itself, an area in which I found very significant gender differences.

> *5 November:* I find it's increasingly difficult to write now. I'm not sure why. Journals are often like that w/me—I start very excited, full of thoughts and ideas but gradually that enthusiasm fades and I have to make an effort to write. I usually stop writing then because I feel like it is not serving its purpose. I can't stop writing here, though, and maybe it will be good for me. (to stick w/it) Perhaps I have reached a barrier but can get over it if I don't give up. I'll try.
>
> I've had so much studying to do in these past weeks that I've been feeling burned out. To write during that time would have only added more stress. I think that it's good that I realized this and took some time away from the journal.
>
> I think I'm ready to begin again.

Carrie, too, is worried about the amount of homework that she has to do, but notice the difference in tone between her handling of her worries and that of Tom or Ted:

> *21 September:* All I can do is think about how much work I have to do. Ever since the first day of classes I've been so weighted down by work that when the weekend finally comes, I don't feel good about myself when I go out. Thank god I don't have classes on Fridays. Usually I try to finish the readings I couldn't find time for throughout the week. Every Thursday I write a list of all the homework I have to do for Tues. The list just keeps on getting bigger and bigger.
>
> *19 November:* I'm striving for self actualization—what is keeping me below this level? I want to be all that I can be. I want to do my best in school. I want to be the best friend of all who deserve my

attention. I want to use my time wisely: every minute devoted to doing something. I want to do all I can now that will help me in my future.

So many unanswered questions hang like dirty socks on the shower curtain rod. If I don't start getting my life in order soon, those socks will leave a permanent stench in the bathroom that no air freshener or even ammonia could break up, it could only cover the underlying problem of a confused and disorganized mind. . . . I've got to exert myself, drown myself with my books. Stimulate my mind with books and lectures. Uncover parts of my brain and memory to find interesting, invigorating methods of conveying my thoughts.

In contrast to the men and in keeping with women's journaling traditions as interpersonally focused and as a means of self-construction, my female students tended to write more extended and reflective entries regarding their social, academic, and personal lives than did the men. Understanding the journal as part of a discursive network, which it has been for women since the eighteenth century, some of my female journalers even drafted important letters in their journals, which they then copied out and sent, usually to family or close friends. *None* of the men chose to do this. The women as a group devoted considerable space to examining and connecting their personal and interpersonal experience and their academic experience, and to finding ways to connect their voices and experience to academic texts and discursive practices.

Let me take you into Carrie's, Jennifer's, and Sarah's journals to sample some of their entries. Carrie's journal starts with two drafts of a piece she finally turns in much later about her wealthy, distant mother who beats her and how she still needs to connect with her. Also among her early entries are several drafts of a letter to her father whom she loves dearly.

Entry 5: I just can't stop smiling. Seriously, I haven't been this happy for god knows how long. In fact I don't think I've been this happy in a year. [She has met Bobby who becomes her boyfriend.] *Entry 8:* So many feelings and thoughts are unspoken. Why don't people just come out and say what they are thinking? I must have encountered 100 people today. Some of those acquaintances were accompanied by hellos, some simply with smiles or nods. What do all these daily rituals mean . . . I see friendly smiling eyes in the distance that belong to a boy I know. As our distance shortens my

body tenses. What will I say to him, him to me. "Hi," he comfortably says, "you look really nice today." Stumbling for something
to say, I turn purple and red. What makes me look better today
than yesterday? Is he just being friendly. I mentally review my
appearance. I wonder what I'm wearing: too sexy, too conserva-
tive, too boring? We pass each other by, both thinking about the
immediate encounter? Does he like me? Does he hate me? Does he
care? Why do I care?
Entry 15: The rain jubilantly bounced off the damp hood of my
blue Cataract. My nose seemed like a cold iron plate. The top of
my Tretorns were sopping wet, the tips covered with mud. My
toes were numb. My whole body was as numb as my toes, but it
wasn't from the weather. It was a happy ethereal feeling I'd never
felt before. Sloshing thru puddles like a 7 year old, I noticed that
my inside of my mouth could feel light sprinkles of water. I then
noticed why. My lips had been spread apart into a wide uncon-
trolled smile. I felt as if I crossed streets and skipped down the
sidewalk oblivious to all the bewildered stares and honking horns.
My body floated across the streets and sidewalks like a red sun-
touched leaf blowing in the wind.

Many of these "thick descriptions" of personal and interpersonal
events or relations go on for *several* pages. Notice the predominant focus
on connecting internal and external events in the women's journals,
while the men choose to write about more externally dramatic events,
like winning the intramurals or getting arrested for speeding or drugs.
One striking thing about Carrie's journal and many of the other
women's journals is the narrative and textual quality that their own
lives take on in writing. For many women in this class, personal experience was seen precisely as some kind of text that needed to be written to
be understood, and indeed, many more of their journal topics were
developed into more formal papers. As another woman in the class,
Christina, put it in her journal: "Writing. A release. A desire to express
captured feelings, verbalized thoughts. I need to write. I need to corre-
late my thinking and my acting—on paper the two seem to flow
together."

Jennifer, the second woman whose journal we'll look at, sets out
only to talk about reading and writing (her own and that of others)
because she is already keeping her own personal journal. Nevertheless,
the focus on human relationships, caring, and communication that we
saw in Carrie's writing is ever-present in Jennifer's journal as well. And
while this journal for her is not a personal journal, she still discloses far

more about her personal situation, feelings, and ideas than her male counterparts generally do. In her first entry, for example, Jennifer introduces her boyfriend John.

> *8 September:* I got a call from John, though, which made the night worthwhile. I had a feeling his name would turn up in here sooner or later. Perhaps that's the price you pay for being in love. Is it expensive to be in love? (besides phone calls, stamps, and gas I mean?)
> *10 September:* Perhaps my first paper will deal with the book "The Color Purple." I became very involved in it. Or perhaps something with a theme similar to what that story was about (my own story). I feel personally involved with the theme of LOVE at this stage of my life.
> *12 September:* The ring on her finger could be the ring on mine. But I'm too young—is she???
> *24 November* [Thanksgiving Break]: Boy it's great to be home. . . . Steven is so tall, Jim's sense of humor hasn't changed, and Chris seems so self-confident. Of course my parents are as loving as ever to me—good paper topics.

Jennifer, like Carrie, frequently renders her life experiences in the journal as possible texts or possible stories. While Carrie makes small moments into rich, well-elaborated descriptive narratives, Jennifer writes of composing her own story of love after reading *The Color Purple* and refers to the members of her family as "good paper topics."

Sarah's daybook section of her journal, the final woman's journal we'll discuss, also demonstrates the traits that seem to characterize women's journal writing: the presence of frequent drafting based on journal entries, letter writing and self-induced freewriting, a focus on relationship, reflection, and communication, and the intriguing strategy of rendering personal experience as a reflective, textual narrative, of "composing the self." For example, Sarah's very first daybook entry starts with what appear to be two random renderings of an early life experience:

> *12 September:* I remember standing on the plaid couch in our musty basement watching Gilligan's Island. I had the chicken pox and mom brought me a glass of Hawaiian punch and pretzels.
> Maribeth and I used to ride her dog Clipper (a black lab) all around the neighborhood. We thought he was as big as a horse. We'd play on my blue and orange swings for hours. We both had

navy blue Keds and would listen to "Hey Jude" on her parent's stereo. Maribeth wanted to carry a purse filled with make up to school on the first day. Her mom wouldn't let her and stopped her on the way to the bus stop. Painted faces from the Lionville Elementary School fair.

Or consider this excerpt from an entry concerning a weekend with Rush, Sarah's boyfriend, up in the White Mountains. It also has that descriptive narrative textual quality.

1 October: Rush and I took off early Saturday morning for the White Mountains. We packed a picnic lunch and ate it on two smooth rocks in the middle of the river. Oh how could I forget the delicious cider that we picked up alongside the road. *Pictures.* We snapped away so many of them I can't wait to see them. We jumped from rock to rock downstream along the river, [an] array of colors dotted the mountainside. The sun went down and the clouds began to move swiftly across the sky.

Sarah's entries often take the form of freewriting. She allows herself to move freely from large questions about career choice and relationships ("Why can't two people who love each other get along? Why?" (15 October)) to the smallest of irritations, such as stubbly legs. Like those of many of the women, her entries often give the sense of a powerful cognitive and affective collage. One sees a multiple self in the process of constructing itself:

12 September: I wish I had a camera around my neck right now and I could just take off—somewhere where no one else has been—they'd have been there physically—it would look different to me—it would be my world—seen through my eyes. I know we have to live each day at a time—live for now—But I like to sit and daydream, what will my life be like 10 years from now. Will I have kids? I want little boys. There's so much to take advantage of around me and I don't want to let it slip by anymore. Rush and I should go on the Cambridge Exchange. We could do that next summer. If you could go back in time, when would it be? 50s? 20s? My legs are stubbly—yuk—what would I be like if I grew up in a city environment? Maybe I could write an English paper about that. I want my hair to grow.
2 December: Why do I feel this way? One minute happy— depressed the next. This huge house was being moved up Main

Street. It was wild—I looked out the window and a house was staring me in the face. Why do I blow things off? I've been doing better lately. Right now all I can think of is going home for Christmas. I'm getting those stupid feelings again with Rush. Am I being too affectionate? A stupid girlfriend? How should I act? I should act the way I want. I'm tired of being put down.

Attitudes toward the Journals

That the students implicitly drew on gendered traditions (often from popular culture rather than academic culture) in their writing journals suggests that they have a gendered conception of the journal generally, and indeed, that they see the journal as a gendered genre. Their understanding of the journal as a gendered form is based both on their knowledge of the popular associations with the genre(s) and on their own nonacademic experience with journaling. What was most striking to me was that both the men and the women in my class tended to see the personal writing journal as a feminized type of writing and that the men, in particular, tended to be suspicious of its academic/masculine value.

One indication that the men did not value the journal as much as the women is that they simply didn't use their journals as much. In fact, the average woman's journal (119 pages) was over twice as long as the man's (48 pages). Seven of the eleven women in my class had journals over a hundred pages long, while the longest man's journal was eighty-two pages in length. For a more specific illustration of the disparate lengths of the journals, let's look at the six journals I'm using as representative: Tom's, Steven's, and Ted's numbered 82, 27, and 33 pages respectively; Carrie's, Jennifer's, and Sarah's were 130, 120, and 73 pages long.

Even more telling is the fact that over half (at least seven of eleven) of the women were actually keeping their own personal journals *in addition* to the journals they produced for class. None of the men who completed the class reported having kept journals previously, except those who had been "forced" to do so in previous classes. As one young man, Ted, put it in the epigraph that started this chapter, "It's been eight years since I kept any kind of a journal, since seventh grade English. I can't say that I miss doing it, I used to hate it—five pages a week."

These differences in length, use, and function are clearly apparent in the comments the men and women make about their journal writing and in their attitudes toward their journals and toward writing generally. These attitudes have already been prefigured in several of the student quotes. Simply put, while both the men and women considered their journals as jobs to do—which they were—the men overwhelmingly felt that their journals were a chore. They were a responsibility foisted upon them from outside that they were not particularly committed to and that, often enough, they considered a waste of their time. Steven, commenting that his journal needs improvement, writes, "So what the heck. I'll do some mindless free righting (bad) writing."

Tom also writes constantly about having nothing to say in his journal. In fact, many of his entries start with some variation on this theme:

Entry 4: Not much happening today. No writing, just reading, so I guess I'll freewrite for five minutes. [Tom tries but finds it's too noisy in the library.]

Entry 5: Nothing to say whatsoever. I haven't really thought about what I'm going to write my next paper on, but I have a feeling I better start quick.

Entry 12: The only thing that was anything near worth writing about was Andre Guerron and the UNH Wildcats and they lost. Last Saturday I didn't write anything. I know that's bad, but what kind of writing is this? I'm writing about nothing that means nothing to no one. I hate doing things for no reason.

Entry 55: Nothing much happened to me today and I think this journal entry is going to be an indication of why I need a vacation. It's not only myself but also everyone else. We all just seem to be going through the motions. . . . I'm just writing right now just to fill space and I think that's bad.

Entry 67: I'm so sick of writing that all I want to do is get to the bottom of the page, but I don't even think I can get there. [Tom writes about the music he's listening to and thinks he might write a paper on some song lyrics, so one might think he's gotten something from the writing. But when he reaches the bottom, he writes "I made it!" and stops abruptly.]

Tom probably got more from his journal than he realized. For one thing he obviously needed to release all that academic pressure he felt, and release it he did, which certainly helped clear his mind for more productive tasks. Interestingly enough, although he protests he has nothing to say, he usually goes on to fill a full page or more. Even so, it was arduous work, and he clearly felt it was not as effective a writing tool as it could have been. And Tom wrote more than any of the other men in the class.

Ted's comments on his journal and journal keeping tend to bear an uncanny resemblance to Tom's and Steven's. In addition to the blunt, but honest, comment on hating to keep a journal for his seventh-grade English class, Ted repeatedly comments on his troubles with "freewriting," which he associates with the journal. Ted is also the fellow who, deciding to abandon the idea of writing a paper on a wild weekend he had spent during the summer, reports that some stories can be told, but not written. He does not, in other words, see his life as particularly textable.

Echoing Steven's feeling that freewriting in the journal is essentially useless, Ted starts an assigned freewriting exercise in class with: "Freewriting again. Ten minutes of non-stop writing. At least I can use this for a journal entry" (24-25). Like Tom, Ted has trouble with finding anything to write in his daybook, resisting life as text, and feels the need to carefully control his writing. Paradoxically, Ted feels uncomfortable with his freewriting but feels he could do a more formal or public class paper without any difficulty. He writes: "This is not working. It was supposed to be a freewriting type piece. But I can't do it. I'm constantly editing myself in my head. I might be able to do a paper on this subject because I like the topic but I can't do it in the freewriting style" (11). At another point he thinks maybe he'll write a paper on songs and song lyrics, so he starts to jot down ideas but then stops, remarking "Not getting anywhere with this freewriting shit so I'm cutting myself off" (9).

In fact, the men's attitudes toward their journals are amply demonstrated by the fact that they generally wrote less and less as the semester went on, as Steven did, or like Ted, simply stopped writing shortly after the middle of the term. Clearly, although the men did sometimes say it was good to release pressure in the journals, journal-writing assignments were not perceived by the men as being nearly as useful or pleasurable as they were by the women.

The women usually did find their journals to be valuable and useful to them, and tended to enjoy freewriting. In fact, they seemed to find reading and writing generally to be valuable activities. Christina writes at one point, "since I was a little girl I have always loved reading and writing. To others it might have been a chore—but to me it was purely a pleasure." She later makes the specific connection between writing and understanding her life mentioned earlier. We have seen Jennifer working through her journal slump by trying to find new strategies to make the journal work for her.

Here are some other comments women made about their journal keeping. Carrie writes, for example, in response to Joan Didion's "On Keeping a Notebook," "She brings up a very interesting question, why does she keep a notebook? I write in a diary myself which is not too different from a notebook. I don't write daily accounts of happenings. I write down how I'm doing and how I feel about others close to me."

Jennifer deliberately looks for ways to renew the value of her journal, and finds pleasure (and insight) in her freewriting entries, as we can see in the following passages:

> 20 November [Jennifer tries freewriting to help her get going in the journal. She writes about working in a bookstore]: I had a great time. There are so many books I want to read. I just got the inspiration I think I needed to keep a journal. I've been waiting for something related to my writing or reading to note in here—I want it to be "relevant." But isn't everything I do or hear or say relevant to my life and therefore to my writing?
> 30 November: I'm beginning to enjoy the journal writing. It's like a personal challenge to write every day. A challenge with an instant reward.
> 2 December [Jennifer is responding to freewriting]: I loved it—trying to recall the minute details of the Christmas tree brought back so many memories. I realized it's the little details that make it so special and unique to our family.

Sarah is even more adulatory about journal writing, freewriting, and poetry writing than Jennifer because she sees her life as a sort of continuous fluid text writing itself from inside her, as we see in her response to Didion's piece on journals below. While Tom, Ted, and Steven would prefer to write papers (public, formal texts) rather than journals, Sarah clearly prefers the private, personal, and connected nature of the journal and freewriting to more public formal writing. She feels she can put herself "into the poem." Indeed, for Sarah, in the final excerpt below, the boundaries between life and text are so fluid (as they are for Christina, who also sees writing as necessary for her life), she can't tell which to write about. In contrast to Ted, who prefers formal academic writing to writing in his journal, Sarah finds in her journal an opportunity to negotiate between the word and the world and her relationally-based, present and possible selves, while her academic writing is a source of real concern for her.

> 10 September: Like Joan Didion, my journal contains various quotes, short paragraphs and lines. I write down how I feel, not factual information. I write on how I perceive a certain event or what I get out of a quote. No one would understand or get anything out of my journal. It's about how I see the world and about

how *I* feel about certain things. I love it. I never realized until I met a special friend last year, how different people's thoughts are. You take a situation and I could look at it completely differently than another person. For example, looking back in my journal, I found an entry, "Bert's Barn, memories of a big red house. it sits on the dunes. Seagulls soar overhead as laughter is heard in the house. Family. The beach. We're all together."

Now like Joan has her own thoughts about her writing . . . these lines mean something special to me. Bert's Barn is our family's (relative's) beach house. It's a reunion spot. If anyone else read this they'd interpret it differently.

In my journal I daydream a lot of the way I want to be or would like my life to be like. Reading Joan's essay, made me realize just why I keep a journal, too. It's something private for me and only pertaining to me. They're my thoughts. Thanks Joan, for helping me remember that.

26 November [Sarah freewrites on how hard revising and editing are] I love to write in journals and freewriting but making papers the best just isn't my cup of tea. It seems as though I always mess things up instead of making them better. I really like poetry. I really love to write poems. I guess it's because I can really feel the words—I put myself into the poem.

In sum, the journals proved valuable in different ways for the men and the women. The men's interests, as represented by what they were willing to write down, tended to cluster around their academic and social responsibilities or burdens. Thus, their journals served to identify those responsibilities or burdens, explain them, plan for them, and vent frustrations connected to them. Occasionally, they brought other parts of their lives into the texts of their journals, usually in the form of sports activities or dramatic, action-packed adventures. The men, however, felt less comfortable with their journals overall, especially with "freewriting," or what they considered to be personal writing (writing about feelings other than anger or frustration; writing about relationships). They tended to code or mask their personal connections to experience or ideas. When they did make personal connections in their journals (as they all inevitably did), the men usually stopped writing or pulled back in some way from that connection. From their own remarks, it appears they did not want to lose control over what happened on the page. They did not want to risk too much self-disclosure.

Thus, the men felt the journals were often a chore, in part because they had a difficult time figuring out what they could write in them that would not compromise their authority. They were loathe to relinquish their sense of control over both objective information and subjective experience.

While the men tended to prefer the experience of authority, then, the women tended to prefer the authority of experience. The women felt much more comfortable with their journals because they tended to see their lives as texts that needed to be written and read to be understood. They used the journals for freewriting and other personal writing, including letter writing, drafting papers, and problem solving, among other things, and found them to be both pleasurable and valuable.

While it is difficult to generalize about the relationship of gender and journals from six students in one composition class, I do not think my findings are anomalous. For example, I see the same characteristics in the women's studies journals that I have found in composition classes.

Women's Studies Journals

In the Women's Studies classes I teach (usually composed entirely of women), journals often play an essential role in student efforts to integrate scholarly knowledge about women and women's issues with their own knowledge and experience. Students discuss the issue of women's discursive muteness and are encouraged to use journals as an intellectually empowering form that is not alien to their discursive traditions. And use it they do. In addition to writing short papers every other week, and preparing a final formal paper or project, the women generally turn in journals that are well over a hundred, and often two hundred, pages long. I have actually received journals of up to *four hundred* pages in length, from students like Tricia. Here is Tricia writing about her journaling:[4]

27 September 1989: This class journal gives me [an] opportunity to document my growth. I know it's supposed to be thoughts related to this class—but this class is so much related to my life, so I can't help but let myself and my life spill over onto these pages.

20 October 1989: I write what I want to write, and I admit some of it—well you'd have to stretch it to really make it relevant to this course. But then, not really. Women are a part of life. Their experiences aren't all with children or work or bodily appearance, or "issues." They are—like me, not always getting enough sleep, holding conversations with friends who are in pain, remembering the loss of loved ones. Sometimes I wonder if I am wasting your time by including these comments, etc. But this is my journal—a place to keep my thoughts. My thoughts aren't always zeroed in on chapters from the text, and my thoughts aren't always rational or coherent. But I find that jotting down even far-fetched examples from my personal life helps me understand the class material better *and* helps me deal with my own life. That's what education means to me. I don't cease being me when I walk into the classroom. I have to stay in touch with myself even as I struggle through Chodorow's and Lever's theories. What good would I be to humankind if I deny the expression of my own experience?

5 November 1989: I was thinking about what we were discussing in class—whether or not journals are written with an audience in mind. I don't mean to be nit-picky, but I think that is the wrong word to use—audience I mean. Reader would be more appropriate. Audience stirs up this image in my head of a performance, and a performance is not what I intend to achieve as I write. I don't think the other women who wrote journals intended them as performances. . . .

From page one of my journal I have been conscious of the fact that my entries would be read by you—my professor. I guess I write this journal to you. But you are not my audience. I don't have to put on costumes or assumed roles. I have just written what is me—my thoughts, feelings, memories, perceptions, and misconceptions at times. I will admit that I have been more brave in revealing more of myself than I would have had we simply had conversations. Writing allows you to free yourself of your usual inhibitions. But that's not the same as performing.

Still I realize that I write this journal to me. I just happen to share it with you—a course requirement. I guess I believe that every person is really more than one person, and sometimes one part of a person will know something before the rest of the person. A journal helps to inform a person—the whole person—what all the parts of the person know. I'm not schizophrenic, but I don't always know myself very well. This journal is acquainting me with parts of me. I read what I think about things—comments I made; and I re-think what I wrote, and sometimes I revise the way I think.

Many of these students try to tell the truth about their experience as women, as they try to construct and reconstruct themselves as subjects of knowledge through language. Coming to voice is a central epistemological metaphor for intellectual development, as Mary Field

Belenky, Blythe McVicker Clinchy, Nancy Rule Goldberger, and Jill Mattuck Tarule show in *Women's Ways of Knowing*. Many of my students, however, have been silenced or, at best, discouraged from expressing themselves, not only by the all-pervasive mutings of education and socialization, but also by sexual violence. Every semester I find that at least a quarter to a third of my female Women's Studies students are survivors of incest or early sexual abuse. At least half, if not more, of the members of the class have experienced some form of sexual violence, a violence that silences them. Like untold numbers of women in the past, many of these students have literally used their writing and their journals to break their silence for the first time, to construct a self, to find their voices. Nonetheless, this does not mean that they write antifamily journals or "journals of man-hating and sexual development," as women's journals have been called in certain quarters. Carolyn and Tricia are two good examples. Here is what Carolyn wrote on 11 September 1988:

> I don't think about *writing* it when I'm writing in my journal—never occurred to me to wonder "who" I am writing to, or to name the journal as though it were someone else—although there *are* times that I address parts of my own self that seem inaccessible. I'm not sure they listen, let alone respond. Regardless, journal writing is my major addiction: I would surely die without it.
>
> What I did last night, when I felt too self conscious to write, was unpack my journals from the box they are overflowing, and set them out on a shelf. Not aesthetic, by any means: a solid row of wire spirals—but all these years (five, next month) I've hidden my journals in the closet did not prepare me for the visual heft of 28 volumes lined up on the shelf. I am awed—keep looking over there at the visual indisputable evidence of my existence—considering where I started from, I feel I have literally written myself into existence.

Tricia wrote on 28 October 1989:

> But as we discussed in class on 10-4-89, "Poetry is not a luxury." I don't remember who you said said that, but I do know that those words are so true. Poetry was my lifeline for so many years. It served as anchor to bring me in touch with reality. It served as a casting line to dare me to reach out and grow. It served as bait for others to see that there was more to me than what was showing on

the surface. It served as a net to gather all my experiences and feelings to be sorted in a way that would make sense and make a profit for me (the profit of real relationships and ever improving self esteem.)

These women understand, as did the early twentieth-century diarist Evelyn Scott, that "Knowledge is the condition of my being" (Moffat and Painter 1975, 101).

Miscellaneous Support

Several miscellaneous bits of information and experiences I have gathered over the years also suggest that the trend toward the gendering of the journal is quite real. For one thing, I have repeatedly received journal entries, poems, even final papers written by women as encomiums to their journals, and to the intellectual and personal pleasures they find in writing them. For example, at the end of fall semester 1988, I received a gift from one of my women composition students. It was a blank journal (actually, the one I'm currently using) and inside was a photocopied set of some of the student's journal entries along with the following inscription: "Cindy, Thought I would share this with you. I opened this journal after seven years. I decided to pick up where I left off. Thank you for the inspiration. Love, Jane." I have yet to receive a single paean of praise for the journal from one of my men students, although many will admit, sometimes grudgingly, that the journal was good for them. The only exceptions I have come across are either men who want to be writers and find their journals useful as writers' notebooks or, occasionally, men who have been radically marginalized by specific events, their ethnicity, their sexual orientation, or some other factor.

I have also found that at the end of every course, several of my women students will immediately ask for their journals back. If I do not return them quickly, I get phone calls, even letters requesting that the journals be returned. My men students generally want their graded papers back, but rarely request their journals.

In addition, I have shared the results of my research with some of my classes, and the men and the women alike almost universally share the perspectives of the men and the women evoked on these pages. When I ask for comments, the men often tell me they are glad their discomfort is shared by other men. The women are pleased to find out that other women secretly find pleasure or even life in their journals, as they do. During one of her weekly writing conferences last year, one young

woman who was very quiet in class confided to me that she had always
kept a journal. When I asked why, she responded, just as Marie
Bashkirtseff had a hundred years ago, "Well, what would happen if I
died. I know it's morbid, but there would be nothing left of me if I
didn't." This fall, another student, for whom I was directing an indepen-
dent study, included a letter with her final project. The letter began:
"Enclosed are copies of my life, which is my journal work. The other
pages are the facts that I'll use at the beginning" (11 August 1989).

In sharing my research with faculty groups, I inevitably hear anecdotes whose thrust is remarkably consonant with my own findings
regarding the journal. For example, I was working on some curriculum
plans with three colleagues from my institution one afternoon, and we
began to discuss my research. Each of the instructors immediately
offered confirmation of the discomfort many males feel with the journal.
One colleague, Jean Zipke, reported that one of her male students
refused to write a journal for her class. When pressed to do so, the student finally turned up with a series of "love poems" he had written the
previous year to a girlfriend. Gail Rondeau, another colleague, reported
that one of her male students had also flatly refused to do a journal and
had figured out that he would have sufficient points to pass the course
(barely) without one. He preferred the "D" to doing the journal.

Jerry Duffy, an instructor at the University of New Hampshire in
Durham, came up to me after I had given a talk on my work, and
reported that one of his students had actually written a paper about
receiving a blank journal book from his grandmother and feeling considerable tension over whether or not he ought to write in it, as keeping
a journal was something that girls did. Finally, he did write in it and
found, as my colleague reported, that it "helped him record and sort out
the feelings of a troubled adolescence." Even though the student found
the journal useful, he didn't broadcast the fact that he was writing one.
And while writing up that anecdote, Jerry Duffy came across another
series of echoic remarks by another student in a paper about trying to
become a writer. Not only does this student derogate the diary, he also
fears its feminizing influence and the possibility that his disclosures will
show him to be unoriginal.

Sure, I keep a journal too, but I fear it has almost degenerated into
a Diary (a label which has always suggested to me something an
emotional pre-adolescent keeps, furiously writing out her
thoughts every time the captain of the football team looks at her or
whenever she develops another pimple). I have kept my Journal
for three years but I firmly believe it has only served to turn me

into an overly-introspective individual. I rarely use it to write down original cogitations and meditations because it seems as though so many thoughts have already been written about at length. (Student paper, 2 April 1987)

Over lunch last year, Bob Connors, a noted rhetorician and a colleague of mine at the University of New Hampshire, explained that while he had kept a journal for a short time during his college years, he, too, was worried about it being too much like a diary. In fact, he scratched out the label *Diary* that appeared in large letters on the front of the blank book, and wrote *Journal* over it.

But I wanted more than anecdotal support for my findings. Therefore, I administered a writing-experience questionnaire to all sections of the composition course that began the fall semester of 1986. The results of my gleaning appear in the next section.

Results from the Writing Experience Survey (WES)

The Writing Experience Survey is a three-page questionnaire frequently given out at the beginning of the semester to entering composition students. It provides instructors with a detailed profile of a student's previous writing and reading experiences, both in school (usually high school) and out of school (in the workplace or at home). The WES is also used in the classroom to initiate students' assessments of the varieties of their own literate behaviors as well.[5]

Certain questions on the WES ask specifically whether students have kept journals in school or personal journals/diaries at home. Students are also requested to state their impressions of both kinds of journal experiences. My colleagues and I also asked about other kinds of personal writing (letters, poetry, and so forth) that students might have done in order to see what kinds of personal writing might or might not be identified as *journal writing* or *diary writing* by individual students.

I checked the responses to these questions from seventy-six students (forty-one females and thirty-five males) enrolled in four sections of Freshman English that fall. The information they yielded was quite rich and deserving of a full discussion in itself, but here I will only look at two major patterns of response that confirm my hypotheses.

First, I found that, while almost equal numbers of males and females had been required to keep some form of writing journal in school at some previous time (twenty-four of the women and twenty of the men (see Table 5.1, page 183), far more women than men kept personal journals or diaries, just as was the case in my class. Indeed, as

TABLE 5.1
Number of Male/Female Students Keeping Class Journals and/or
Personal Journals

Females/Section		Class Journal	Personal Journal
Zipke	n=12	9	8
Gannett	n=8	3	4
Lambert	n=10	6	7
Rondeau	n=11	6	9
TOTAL	n=41	TOTAL n=24	TOTAL n=28
Males/Section		Class Journal	Personal Journal
Zipke	n=11	6	2*
Gannett	n=9	5	1*
Lambert	n=8	4	0
Rondeau	n=7	5	1
TOTAL	n=35	TOTAL n=20	TOTAL n=4*

*Two of the four "personal journals" were actually logs of sports activities. A third was a sailor's journal.

Table 5.1 shows, a majority of women (twenty-eight of forty-one) had done some kind of writing on their own that they were willing to identify as a journal or diary.

However, only four of the thirty-five men responding reported having kept a journal or diary on their own. Their responses are very interesting. Two of the four men had kept what were essentially logs of one kind of activity or sport, another important male-affiliated diary tradition. Respondent Z-4 (age nineteen), for example, writes "No" when asked if he keeps a personal journal, but then goes on to say, "For three years I kept a running diary of mileage and times. My coach suggested it and I benefited from it." Another student, G-6 (age eighteen), responds "Yes" to keeping a personal journal that records his climbing activity over the course of a summer. "It was a journal of climbs in New Hampshire I have done. Only one summer. 1985. I wanted to keep a list to see if my climbing was improving. My ethics and style. And I kept it to recall experiences and people I met." Notice that both of these journals were discrete both in duration and in focus; the journals were undertaken primarily in order to improve performance and skill in sport.

The third man who kept a personal journal, Respondent R-3, was also an interesting case. He had been in the United States Navy and had kept a journal during his time at sea. The isolation during time at sea, the need to fill time with quiet activity, and the wish to chronicle his travels may all have motivated his journal, as such factors have motivated sailors' journals over the centuries. He writes, "I had a day to day book back about two years ago." He can't remember, however, precisely why he started it, and notes that he lost interest in it after he got back on dry land: "Once I lost the interest I soon after lost the book."

Indeed, only one out of the thirty-five men polled, Z-11 (age seventeen), kept what might actually be termed a personal journal. And he used it in precisely the same way Steven, Tom, and Ted, my former students, had: to release pressure. Here is what he writes about his journal: "I write down many of my problems. I write in it sporadically. It may be hours or weeks between entries. I needed a way to let out frustration."

Thus, with the exception of respondent Z-11, who used his journal to write about his personal problems, the few journals that the men in this sample kept were either logs of activities, or listings of day-to-day happenings. They were kept for brief, discrete periods of time and motivated by a specific pragmatic purpose. They were not intended to be *personal* journals.

It will not be possible to explore all the women's descriptions and impressions of their personal journals here in detail. Suffice it to say that many of the women who reported keeping personal journals describe them in the same ways that Sarah, Carrie, Jennifer, Christina and the other women do. While a few of the women responded by saying that they tried writing a diary or journal and were either too lazy or didn't find the journal useful, most of the women who had kept or were keeping personal journals found them valuable. They often say, for example, that they want to safeguard their memories, or keep records of their lives or the changes they had been through or would go through. Many also report self-expression as a primary function of their journals. Several of the women also report that they have been keeping their journals (sometimes continuously, sometimes sporadically) for several years. One student, R-3, says that she has been keeping a journal ever since her eighth birthday, ten years earlier, while another student says that she has been writing one ever since she learned to write (L-10). Another woman, G-5, writes: "A diary, my everyday events, no matter how boring or exciting, my feelings, my goals, also my dreams and secrets." As for its value, she writes, "I love my journal. It keeps everything, every moment or feeling that has affected me." Her response was echoed in several of the other women's remarks. One, R-1, said simply that her journal was "priceless."

Most importantly, the men's and women's attitudes about and experience with personal journals or diaries carried over into their attitudes about keeping class journals. We have no way of knowing exactly what kinds of journals had been required of the twenty-four women and twenty men who reported keeping journals in school, but they were in all likelihood quite various in nature. From the comments students made on the survey, it appears that some were daybooks, some were freewriting journals, and others were reading logs. Some students said they had been assigned topics to write about, while others reported writing about whatever topics interested them. Nonetheless, however wide the range of previous journal experience, gender would remain a critical determinant of whether the journal was perceived positively or negatively by my first-year composition students.

Table 5.2 and Figure 5.1 show how dramatically the males and females differed in their attitudes toward the journals they had kept for school. I gave "positive" ratings to those who made only positive remarks such as "Great, very helpful" or "I enjoyed it." Mixed responses were answers such as, "Sometimes tedious, mostly enjoyable" or "OK. Somedays I had something to write about, some days I didn't." Negative responses were usually short and to the point: "I never took it seriously" or "I hated it—thrown out of class for writing what I felt." Again, as was the case in my class, eighty percent of the males had mixed or negative responses (fifty percent made *only* negative comments). The females made almost diametrically opposed remarks, with nearly seventy percent reporting only positive impressions of the journals.

Another interesting thing I discovered is that the men and women who disliked the journals did so for differing reasons. Just like Tom, Steven, and Ted, the men tended to say the journals were "a waste" or "boring," or that they didn't like writing personal things. The few women who were uncomfortable tended to say rather that their journals were "*too* private" or "too personal to be graded." They were aware, that is to say, of the tension between their nonacademic journaling and most academic discourse.

These journal attitudes and habits appear to be well in place long before students come to college. In 1987, when my son was a fourth grader, he came home one evening and reported his extreme dislike of the class journals all the students had to keep. Since he had kept a little notebook/travel journal when he was five and six years old, I was somewhat surprised by this sudden reversal in attitude. When I asked him why he disliked the journal so much, he said simply, "All the guys hate it." When I talked to his teacher, Joan Zelonis, she reported that the older children were less and less interested in self-disclosing writing, particularly the boys. She remembered auctioning off some blank books for the children to

TABLE 5.2
Gendered Attitudes to Class Journals by Sections

Females		Positive	Mixed	Negative
Zipke	n=9	5	3	1
Gannett	n=3	2	0	1
Lambert	n=6	6	0	0
Rondeau	n=6	3	2	1
TOTAL	n=24	16	5	3

Males		Positive	Mixed	Negative
Zipke	n=6	2	1	3
Gannett	n=5	1	2	2
Lambert	n=4	1	1	2
Rondeau	n=5	0	2	3
TOTAL	n=20	4	6	10

FIGURE 5.1

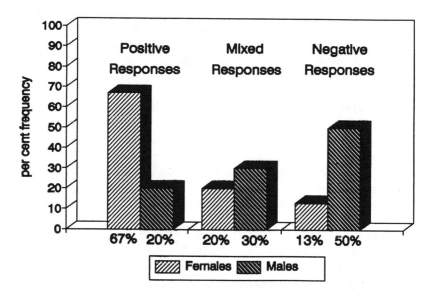

write in, and hearing comments like "What would he want that for—boys don't write diaries!" (personal communication, 25 March 1987).

Intrigued, I asked permission to survey her class regarding their perceptions of and experiences with journals and diaries. Their responses showed that already, by the age of 10, they understood diaries and journals to be related in complex and confusing ways to both academic and popular-culture literacy practices (Gannett 1991, 17-19),[6] and that boys were learning, as Jane Dupree Begos has put it, that "[d]iaries are sissy things" (Begos 1987, 69). Both males and females identified only females (sisters, mothers, or other female relatives) as people they knew who kept journals, and none of the six boys responding reported that they had kept or were keeping a personal journal, while six of the nine girls had already begun to keep a journal or a diary. Some of the girls also reported reading each others' diaries as part of their journaling experience (Gannett 1991, 18).

Indeed, the gendering of literacy practices called journals or diaries may accompany the acquisition of literacy itself. Writing researcher Ruth Hubbard, from the University of New Hampshire, who conducted her doctoral research at a nearby elementary school, shared the following story with me. One of the first grade teachers who participated in Hubbard's research project gave out blank books for her students to write in over the summer if they wanted to. The following fall, four or five students came back with the journals they had written over their vacation. All of them were girls—in the first grade (Ruth Hubbard, personal communication, May 1988).

The Journal Legacy for Men

The journal legacy for men includes the general forms and functions of public writing based primarily on discourse models built on the inscription of power and control over language, knowledge, and discursive rights. These linguistic and epistemological models are maintained by strategies such as the privileging of specific rhetorical modes and forms of logical development (formal logic and agonistic structures like debates or certain forms of argumentation), aggressivity (interruption and topic control), selective nondisclosure and territoriality (strictly defined boundaries separating genres, texts, and life, speakers and listeners, writers and readers).

Most of the young men I studied were not specifically aware of the rich literary/literacy traditions of educated men's journal keeping, such as the famous (or infamous) secular personal journals of Pepys, Boswell, Johnson, and Byrd. They were not likely to have been exposed to Bacon's advice that all young men should learn to keep journals to cultivate the critical habit of observation and intellectual reflection. Nor had they been frequently exhorted to keep tabs on their souls in the form of a spiritual journal unless they belonged to a specific religious sect such as Mormonism.

Yet they have inherited all these traditions and more. Young men, like my student, David, interested in developing as writers or thinkers, will often know or at least feel comfortable with the tradition of the commonplace book or writer's notebook as a place to keep observations, anecdotes, transcribed conversation, epigrams and quotes, lists of readings and responses, and notes for writing.

They have also inherited the varied traditions of public logs, military and scientific journals, and daybooks for listing daily plans or activities. The logs of schoolwork and daily events my men students wrote are in keeping with a tradition at least as old as John Evelyn's *Kalendarium* and probably considerably older. Their running logs and climbing logs parallel other early protojournal types: seafarer's and explorer's logs, logs of commerce that function similarly to record and monitor one type of activity and to improve productivity. Maybe the running logs and climbing logs do for the body what the spiritual logs used to do for the soul.

Even the travel and military journals of earlier centuries find their updated echoes in the latterday tales of run-ins with police, road trips, wild weekends, and dramatic moments in sporting events. They are in good company. Even Byron, the great Romantic poet, wrote: "the journal, where love and all else are concerned, remains more a field of action than introspection" (Mallon 1984, 221).

Finally, they have inherited a degraded and degrading notion of the diary as a feminized form. This is due in part to changing literacy practices and to the "separate-spheres" ideology of the nineteenth century. More generally, however, it is the result of the long-term cultural muting of women's discourse and experience by means of the creation of the public/private dichotomy. Thus, they have learned both contempt for the term *diary*, which has been twisted over time to mean writing that is trivial, nonintellectual, and hyperemotional, and a certain fear of the supposedly feminizing influence of a genre whose safety and flexibility might encourage or invite undue self-disclosure, thus rendering certain aspects of the masculine identity vulnerable. As we saw in the preliminary studies I have reported, men were much less likely to participate in a journaling tradition outside of school; they did not enjoy writing the school journals to the extent that they saw them as diaries; and they were also less likely overall to perceive their academic journal-keeping experience as valuable or productive as the women did.

The Journal Legacy for Women

Unlike men, women have inherited a marginalized and frequently privatized relation to language and discourse generally and to textuality specifically. As members of a muted group of speakers and writers, they may partake of or even subscribe to the dominant models of discourse, but historically they have had only limited rights to shape or use dominant discourse practices. Because of (or in spite of) their muted discursive status, women's language and epistemological models tend to focus more on connection, collaboration, and interpersonal relations with others. Given these functions, the structures of women's discourse, to the extent that they can be separated from those of the dominant discourse, are often collaborative and overlapping rather than interruptive. They allow or encourage fluidity of public/private distinctions, genre boundaries, and speaker/hearer, writer/reader roles.

Like men, women have inherited a rich set of journal and diary traditions that are centuries old. Unlike men, however, women are the immediate heirs to a flourishing and highly visible (albeit invisible to much of the university) popular-culture tradition of women's journal keeping. Although women have written in all forms of the journal/diary along the public/private continuum, their journals have tended to perform familial, domestic, and social discourse functions. Their journals paradoxically served the discursive needs of both the dominant community and their own muted group. The journals of my women students still show the strong traces of journals women traditionally wrote to chronicle family and social life, to record and monitor domestic productivity, to act as letters for family and friends when speech communities were disrupted by immigration or resettlement, to interpret interpersonal and social relations, and to integrate and explore their spirituality.

At the same time, women have inherited the tradition of using the journal as a relatively safe and secret "place" in which they might begin to escape the muting of their discourses. In the "wild zone" the journal can provide, women have for hundreds of years explored their world and *the* world without interruption or judgment. Often deprived of more public/academic ways of becoming knowing selves, women have been writing to themselves or to *dear diary* for centuries. Thus they harness the dialogic power of the journal to provide what has been called a "recursive audit of meaning" (Berthoff 1984), in an effort to discover themselves as subjects, to learn how to work through language to inscribe themselves into the world textually, and to learn to identify and develop an array of private and public voices.

Women's journal and diary traditions, while not sustained in the same public ways as men's, have still provided ample published, and even more unpublished, models to support and encourage female diarists. Starting with Fanny Burney in the eighteenth century, the availability of young diarists like Marjorie Fleming in the early nineteenth century, Marie Baskirtseff in the late nineteenth century, and Anne Frank in the twentieth century, assured girls that diary writing and reading were practices amenable and appropriate to young females. The diaries of writers like Virginia Woolf, Anaïs Nin, and May Sarton continue to invite women to journaling even as they provide interesting reading. In addition to the published models, many girls see journal keeping modeled informally by peers, sisters, mothers, grandmothers, or other female relatives. Girls are more often encouraged to keep diaries from an early age and are often given diaries by a family member or friend. (My daughter, at age seven, has received three diaries already. My son has never received a single one.)

Unfortunately, however, like young men, many young women are also unaware of the rich history of the journal/diary, and have been trained to see the diary as being neither academic nor intellectual, but rather quotidian and mawkish—in short, to see the diary as something of an embarrassment. Nevertheless, their familiarity with the current strand of popular diary traditions offers direct evidence that contradicts this view and predisposes them to use and to find considerable value in many kinds of academic journal assignments.

Clearly, male and female students tend to draw unconsciously on overlapping, yet gendered, traditions of journal/diary writing and to see journals and diaries as gendered kinds of writing regardless of whether they are practiced in academic settings or not. These ideas inform their sense of what can be written in a journal and how it can be written, as well as whether it is acceptable to keep a journal or diary at all. What they "know" about journals and diaries clearly affects their attitudes toward journal keeping in the classroom.

6

Gender, Journals, and Academic Discourse: Capacious Hold-All and Pandora's Box

What sort of diary should I like mine to be? Something loose knit and yet not slovenly, so elastic that it will embrace anything, solemn, slight, or beautiful that comes into my mind. I should like it to resemble some deep old desk, or capacious hold-all, in which one flings a mass of odds and ends without looking them through. I should like to come back after a year or two, and find that the collection had sorted itself and refined itself and coalesced, as such deposits so mysteriously do, into a mould, transparent enough to reflect the light of our life, and yet steady, tranquil compounds with the aloofness of a work of art.
                                    —Virginia Woolf

I chose this passage from Virginia Woolf's diary to begin my final chapter for several reasons. It continues the practice in this book of granting literary or scholarly authority to privatized, nonacademic genres of texts and acknowledges Woolf's diaries as successfully combining the best of dominant/muted, public/private discourse traditions. Most importantly, her description helps to center my understanding of the journal/diary and its roles inside and outside the academy.

As I reread what I have written to draw the book to a close, I hope

I have written something "loose knit, but not slovenly," that I have created something of a "capacious hold-all" containing a collection of ideas
that I will begin to try to "refine and coalesce" to help reflect, however
opaquely, "the light of our life" as writers and speakers inside and outside the academy. As Nina Auerbach writes, "The best of our writing is
entangled in the messiness of our experience" (Bauer 1990, 385).

At the most general or theoretical level, I have come to view the
journal in a way that is consonant with Virginia Woolf's conception of it.
As I see it in my mind's eye, journals of all kinds fill a desk with big and
little drawers and many filing slots. Some are labelled clearly: ship's log,
accounting ledger, spiritual journal, travel journal, writer's daybook,
dialogue journal, double-entry journal; others are as yet unnamed. The
desk overflows with texts, some neatly filed, most shoved into the near-
est slot or drawer, many piled in bundles on the writing surface itself.
Thus, I see the journal as a complex set of forms, styles, and functions
that vary over time, that span the personal, familial, social, and public
domains of discourse, and that implicitly inform our current views of
academic journaling. But I also see the journal as the container itself, as
a locus, a site of writing, a palimpsest variously written over by different ideas of the self, the world, and the word. To carry forward some of
the primary metaphors that have informed this text: the journal is both
seed and container, Aunt Jane's quilt and the sewing, a grandmother's
desk or hold-all trunk, a Pandora's Box.

The Journal as Pandora's Box

Because the journal inhabits the overlapping borders of public and
private discourses, of academic and nonacademic discourses, of
socially-constructed masculine and feminine discourses, it is not only
interesting as an object of inquiry itself, it can also be seen as a place
from which to reflect on these other linked sets of discursive practice,
which are themselves linked to particular linguistic and educational
models, and to particular discursive communities.

We've seen how the journals of men and women have been marked
in various historical periods and cultures with the dominance and difference of gender. Women's journals have been privatized and marginalized, their discursive strategies and sense of self-as-subject tend toward
the muted and the multiple, tend toward connection and collaboration.
The linguistic/discursive/sexual oppression of women has also made
them keenly aware of the power of the constructive and reconstructive
power of language as well; language can liberate, language can heal.

Men have historically held a dominant and dominating relation to language, building models based more frequently (but not exclusively) on the allocation of public verbal power, by means of hierarchy, exclusion, and displacement. Men's journals have more often been public forms of writing in intention, topic, and audience, composed as demonstrations of knowing, autonomous selves built upon boundaried notions of self/other, text/life, speaker/hearer, and writer/reader.

In trying to understand how the university has received, defined, and practiced the journal, I have come to a less than startling understanding. The ambivalent reception of the chimeric set of writings we call journals or diaries is not simply due to this form's status as private rather than public, or relatedly, to its status as nonacademic—and, therefore, not intellectually valuable—rather than academic. Rather, these two statuses derive in large part from the feminization and consequent derogation of the diary. The *diary*, because of its association with women's experiences, voices, and perspectives, has been labelled a problem, a Pandora's box. The metaphor of the journal/diary as Pandora's box is quite instructive. According to Hellenic mythology, Pandora, a vain and silly girl, is seduced by her curiosity to open a box filled with all things good and evil; in essence, she was a "troublesome, treacherous source of human woe" (Spretnak 1984, 18). Using that metaphor, it becomes easy to see diaries or journals as texts written by troublesome, vain, and silly girls who let all kinds of secrets out. This notion sees the journal as a Pandora's box, which, when opened—or written, or read—releases taboo, evil, and toxins along with the good. Because of the diary's association with women's experiences and women's voices, this insight has served to remind me that whatever it is we call academic discourse has hardly been neutral with regard to gender (or to a host of other issues).

The academic discourse community: it is a very neutral sounding term. And as it was defined by Patricia Bizzell, one of its leading explicators, just a few years back, it sounds only slightly less neutral:

But the academic community is a community united almost entirely by its language, I think: the academic community is not coterminous with any social class, though it is more closely allied to some than to others. Like any other language community, the academic community uses a preferred dialect (so-called Standard English) in a convention-bound discourse (academic discourse) that creates and organizes the knowledge that constitutes the community's world view. If we see the relation between dialect, discourse conventions, and ways of thinking as constituting a language community, then we can no longer see dialects or discourse conventions as mere conveyances of thoughts generated prior to their embodiment in language. Rather dialects and discourse generate thoughts, constitute world view. (Bizzell 1986, "What Happens," 296-97)

But whose world views are these? Whose convention-bound discourses are these? The academic discourse community (or communities as we now say, referring to the specific knowledge communities often associated with particular disciplines) has been for all but 150 of its more than 1000-year history, an essentially exclusive preserve of males. Thus, many of the traditional scholarly and pedagogical discourses of the university have clearly been constructed on the historically masculine model of territoriality, dominance, and display in a concentrated and distilled form.

As Walter Ong shows in his well-known book, *Fighting for Life*, the original academy was built on masculine models of language and knowledge based on territoriality, competition, and aggression (Ong 1981). Ong tracks academia's agonistic heritage at great length: the ceremonial enmity and contest of teacher and pupil, the focus on disputation and oral defense, on argumentation, the learning of Latin as a male puberty rite, and the common use of severe physical punishment to ensure learning are all a part of this multileveled heritage in their manner, milieu, and content (Ong 1981, 119-34). Indeed, Ong accounts for the recent major changes in the academy and academic discourse as being consequences of the entrance of women therein during the nineteenth and twentieth centuries.

Robert Connors, working from Ong's study of the academy at large, has articulated some of the ways in which rhetoric itself has been what he calls "feminized," that is, affected by the presence of women in the academic world since the nineteenth century (see also Presnell 1989).

The primary effect of coeducation was the quick decline of public contest as a staple of college life. As Ong argues, the agonistic impulse is purely a male-against-male phenomenon. Males perceive it as noble to struggle ritually—either physically or verbally—with other males. . . . But to struggle in ritual contest with a *woman*? It was unthinkable. . . . Real men don't fight women. And thus, when women entered the educational equation in colleges, the whole edifice built on ritual contest between teacher and student *and* student and student came crashing down. (Connors 1986, 21)

The lecture-recitation format for classes was partially replaced by discussions, lab classes, and seminars that "minimized agonism" (Connors 1986, 21). Debating societies broke down, and agonism was increasingly funneled into the available male enclaves, like sports and fraternities (Connors 1986, 22). In rhetoric and composition specifically, the entry of women was accompanied by certain critical changes in the "academic discourse community." Connors lists four primary shifts: 1) the shift from oral polemical rhetoric to written composition as a pedagogical focus; 2) the shift from argument to multimodal approaches, including exposition and narrative; 3) the rise of more personal as opposed to abstract writing assignments; and 4) somewhat more nurturing, as opposed to purely judgmental and combative, teaching styles (Connors 1986, 23).

These changes of the last hundred years or so, whether deliberately accommodative or not, certainly have made it possible for women to negotiate the discursive field of the university. But again, it must be remembered that women, like other marginalized discoursers, have always had to be in some sense "multicultural," or perhaps "multidiscursive," to be able to function within the dominant male discourse communities, within muted frameworks, and outside in the "wild zone" of women's discourse.

Women have more recently been aided by what Bizzell terms "personal-style" pedagogy (Bizzell 1986, "Composing Processes," 53). This style is linked with the writing-process movement of the 1960s and 1970s, a movement that is considered essentially non-agonistic because it values process over judged product, rewrites the roles of both teachers and peers as collaborators and readers, encourages students to choose their own topics (which may well come from personal experience), and allows for some student control of writing processes (Connors 1986, 38-39). Personal-style pedagogy has promoted more personal "connectivity" both in terms of style and of content, a feature that we have seen is often associated with women's discourse models (see Caywood and Overing's book, *Teaching Writing* (1987) for a good discussion of the links between process pedagogy and gender equity). It is no accident that the journal makes its explicit reentrance at this point as a powerful, expressive prewriting tool and later as a fulcrum for the current "writing to learn" across the curriculum movement. While the journal was certainly not brought into the composition or rhetoric curriculum specifically to validate women's writing traditions, or to help women work through to their public voices and gain confidence as writers, these were, in fact, some of the consequences, as we've seen. (It is important to note, also, that journals were entering the college curriculum during the 1960s and 1970s through the side door of Women's Studies. These journal pedagogies consciously exploited the journal as a means of validating and reclaiming women's ways of knowing and writing.) Throughout the 1970s and 1980s, some feminist composition scholars, such as Florence Howe (1971), Joan Bolker (1979), Margaret Pigott (1979), Janet Emig (1977), Susan Meisenhelder (1985), Ellen Berry (1987), and Donna Perry (1987), were also aware of the special intellectual empowerment journals offered to women.

Certainly, too, the efforts toward pedagogical reform in the 1960s were part of the larger political and social criticism of the academy and other major cultural institutions of that era. Patricia Bizzell points out that the early work by Gordon Rohman and Albert Wlecke on journal keeping and meditation as composing strategies met considerable institutional resistance:

> [T]his resistance was seen as discriminatory social sorting, with white middle class men being educated for positions of power and all others being disenfranchised. Academic expository prose was implicated in the indictment of the academy as an institution of political oppression. . . . Instead of forcing students to *master* it, and the concomitant complexities of formal Standard English, writing teachers began to believe that they should be helping students to free themselves from its baleful influence if ever their writing were to improve. (Bizzell 1986, "Composing Processes," 52-53. Emphasis added)

While academic discourse was indicted in the 1960s because of its sexist and elitist bias, it was soon out on bail. By the mid-1980s, process models of composition were themselves under fire for presumably being too dependent on Romantic notions of individual expressiveness based on discovering an authentic voice or self, and therefore not taking into sufficient account the social and historical contexts of writing (Berlin 1988; Gradin 1990). At the same time, the idea of a unified academic discourse community was being replaced by the concept of multiple discourse or knowledge communities that were discipline-based. Yet the underlying discourse model did not seem to change significantly. As Bizzell put it: "mastery of academic writing [had] become once more an acceptable goal of composition pedagogy" (Bizzell 1986, "Composing Processes," 60). Kurt Spellmeyer, in his recent article on the uses of the essay in the academy, agrees that this view of composition and its pedagogies is built on an agonistic mastery model. In his words, the "prevailing tradition of discipline specific writing encourages both conformity and submission" (Spellmeyer 1989, 266).

Unfortunately, and somewhat ironically, because of its immediately visible link to process pedagogy, the journal has come under subtle attack by some of the people most concerned with understanding the links between academic genres and the larger literacy practices that inform them. Both David Bartholomae (1986) and Patricia Bizzell (1986) seem to question the value of the journal to cultivate the habits of thought associated with academic discourse. Bizzell questions the journal most explicitly:

> [S]hould all students be required to learn such conventional academic genres as the case study or the literature survey, or be allowed to pursue the "same" intellectual work in genres with which they feel more comfortable, such as the journal? Advocates of requiring students to practice academic genres argue that knowledge of them is necessary for college; advocates of other forms argue that the criteria for success in college must change.
>
> If, however, the discourse conventions are seen as generating, and not merely conveying, certain kinds of complex thinking, then the "same" intellectual work is not possible in different genres. For example, the journal might be a genre that generates personal connections with classwork, such as expressing religious revulsion for genetic research, but that discourages other kinds of thinking, such as surveying religious resistance to scientific research through the ages. According to this line of argument, students would need to learn other, more academic intellectual work. (Bizzell 1986, "What Happens," 295-96)

Clearly, in this passage, the journal is being narrowly defined and somewhat disparaged for what Woody Allen might call its "jejeunosity." But I strongly suspect that this judgment of the potential intellectual value of the journal has more to do with its noncanonical, feminized status and with its immediate origins in the personal-style pedagogy of the 1960s, which is undergoing critique by social constructionists, than with any inherent incapability of the journal to foster complex thought.

In fact, when one of my colleagues read the present section of this book, she wrote the following comment on a post-it and stuck it on the page:

> I see the journal as a place where *complex* thought can be *developed*—as a genre that permits and encourages complex thought. The notion that the "agonistic academic genre" is the site

of "real thought" is absurd—as a "linear" form, it is necessarily a reduction of complexity to a "line of thought" linearly developed into an "argument." If the journal has any characteristic at all, it's that it has the "inherent complexity" to foster complex thought! (Carol Barringer, personal communication)

While I cannot imagine the journal ultimately "displacing" other kinds of academic writing in the male discursive territory, neither can I see it as discouraging complex habits of thought unless it is misused or misunderstood. When Bacon gave advice to young men to keep journals as they made their Grand Tours, he did so because he understood the journal to be particularly appropriate for developing critical observation and reflective skills. When Henry Slingsby decided to keep a journal in 1638, even before Evelyn or Pepys, his decision was motivated by the habit of mind developed in the essays of Montaigne, which his son had brought home with him from his schooling in France. That same habit of mind was what distinguished Montaigne as the father of the modern critical essay. The university commonplace book was common for centuries before writing even became an important part of the rhetoric curriculum.

The issues surrounding the role and place of the journal in the university are representative of the larger question of whether we are continuing to reify the traditional, primarily male-generated, academic discourses and privilege primarily agonistic ways of knowing the world. David Bartholomae suggests that when students enter school, particularly students with only basic academic skills, they in essence "invent the university" (Bartholomae 1985, 134). I agree. But I think we need to work to ensure that what university students invent is not the relatively exclusionary, sexist, racist, and elitist world that the academy has been for a thousand years. It is still easy to show that the prevailing models of discourse, even those generated by our most thoughtful scholars, can be implicitly saturated in agonism.

For example, in "Wanderings: Misreadings, Miswritings, Misunderstandings," David Bartholomae tracks the "approximate discourses" students generate as they try to become more skillful in the ways of academic discourse. His premise, that these approximate readings and writings are signs of growth toward academic discourse, is amply proved in his piece. But the process he insists that *all* his students are or should be going through is an utterly agonistic one. A student's reading of a text requires an "initial act of aggression and translation" (Bartholomae 1986, 92). Reading is "the effort to justify or account for (and usually by speaking or writing) a position we have taken by *speaking over or*

against the words of an author who gave us our beginning" (Bartholomae 1986, 91; emphasis added). Indeed, Bartholomae consciously
asserts a few pages later that "The language of reading instruction, like
that of writing instruction, is loaded with images of mastery and control" (Bartholomae 1986, 96). These images of aggressive struggle recur
frequently in his text: recent literary criticism, according to Bartholomae,
casts the reader "in an agonistic role, struggling against teachers and
canonical interpretations" (Bartholomae 1986, 113); discussing Harold
Bloom he mentions "the violent dynamics of the classroom" and the
"struggle for authority" (Bartholomae 1986, 113); education "is a scram-
ble for power and for violation" (Bartholomae 1986, 114), and so on.

I suggest that while the presence of women in the groves of
academe, both as scholars and as teachers, continues to dilute or to
change the male discourse forms of the university somewhat, the traditional academic forms are still strong drink for many women (Annas
1985; Churgin 1978).[1]

An enormous amount of literature on gender and classroom interactions suggests that in many classrooms, discourse patterns (both in
pedagogical styles and in peer interactions) that derogate and mute
women predominate (Brooks 1982; Richardson et al. 1980. See also the
extensive annotated bibliography in *Language, Gender and Society* (1985
Thorne et al. 1983)). These obstacles only lower the temperature in the
already "chilly climate" of classroom interactions which we discussed
earlier.

Pamela Annas, among others, has pointed out that even in the
pedagogy of writing courses that allow or assign "personal writing,"
writing that allows for real connection between the writer, the word,
and the world, the implicit goal is to move from personal writing to academic writing, which assumes that *mastery* of academic writing is finally
different from, incompatible with, and superior to, personalized and
connective writing. Hence, the journal, which is still primarily seen as a
solely personal or private discourse, is granted only the most limited
kind of academic value.

We have been trained to teach expository writing in a particular
way—one that values writing that is defended, linear, and "objective." Indeed many writing classes seem to be designed to teach the
use of abstract, logical, and impersonal rather than sensual, contextual, and committed language. How many of us teach writing in a
way that moves during the semester from image to argument, from
the particular to the abstract, and that attempts to "wean" students
from subjectivity into objectivity? (Annas 1985, 360)

Indeed, Annas has a rather different educational goal in mind:

> The kind of writing I finally want these students to be able to do brings together the personal and the political, the private and the public, into writing which is committed and powerful because it takes risks, because it speaks up clearly in their own voices and from their experience, experiments with techniques of argumentation and skillful organization, and engages, where appropriate, with the insights of other writers. (Annas 1985, 370)

As Susan Meisenhelder puts it, in her critique of several texts on writing and teaching, "Beneath each of these metaphors is a conception of "powerful" public writing as equivalent to "forceful" writing, writing that "disarms" and "defeats" the reader (Meisenhelder 1985, 186). These models rely not only on the ancient forms of ritualized rhetorical combat between men, but also recapitulate or at least are complicit in a patriarchal model of experience with its violent suppression of women's bodies and voices (Meisenhelder 1985, 185-88). Like many others, therefore, Meisenhelder argues that we need to develop or incorporate conceptions of potent writing that are are not built on the agonistic core of combat, violence, and mastery. Sally Gearhart, in "The Womanization of Rhetoric," offers a similar analysis and proposal:

> Over the centuries rhetoric has wearied itself in the ancient and honorable act of finding the available means of persuasion, the better to adapt a discourse to its end. Of all the human disciplines, it has gone about its task of educating others to violence with the most audacity . . . the act of violence is in the intention to change another. . . . [Rather than employing] the conquest model of human interaction . . . it is important [that we understand] the whole communication environment . . . as a matrix, a womb. (Gearhart 1979, 195)

Clearly the ways of knowing that the academy induces in all those who enter to study or to stay as scholars and teachers can be, and should be, sufficiently broad to embrace the epistemologies of women, who now constitute over half of its members at the undergraduate level, and to welcome the discursive and epistemological traditions women can contribute. Feminist scholars in all disciplines have shown the need for incorporating not only new material about women into the classroom, but also new ways of knowing, speaking, and writing into scholarship and into the classroom.[2]

Ultimately, it seems to me that what we need to do is work to understand and then move beyond the simple dichotomies that serve to separate and marginalize women and other groups in the academy. I agree with Dale Bauer when she writes, "Rather than opposing the public and private voices or opposing masculine and feminine, we need to see how to negotiate that position in order to speak a multiplicity of voices into the cultural dialogue" (Bauer 1990, 388). In the next section, I want to discuss some of the ways we might use the scholarship on journals and journal pedagogy to help us work toward this goal.

The Capacious Hold-All Within and Across Disciplines

To use language is always to seize the world in
a particular way and at the same time to be
seized. To teach language is never to dwell in a
sanctuary free from questions of power, but to
labor in its very smithy.
    —Bob Morgan, "Three Dreams of Language"

Power is the ability to take one's place in whatever discourse is essential to action and the right
to have one's part matter.
    —Carolyn Heilbrun, *Writing a Woman's Life*

My daily life as a teacher confronts me with
young men and women who have had language and literature used against them, to keep
them in their place, to mystify them, to bully
them, to make them powerless.
    —Adrienne Rich, *On Lies, Secrets and Silence*

In this last section I want to suggest some ways we might use the journal to help all students, male and female, read and write and think more effectively as well as to understand their own discourse communities and those of the university. Like Bartholomae, I think "students need a curriculum that dramatizes the politics of reading and writing," and that teachers need to let students know "What's at stake?" and "What's going on?" (Bartholomae 1986, 100). In order to provide a curriculum that sensitizes students to issues of dominance and difference, however, we may find it useful to tap into our own implicit assumptions about knowledge and academic discourse. Perhaps we need to examine our "pedagogical unconscious," the ways in which our teaching practices, as Stephen Jay has put it, are "tied to our constitution as social subjects" (qtd. in Bauer 1990, 388). For me, at least, examining my assumptions and experiences with journals and diaries as a teacher, a scholar, and a woman provided me with a new lens or mirror from which to view not only the journal and academic discourse, but also to see myself as a socially constituted subject, a gendered discourser. Allow me, then, to make a series of suggestions that my experience in studying and using journals in the classroom has led me to. These strategies or claims are not intended to displace other uses of the journal that I have mentioned already, nor are they intended to be exhaustive. Rather they are intended as openings for further work and discussion.

1. Needless to say, I think journals ought to be introduced to learners and to prospective teachers in their historical and social contexts both inside and outside the academy. Rather than ignoring what our students know about journals, we should acknowledge their literacy and discursive experiences, and tap into their knowledge of journals and diaries to help them write more effectively, and to create some discursive common ground. As Kurt Spellmeyer points out, citing Mikhael Bakhtin, discourse communities are never monolithic, but always at least partially "heteroglossic"; thus, students should be encouraged to find ways in which the conventions and practices of their "home discourses" overlap with those of the university:

> Because languages "intersect with one another on many levels at the same time, entry into a community of discourse must begin, not with a renunciation of the 'home language' or 'home culture' but with those points of commonality that expose the alien within the familiar, the familiar within the alien." (Spellmeyer 1989, 261)

Spellmeyer makes a powerful case for recognizing the value of the reflective essay, which, as we know, is close kin to the journal in its development, its forms, and its functions. His case for the essay as the last discursive common ground of the university is a compelling argument for our revaluation of the journal, as a "common place." Arguing against the "institutional rigidity of discourse," Spellmeyer claims that "by disguising authorial fallibility and bias, as well as the uncertainty of the discourse itself, more 'serious' forms of writing typically perpetrate an unequal relationship between the writer and the audience, and between the writer and the subject under scrutiny" (Spellmeyer 1989, 264-65). What is so important, and unique, about the essay/journal is that it announces its own "situatedness"; it "dramatizes the process of appropriation concealed by other genres" (Spellmeyer 1989, 264, 265). By resisting the "coercive power of authoritative language" (268-69), the essay/journal transcends the "propriety of discrete communities"

(Spellmeyer 1989, 268-69), and thus it can bind the discourses of the academic community together, provide a common ground for the language communities of the academy. Spellmeyer writes:

> [The essay/journal] with its tolerance for essayistic introspection and digression, is probably the last opportunity most students will have to discover the relationship of mutual implication, a relation fundamental to all writing, between the self and the cultural heritage within which selfhood has meaning. To put it in simplest terms, we do not deny the socially constituted nature of either learning or identity when we ask our students to write from their situations, but I believe it is both dishonest and disabling to pretend that writing, no matter how formal or abstract, is not created by persons, from within the contexts—historical, social, intellectual, institutional—of their lived experience. (Spellmeyer 1989, 269)

Or, as Tricia, the women's studies student whose journal I discussed in the last chapter, put it simply, yet profoundly: "That's what education means to me—what good would I be to humankind if I deny the expression of my own experience?"

2. Discussing different journal types and their uses and functions will allow students to understand and reconnect with valuable journal traditions they have all inherited and help them understand how they might be useful for intellectual and academic work. I have found that reconnecting men with the rich heritage of journal writing available to them can alleviate some of the discomfort and anxiety they have experienced when faced with the journal assignment and help make their journaling more productive. At the same time, I think it is critical to acknowledge women's muted journal/diary traditions and to recuperate the diary as a potentially valuable literacy practice with genuine intellectual merit.

In my writing classes, I find that having students share their associations with the terms *journal* and *diary*, along with discussing their experiences of reading or writing journals outside of school, helps them understand their own gendered assumptions and helps them to find common ground within various journal traditions in addition to helping them to learn to appreciate the differences in their nonscholastic literacy experiences. Sometimes, they even become more willing to try certain types of journal writing that are less familiar to them.

Some of the questions I often ask them to write about or discuss include: What's the difference between a diary and a journal? How are they similar? When do you think the two became differentiated and why? Who do you know that keeps a diary or journal? Why do you think the diary is considered less important than the journal? Why would anyone want to keep some verbal record of their life? How are journals like letters or autobiography or fiction, in terms of style, structure, and audience? Why is it that men write running logs and daybooks while women tend to keep extended reflective personal documents? Under what circumstances do men keep personal journals? As well as writing more productive journals, students often find these topics interesting to research and discuss because they connect and validate students' larger literacy practices in the context of academic literacy.

3. Having students keep journals and learn about the interesting history of journals and diaries can easily be used to initiate discussion of dominance and difference in discourse itself. Students can consider the nature and relative power of public and private discourses, the relation between canonized forms of writing and marginalized forms, the relation between writing and life, writing and thinking, and certainly, gender and discourse.

One of the most common complaints about the journal/diary is that it is "too personal" in the sense that students write about uncomfortable or unpleasant things, including dysfunctional or alcoholic families, racism, sexism, physical abuse or negligence, and sexual abuse. We have been trained to make the common misguided assumption that therapeutic writing, writing to heal, is unrelated to writing to know and that it has no place in the academy. I have tried to show throughout this work, as have others (Pamela Annas, Mary Belenky et al., Shari Benstock, Carol Barringer, and Louise DeSalvo), that writing to heal and writing to know, to become a self capable of knowing, are necessarily correlated, particularly for marginalized groups like women, whose oppression has been linked directly with sexual and discursive violence. While I don't want to privilege "writing to heal" above all other rhetorical functions, I think we should ensure that such writing has a place in the university, indeed at every level of schooling. In fact, I think it rather odd that so much of our theoretical language comes directly from models of healing, from the fashionable discourses of Sigmund Freud, Jacques Lacan, and Carl Jung, to name just a few, and yet when we see students (male or female) discovering the healing and restorative functions of language, we try to exclude, deny, or trivialize those discourses. A recent article by James S. Baumlin and Tita French Baumlin in *College English* (1989) reminds us that writing to heal, or "iatrological writing," is both an ancient and an honorable aim of rhetoric. Since the time of Plato and Aristotle, they suggest, rhetoric has been interested in "the emotional, as well as the moral and political health of its audience" (Baumlin and Baumlin 1989, 247). They sum up their discussion this way:

> The most crucial of our propositions—that we expand our traditional definition of rhetoric to include iatrology—is thoroughly classical in origin; we know, however, that it flies in the teeth of much contemporary rhetoric. Still we offer it not to refute present theory so much as to heal it, to restore to rhetoric the wholeness it loses whenever psychology, or health, or the mythic is banished from its system. . . . One uses language in many ways: to express, to create, to praise, to blame, to analyze, to explore, to doubt, to destroy, to curse . . . to care and heal. The task as we see it, is not to choose one over the rest, but to admit the place of all these functions in discourse. And this, we believe, serves to restore iatrology as an aim of rhetoric. (Baumlin and Baumlin 1989, 259)

I hope it is obvious that certain strands of the journal and diary tradition offer a useful reentry point for such a worthy aim.

4. Within disciplines, instructors certainly can choose specific kinds of journals for students to keep which are consonant with habits of mind particular to that discipline. Teachers who want students to keep a specific kind of journal in their classes—a double entry journal, a commonplace book, a science/observation/laboratory notebook, a current events log book, or even a freewriting journal, might consider providing excerpts from several journals written by men and women at different times or in different cultures to give students a full sense of the possibilities and conventions of that form and function.

5. Assigning excerpts or whole journals as *reading* can do much more than simply introduce students to journaling. Literature and composition students can read the commonplace books and writing journals of several authors not only in order to understand the process of literary creation, but also to gain a knowledge of the relation between reading and writing, the social and historical conditions in which writing and reading take place, and the often complex relation between the public and the private writing of a specific writer. History students could, and often do, read first-hand accounts of expeditions, military campaigns, and other major historical events not only by famous public figures but

also by private chroniclers to compare these personal accounts with public, received views, and to get a sense of the real texture of the quotidian in times past. In psychology, the famous journals of Freud and Jung, as well as those of Marie Bonaparte, Karen Horney, and Joanna Field, offer insight into the lives of the people who gave critical shape to the field and show the development of important psychological concepts and questions, in addition to demonstrating the limitless curiosity and the cumulative critical reflection characteristic of almost all thinkers' journals. Reading famous scientists' and artists' journals can similarly help students understand the actual process of the development of academic disciplines, and experience how questions, observations, feelings, and acts of the imagination are harnessed synthetically to produce the basis of knowledge in each discipline.

6. John Schilb suggests another way in which the reading and writing of journals can have pragmatic value for improving students' writing. Reading journals and diaries, for example, can help students answer Jean-Paul Sartre's all-important question, "Why Write?" As Schilb points out, students often think that writing is something you *have* to do; for others, for grades, or maybe, if you're very good, for money or fame. They are thus alienated from the act of writing and its value. Students can learn (or remember) the value of self-sponsored writing and learning by reading the journals written by ordinary people, like themselves, who write because the writing itself is valuable. Like the Nebraska pioneer, Mollie Dorsey Sanford (1976), with whom this book began, they can consider writing, not necessarily with the goal of being *Writers*, but with that of being "more than a mere machine." And to the extent that students come to value reading and writing, their learning and our teaching are made simpler and more pleasurable.

7. One specific suggestion comes from Dure Jo Gillikin (1985), who finds that she can teach students how to do close textual analysis and historical literary research by having students work extensively with one anonymous unpublished journal. Students have to work together to discover the author, the historical period, and specific location and social context in which the journal was written. Since students have to actively piece together the meaning of these texts, they can come to appreciate the active role readers have in creating the meanings of all texts, particularly modern fictional pieces, which are often written without many explicit contextual and structural cues just as journals are.

8. Certainly, the reading and writing of journals offers a superla-

tive set of opportunities for discussing and working through the powerful and problematic issue of voice. Reading longer excerpts of some
diverse, resonant voices can help students connect with the literary,
public, and academic possibilities for their own voices. In making this
suggestion, I am not simply hearkening back to the quasi-romantic,
expressivist notion of "personal voice," but rather locating the effort to
find a voice in the social and historical conditions that have governed
the range of possible voices for men and women. The journal is very
important in this regard, especially for women, who have had few
opportunities for developing public voices until very recently. Many
women trying to acquire public voices, from Fanny Burney, one of the
first novelists and journal keepers, to Elizabeth Barrett Browning, Charlotte Perkins Gilman, Virginia Woolf, Katherine Mansfield, right up to
Sylvia Plath, Adrienne Rich, Jean Rhys, May Sarton, and countless others, have used the journal to negotiate that complex and perilous journey. And as Pamela Annas reminds us, "Women students need to stop
learning primarily how to translate their own experience into a foreign
language and instead spend some time learning their mother tongue"
(Annas 1985, 371). What better place than in a "book of one's own"?

Final Questions

In all of these ways, then, we can begin to re-understand Pandora's Box as Woolf's "capacious hold-all." In fact, if we go back to the
original Pandora, the Pandora worshiped long before the Olympian
pantheon was erected, we find that she was called "The Giver of All
Gifts" and that her large jar was indeed a capacious hold-all, holding
memory, mercy, caring and wisdom (Spretnak 1984, 55-57).
    I am convinced that people often write books as much to find new
questions as to find answers to questions they already have. Here are
some of my new questions and concerns. I'll be glad to share them with
anyone who takes a fancy to them.

    1. We need to know a great deal more about the history and tradi-
tions of the journal/diary and the connections between literacy, literature, and schooling. This work is just a tiny part of that project. Since
journals and diaries require at least minimal literacy and minimal
leisure, even though they are the most democratic of forms, they cannot
possibly represent the discursive practices of all peoples in different cultures throughout history. Although some of the studies I have read suggest that the diaries of women varied less across the boundaries of class

than did the men's, considerable work needs to be done to look carefully at the ways in which class and race and other such critical facets of
identity shape or are shaped by diary and journal traditions. However,
I have tried to include black women's diaries in my discussion whenever I could locate them.[3] Certainly, what is out there we need to integrate into our teaching and research in writing, since the journal may be
helpful in bringing discursively marginalized people of many types to
voice in the academy.

2. How are journals actually being used in composition courses
and across the curriculum? How do the powerful, nonacademic traditions of journal and diary keeping affect journal pedagogy and journal
use in the classroom in areas that I haven't been able to address? Some
of the questions we might ask along these lines include:
    a. Do male and female educators use journals to varying extents or
in different ways in their classrooms?
    b. How does the name the specific writing assignment is
given—journal, daybook, log, diary, commonplace book, writer's notebook, notebook—affect students' perceptions and responses?
    c. How do male and female educators respond to the journals
written by male and female students? Can we identify better with and
respond more fully or effectively to journals written in the gendered traditions we each belong to? Or do we respond, as composition teachers,
to journals that best fit our notions of academic discourse? Or in some
other way? And how does gender affect the problematic task of evaluating the journal? Remember, what brought Tom to my door at the
beginning of this inquiry into gender and the journal was, in part, his
concern over the fact that he hadn't written as much as the women,
which he thought might have affected his grade.
    d. Do our students write their journals differently according to the
gender of their teachers? Did my women write up a storm because they
knew I could be trusted to understand the traditions that their writing
participated in? Did my men refuse to disclose very much about themselves in part because I was a woman? Even though several of my male
colleagues have assured me that the same gendering of the journals
occurs in their classes, there will almost certainly be significant effects of
teacher gender we need to explore.
    e. Could it be that my male and female students are both treating
personal topics, though in very different ways? How is the self
expressed and at the same time constructed through the vehicle of the
journal? Although the men's journals did not appear to be very personal
in the common sense of the word, educator and writer Donald Murray's

comment that he "codes" whatever personal material might be in his journal, and researcher Donald Graves's suggestion, made in a personal communication, that the males he had studied seemed to treat personal issues by projecting feelings and thoughts onto third-person characters both seem like interesting leads to follow.

3. How might the discourse communities and models of the academy change if all the forms and functions of the journal were accepted, including those historically affiliated with the diary and with women's writing traditions? What would happen if the journal moved from the margins to the mainstream? What would become of the unique perspectives that the margins afford? Would particular journal traditions continue to be privileged over others? Would our notion of the journal in all its subtle nuance and complexity be coopted by the powerful (albeit not monolithic) model of agonistic academic discourse, or would the essential academic models of rhetoric, rather, be forever enriched?

Epilogue: A Diary Means Yes Indeed

And now, as I finish this public-private work, I can go back to my journal for what Adrienne Rich calls "the relief of the body and the reconstruction of the mind." I end with some recent entries:

[2 May. Almost a month since my last entry. Another chunk of time—evanescent. Just got word that the readers' reviews were "generally favorable"—need desperately to finish this last chapter, finish the semester, and finish my committee work. Then go back and edit, clean, polish, vacuum, index, check every reference and citation, write another article, get the kids in swimming lessons, baseball, and so on. Must prepare for summer school. Write those overdue Christmas cards.

Thursday—in the library. 1 PM. Two hours to cook down/pick at my mess of inchoate notes—a postmodernist's dream of symbolic chaos—need to make some stay against the chaos. One reviewer said he/she was a bit concerned about the breadth of issues I had raised—Could I end it? Good question.

Good air. Sky a fine blue. I have dishes done, beds made, and the most pressing bills paid. The bridal wreath bush is beginning to bloom. Last week I sowed the wild annual garden with nasturtium, sweet pea, dianthus, bachelor's buttons, and astors, some old rusticating zinnias, some leftover cosmos, and a package of faded, rainwashed anonymous seed. The next cycle of the garden that was blooming last year as I wrote the introduction. Please let me finish, that some garden might bloom elsewhere.

4 May. 8:20 AM At the 125 Restaurant. Tim is staining the Breens' house. Ben and Molly off to school. No milk at home so I came to collect myself and fill the well—to generate the pressure I hope will allow me to push the last chapter out. Trying to dissociate myself from bills and selling the house. Can't be much help till I get this book done.

Haircuts all around—they look so nice when they're clean. Ben's going to play first base in Babe Ruth. Good for him. Molly has a French braid momentarily. Feels very chic. Mom bought me a nice card to celebrate the finishing of the book and $50. Told me to take the day off on Mother's Day. That would be her gift. I said I'd try. . . .

During breakfast. My waitress keeps coming back to fill my coffee cup which I am not touching, being too absorbed in making sense of my notes. She finally says, puzzled, "What do you do?" I tell her I am an English professor and she backs away in mock fear. "So you're grading?" "Well, today, I'm trying to write," I confess. "Write what?" she asks, ready to be bored by whatever it is that scholars of English write about. "A book about journals and diaries. About why people write them out of school and in school." "Oh, really?—I've kept one for eight years," she says, brightening. "Especially for my first kid . . . I had a baby book and when it ended, I still wanted to keep writing things down." She gets quiet for a moment. "I'm not going to be able to be with him. I didn't get to raise him. When he's grown, I'll just give it to him—and then he'll know everything. I have to do this, for me and for him. . . . The other book is just for me. It's the one I whine in. But it's not just stupid things though. I think things through, figure stuff out. Some people think diaries are stupid. You know, women aren't stupid." We laugh and I agree. I say, "Can I write all this down in my book? Do you mind?" "No, go right ahead," Debby says and pours me some extra coffee to heat up my cup.

I muse a bit, thinking of all the diary traditions she embodies. I think of Gertrude Stein's "A diary means Yes Indeed." (Moffat and Painter 1975, 19). Yes, indeed.]

Notes

Preface

1. Obviously, journals and diaries in their most popular and current forms, the secular personal journal and the personal diary, belong to the autobiographical tradition in the largest sense, being life studies or personal narratives. Yet, they are often excluded, or mentioned only in passing, in many discussions of autobiography. Some critics and scholars, however, are challenging the traditional definitions and categories of the genre.

Estelle Jelinek, for example, assigns diaries and journals to peripheral roles in the autobiographical tradition in the preface to one of her major works, *The Tradition of Women's Autobiography*:

> I consider an autobiography as that work each autobiographer writes with the intention of its being her life story—whatever form, content, or style it takes. Though I occasionally refer to diaries, letters, and journals (to place them in historical context), I rarely discuss them because I do not consider them autobiographies. I do consider works entitled "recollections," "reminiscences," "memoirs" and the like as autobiographies if the author's intent was to write a life study, to look back over her life or a portion of it. Autobiography is an amalgam of one's self image, one's process of thinking and feeling, and one's talent as a formal writer. Each autobiography, therefore, is unique and defies a formal definition that subsumes all autobiography. (Jelinek 1986, xii)

On the other hand, in works such as *Writing a Woman's Life* (Heilbrun 1988), and in collections such as *The Private Self: Theory and Practice of Women's Autobiographical Writings* (Benstock 1988) and *Interpreting Women's Lives: Femi-*

nist *Theory and Personal Narratives* (Personal Narratives Group 1989), the questions of genre are left open, and the boundaries of various biographical and autobiographical writing practices are questioned rather than defined, or they are left unmarked entirely so as to include as many types of women's personal narratives as possible.

Because of the complexity of these issues and the focus on literary genre that many of these discussions take, I have deliberately avoided any lengthy treatment of the relationships among journals, diaries, and autobiography proper in this work. My intention is not to recuperate the diary as a literary genre or sub-genre, but rather to explore the larger connections between journals and diaries as literacy practices and the gendering of discourse and epistemology. However, much of the current work on gender and autobiography and on women's autobiographical practices does inform my understanding of the gendering of the journal in terms of theory and practice. Important parallels can be found for issues of canonicity, as well as in the construction of the self in language and in the treatment of style and subject matter. In addition to the works mentioned above, I have found the following works to provide useful points of entry for the discussion of gender, race, and genre in autobiography: Andrews 1986; Hoffman and Culley 1985; Jelinek 1980; Mason 1980; Stanton 1985; Sterling 1984; Voss 1986; and Washington 1987.

Chapter 1

1. See, e.g., Abel 1982; Benstock 1987; Berg et al. 1989; Gilbert and Gubar 1988; Green and Kahn 1985; Homans 1986; Jacobus 1986; Malson et al. 1989; Newton and Rosenfeldt 1985; Sherry 1988; and Todd 1980.

Chapter 2

1. While Fulwiler claims Dan Fader was an early proponent of the use of journals in the classroom, it is important to note that Fader's journal took the form of a daily exercise or daily composition book, rather than the student journal as we currently conceive of it.

2. Thomas's critical survey of early twentieth-century academic uses of the journal, while as yet unpublished, will be incorporated into a book she is currently writing on that subject and should be available within the next year or so.

3. The testimony from the Hatch Amendment hearings I quoted on parents' concerns about the use of the journal in school is only a small sample of the grievances registered against this set of writing practices. One person said the journals were used to discuss "sex, religion and anti-social behavior" (Schlafly 1985, 162). Another reported that:

through psychological manipulations, frightening films, moral dilemmas, the use of Professor Kohlberg's moral reasoning, situation ethics, the use of the "Milgrim" shock experiment, "role playing," the use of personal journals, group criticism sessions, and so forth, fourteen year old students are bound to be negatively influenced (Schlafly 1985, 130-31).

One of the most ironic criticisms came from parents and students who were alarmed that students show less certainty and ask more questions when they use journals. One angry student wrote "Life used to be easy—now I have to think" (Schlafly 1985, 192-93), as though that were an inappropriate school activity.

4. These particular responses were generated at the Northeast Regional Conference on English in the Two-Year College in the session "Journals and Writing Empowerment," 12-14 October 1989 in Albany, New York. I simply used the five responses on the top of the pile as a sampling of the comments teachers made on the similarities and differences between journals and diaries.

Chapter 3

1. See, e.g., Gelfand and Hules 1985 in literary studies; the essays and bibliographies in McConnell-Ginet et al. 1980; Thorne et al. 1983; and Frank and Treichler 1989.

2. See also Cixous and Clément 1986; Flynn and Schweickart 1986; Garner et al. 1985; Homans 1986; Jones 1985; Greene and Kahn 1985; Meese 1986; Moi 1985; and certain articles in collections like Benstock 1987, Berg et al. 1989, and Malson et al. 1989.

3. All of the recent collections of essays of feminist perspectives on language and literature (such as Meese 1986; Malson et al. 1989; Berg et al. 1989; Newton and Rosenfeldt 1985; and Benstock 1987) explore the question of differences with and among women in addition to redefining *gender* as a shifting set of relations rather than an absolute or static concept.

4. In fact, a series of multiple and overlapping spheres, such as Lisa Albrecht (1989) has used in defining writer identity, might provide a more accurate representation of dominance and muteness. Such a graphic might include large, encompassing spheres to denote culture and historical period, while internal spheres could mark factors of race, class, sex, sexual orientation, and so on.

5. See also the new anthology *The Rhetorical Tradition: Readings from Classical Times to the Present*, edited by Patricia Bizzell and Bruce Herzberg (1990), which has included rediscovered female rhetoricians such as Christine de Pisan and Laura Cereta from the Renaissance, Margaret Fell, and Sarah Grimke as

representatives of Enlightment rhetoric, and Hélène Cixous and Julia Kristeva from the twentieth century, as well as the work of Cheryl Glenn Seitz (1987) on female rhetors from antiquity through the Renaissance.

6. There are also several new books and articles that attempt to rename and reclaim a fuller range of women's friendships and love relationships, such as Faderman's *Surpassing the Love of Men* (1981), and Carroll Smith-Rosenberg's "The Female World of Love and Ritual" (1986).

7. The social construction of public/private power relations and gender identity through language style and topic is thoughtfully explored in Judith DiIorio's ethnographic study of young working-class male "van culture" in the 1970s, "Sex Glorious Sex, The Social Construction of Masculine Sexuality in a Youth Group" (1986). The members of the van club, the "vanners," she observed, spent much of their time talking about two topics: their vans and sex, through which they constructed and reinforced their sense of masculine identity. Interestingly, the "sex talk" was not private, but rather public, a kind of "collective fantasizing," which DiIorio calls "the collective cock."

> For these young men, sexuality, supposedly the most private and natural of human properties, was neither. Their sense of themselves as sexual beings rested not on their actual behaviors and accomplishments but on the collective public expression of their desires and drives. The vanners created their sexual identities through four major devices: the vans, collective fantasies, public celebration of each other's sexual exploits, and the blaming of women for their apparent failures. (DiIorio 1986, 264)

8. Because CR groups allowed women to talk beyond the "control" of men and allowed women to take each other seriously, they were often seen as dangerous by the men who were significant others. Spender offers several examples of men's responses to this loss of discursive control (Spender 1980, 106-17). I can personally attest to this phenomenon, having encountered considerable hostility to my participation in a CR group from my first husband, who would always grill me after every meeting to find out what I'd said about him. More recently, a comment by one of our deans who came to observe my Women's Studies class, reminded me that most people do not understand the powerful kinds of learning that go on in CR-type sessions. He praised me in his written report for successfully *preventing* the class from turning into an "Encounter Group."

9. Here and elsewhere in this chapter, I am using the manuscript pages of Barringer, which is currently in press.

10. Virginia Woolf wrote: "Father's birthday. He would have been 96, 96, yes, today; and could have been 96, like other people one has known; but mercifully was not. His life would have entirely ended mine. What would have hap-

pened? No writing, no books;—inconceivable" (qtd. in Olsen 1979, 17).

11. Tillie Olsen: "In such snatches of time I wrote what I did in those years, but there came a time when this triple life was no longer possible. The fifteen hours of daily realities became too much for the writing. I lost craziness of endurance" (Olsen 1979, 19-20).

Adrienne Rich: "For about ten years, I was reading in fierce snatches, scribbling things in notebooks, writing poetry in fragments" (qtd. in Olsen 1979, 44).

Innumerable diarists will also comment regularly on the difficulty of finding even the tiniest fragments of time for their diary writing. Mary Richardson Walker wrote in January of 1838, "I have little opportunity to record thoughts or feelings for want of opportunity to think—I am always surrounded with a flock of noisy children, and my head resounds with their noise like an empty barrel" (qtd. in Bank 1979, 92).

12. The title of this section comes from the title of Margaret Homans's wonderful book *Bearing the Word: Language and Experience in Nineteenth-Century Women's Writing* (1986).

13. See, e.g., such books as *The Female Spectator: English Women Writers before 1800* (Mahl and Koon 1977), *By a Woman Writt: Literature from Six Centuries by and about Women* (Goulianos 1973), and *Mothers of the Novel: 100 Good Women Writers before Jane Austen* (Spender 1986).

14. Kolb notes a parallel development to European women's access to writing through Medieval vernacular language that occurred in Japan. She writes:

> In Japan, the development in the ninth century of *hiragana*—the Japanese table of written syllables—gave the spoken Japanese language its own writing system in place of the cumbersome half-phonetic, half-semantic use of Chinese characters, that had been its only means of transcription. "Woman's hand" *(onnade)*, was what the Japanese called their new cursive script, as opposed to "men's letters" *(otokomoji)*, which consisted of the more prestigious Chinese characters plus a second phonetic table of syllables. And while the bureaucrats continued to write formally in the classical Chinese, aristocratic women were allowed to use Japanese written in the new cursive script. (Kolb 1989)

When I asked a Japanese friend who was visiting recently about medieval Japanese women writers she informed me that medieval Japanese women not only wrote in the new *hiragana*, but that it was a woman scholar, working for the emperor, who actually invented it (Yuriko Tsuda, Personal Communication, 6 August 1990). Also, it may not be a coincidence that Japanese women were among the very first to write secular personal journals, as early as the tenth century.

Chapter 4

1. I would like to thank Don Gordon for bringing this cartoon to my attention.

2. For those who want a broader historical overview of certain journal types or access to excerpts from and discussions of individual journals, there are several works I have found helpful. They provide the basis for much of my discussion. They include Robert Fothergill's *Private Chronicles* (1974), one of the first theoretical works on the development of the journal as a literary genre in England, and the three-volume series by Steven Kagle on American diary literature (1979, 1986, and 1988). *Centuries of Female Days: English Women's Private Diaries* (1988) by Harriet Blodgett and *A Day at a Time: The Diary Literature of American Women from 1764 to the Present* by Margo Culley (1985) offer useful feminist perspectives on the role of the diary in both literary and literacy traditions. (See also Cooper 1987; Dunaway and Evans 1957; Huff 1985; and Lowenstein 1982.)

3. For more information on the rich history of the oriental journal forms see Lowenstein 1982, 1987.

4. Other writers will offer somewhat different taxonomies. See Blythe 1989; Dobbs 1974; Dunaway and Evans 1957; Kagle 1979, 1986, 1988; and Mallon 1984.

5. Unless otherwise noted, all citations pertaining to the evolution of the terms *journal* and *diary* are from the *Oxford English Dictionary*.

6. The spiritual journal naturally has links with the much older tradition of women's spiritual autobiography, see Culley 1985 and Jelinek 1986.

7. Interestingly, while Evelyn does mention his family, and his family activities, he never hints at his relationships—his thoughts or feelings about his wife and family—which is very much like the men's journals of today.

8. In several critical respects, diary writing has never become aware of itself as a genre of public literary writing, especially for women, as we shall see in the next section.

9. This trend is apparent in the canon and in criticism of women's autobiography in general. See Jelinek 1986, 1-10 and Benstock 1988, 10-33.

10. For those who might interested in knowing more about Martha Ballard, Laurel Ulrich has recently published a book on her life (1990), based on her diaries. The thoughtful and evocative picture of a woman's life that comes out of the diaries testifies both to the richness and complexity of a midwife's life in eighteenth-century Maine, and to the power of the diary form that catches it day to day.

11. While I cannot do justice here to all the complexities of form and the

historical development of women's journal traditions, let me suggest to the reader Margot Culley's and Harriet Blodgett's work, as well as Penelope Franklin's *Private Pages* (1986), all of which form much of the basis of my remarks in this section. *Women's Personal Narratives: Essays in Criticism and Pedagogy*, edited by Leonore Hoffman and Margo Culley (1985), is also recommended for those interested in further reading. There are several other recent anthologies of women's journals/diaries, many excellent works on women's autobiography, and myriad published women's journals now available.

For example, there are collections of women diarists over time (Culley 1985; Franklin 1986; Huff 1985; and Moffat and Painter 1975), collections of contemporary diarists (Lifshin 1982), collections of frontier and westering women's diaries (Arpad 1984; Fischer 1977; Hampsten 1982; Myers 1982; and Schlissel 1982), and diaries of individual women dating back to tenth-century Japan (Sei Shonagon 1977), through to the twentieth-century diaries of Virginia Woolf (1977-1984), Joanna Field (1981), Anaïs Nin (1966), and May Sarton (1984).

12. Others, however, have made different observations. Cynthia Huff, for instance, found in her analysis of fifty-eight nineteenth-century British women's diaries that they did record in considerable detail the physical and emotional experience of that central rite of passage for women: pregnancy and childbirth (Huff 1987, 63-68. See also Huff 1985).

13. The Burney diaries, the Wynn diaries, and the Woodeforde diaries are all examples (see Blodgett 1988, 38; Dobbs 1974, 190-93; and Mallon 1984, 15-19).

14. In 1837, for example, women were thirty-two times more likely to die in childbirth than now and it was a commonplace for children to die in infancy.

15. I have been able to locate some diaries by black women, such as the diary of Charlotte Forten (1987), extended excerpts from four black women (Frances Rollin, Mary Virginia Mongomery, Laura Hamilton, and Ida Bell Wells) in Doroth Sterling's *We are Your Sisters* (1984), and several more in Culley's *A Day At a Time* (1985), including Rebecca Cox Jackson, the nineteenth century itinerant preacher, and Eslanda Goode Robeson, Joan Frances Bennett, and Barbara Smith in the twentieth century. These diaries will need their own analysis, just as the work on black women's autobiography suggests both similarities to and differences from other autobiography.

Chapter 5

1. See Gannett (1987) for a full discussion of the criteria I used to make my choices and extensive excerpts from each of the students' journals.

2. The essays the students read from *A Writer 's Reader* (Hall and Emblen 1982) included: James Agee's "Knoxville: Summer 1915"; Maya Angelou's "Mr. Red Leg"; James Audubon's "The Passenger Pigeon"; Ronald Blythe's "Aging

and Sexuality"; Frank Conroy's "A Yo-yo Going Down"; Emily Dickinson's "There's a Certain Slant of Light"; Joan Didion's "On Keeping a Notebook"; Annie Dillard's "Strangers to Darkness"; Loren Eisley's "How Flowers Changed the World"; Martin Gansberg's "38 Who Saw Murder Didn't Call the Police"; Lillian Hellman's "Runaway"; D. H. Lawrence's "Pornography"; Norman Mailer's "A Walk on the Moon"; N. Scott Momaday's "The Way to Rainy Mountain"; George Orwell's "Politics and the English Language" and "A Hanging"; John Parrish's "Welcome to Vietnam"; Octavio Paz's "Mexican-American Differences"; Sylvia Plath's "Journal Entries"; William Stafford's "A Way of Writing"; Studs Terkel's "Phil Stallings, Spot Welder"; Kenneth Tynan's "Here's Johnny"; and E. B. White's "Once More to the Lake."

3. I have tried to respect the exact phrasing of the students in their journals wherever it is possible, including fragments, unconventional punctuation, abbreviations, and so on. I have, however, eliminated any references that might directly identify the student.

4. When I asked permission to use excerpts from the journals in women's studies, I also asked if my students would prefer anonymity, a pseudonym, or their own names, and have followed their preferences.

5. A copy of the WES and student responses appear as appendices in Gannett (1987).

6. The page numbers indicated here and in other Gannett (1991) references are manuscript pages and will change when this article is published.

Chapter 6

1. See also the several sessions devoted to gender and composition at the last three Conferences on College Composition and Communication; Annas (1985, 1987), Cayton (1987, 1990), Frank and Treichler (1989), Pigott (1979), Sandborn (1987), and Spender (1989), among others, have documented in detail the roadblocks posed by impersonal, abstract, argumentative, defended academic writing for many women writers.

2. See, e.g., Belenky et al. 1986; Brodkey 1987; Bunch and Pollack 1983; Caywood and Overing 1981; Culley and Portugues 1985; Fowlkes and McClure 1984; Franzosa and Mazza 1984; Gabriel and Smithson 1990; Grumet 1988; LeFevre 1987; Schmitz 1985; and Spanier et al. 1984.

3. See note 15 in chapter 4.

Bibliography

Abel, Elizabeth, ed. *Writing and Sexual Difference*. Chicago: University of Chicago Press, 1982.

Aisenberg, Nadya, and Mona Harrington. *Women of Academe: Outsiders in the Sacred Grove*. Amherst: University of Massachusetts Press, 1988.

Albrecht, Lisa. "Focusing on the Writer—The Politics of Writer Identity." Paper presented at the Conference on College Composition and Communication, Seattle Wash., March 1989.

Allport, Gordon. *Use of Personal Documents in Psychological Science*. New York: Social Science Research Council, 1942.

Anderson, Bonnie S., and Judith Zinsser. *A History of Their Own: Women in Europe from Prehistory to the Present*. Vol. 1. New York: Harper and Row, 1988.

Andrews, William L., ed. *Sisters of the Spirit: Three Black Women's Autobiographies of the Nineteenth Century*. Bloomington: Indiana University Press, 1986.

Annas, Pamela J. "Silences: Feminist Language Research and the Teaching of Writing." In *Teaching Writing*. See Caywood and Overing 1987. 3-17.

———. "Style as Politics: A Feminist Approach to the Teaching of Writing." *College English* 47, no. 4 (April 1985): 360-71.

Anson, Chris M., and Hildy Miller. "Journals in Composition: An Update." *College Composition and Communication*. 39, no. 2 (May 1988): 198-216.

Ardener, Edwin. "Belief and the Problem of Women." In *Perceiving Women*. See Shirley Ardener 1975.

Ardener, Shirley. *Defining Females.* New York: Wiley and Sons, 1978.

————. *Perceiving Women.* New York: Malaby Press, 1975.

Argyle, Michael, Mansier Lalljee, and Mark Cook. "The Effects of Visibility on Interaction in a Dyad." *Human Relations* 21 (1968): 3-17.

Aries, Elizabeth. "Interaction Patterns and Themes of Male, Female, and Mixed Groups." *Small Group Behavior* 7 (1976): 7-18.

————. "Male-Female Interpersonal Styles in All Male, All Female and Mixed Groups." In *Beyond Sex Roles.* See Alice Sargent 1977. 292-98.

Aronson, Anne. "Remodelling Audiences, Building Voices." Paper presented at the Conference on College Composition and Communication, Seattle, Wash., March 1987.

Arpad, Susan S. *Sam Curd's Diary: The Diary of a True Woman.* Athens: Ohio University Press, 1984.

August, Eugene R. "'Modern Men,' or, Men's Studies in the 80's." *College English* 44, no. 6 (Oct. 1982): 583-97.

Ayres, Joe. "Relationship Stages and Sex as Factors in Topic Dwell Time." *Western Journal of Speech Communication* 44 (1980): 253-60.

Baird, John E. Jr. "Sex Differences in Group Communication: A Review of Relevant Research." *Quarterly Journal of Speech* 62 (1976): 179-92.

Bakhtin, Mikhail, M. "Discourse in the Novel." In *The Dialogic Imagination.* Ed. Michael Holquist. Trans. Caryl Emerson and Michale Holquist. Austin: University of Texas Press, 1981.

Baldwin, Christian. *One-to-One: Self Understanding Through Journal Writing.* New York: M. Evans, 1977.

Bank, Mirra. *Anonymous was a Woman.* New York: St. Martin's Press, 1979.

Barker, Diana Leonard, and Sheila Allen, eds. *Dependence and Exploitation in Work and Marriage.* New York: Longman, 1976.

Barnes, Linda Laube. "Gender Bias in Teacher's Written Comments." In *Gender in the Classroom.* See Gabriel and Smithson 1990. 140-59.

Baron, Dennis. *Grammar and Gender.* New Haven: Yale University Press, 1986.

Barringer, Carol E. "The Survivors's Voice: Breaking Silence About Childhood Sexual Abuse." *National Women's Studies Association Journal.* 4, no. 1 (Winter 1992).

Bartholomae, David. "Wanderings: Misreadings, Miswritings, Misunderstandings." In *Only Connect.* See Newkirk 1986. 89-118.

————. "Inventing the University." In *When a Writer Can't Write*. See Rose 1985. 134-65.

Bauer, Dale. "The Other "F" Word: The Feminist in the Classroom." *College English* 52, no. 4 (1990): 385-96.

Baumlin, James S., and Tita French Baumlin. "Psyche/Logos: Mapping the Terrains of Mind and Rhetoric." *College English* 51, no. 3 (March 1989): 245-61.

Begos, Jane Dupree. "The Diaries of Adolescent Girls." *Women's Studies International Forum* 10, no. 1 (1987): 69-74.

Belenky, Mary Field, Blythe McVicker Clinchy, Nancy Rule Goldberger, and Jill Mattuck Tarule. *Women's Ways of Knowing: The Development of Voice, Self and Mind*. New York: Basic, 1986.

Bell, Elouise M. "Telling One's Story: Women's Journals Then and Now." In *Women's Personal Narratives*. See Hoffman and Culley 1985. 167-78.

Benstock, Shari, ed. *Feminist Issues in Literary Scholarship*. Bloomington: Indiana University Press, 1987.

————. ed. *The Private Self: Theory and Practice of Women's Autobiographical Writings*. Chapel Hill: University of North Carolina Press, 1988.

Berg, Temma, Anna Shannon Elfenbein, Jeane Larsen, and Elisa Kay Sparks, eds. *Engendering the Word: Feminist Essays in Psychosexual Poetics*. Urbana: Illinois University Press, 1989.

Berger, Josef, and Dorothy Berger, eds. *Diary of America*. New York: Simon and Schuster, 1957.

Berger, Peter L., and Thomas Luckman. *The Social Construction of Reality*. Baltimore: Penguin, 1972.

Berko-Gleason, Jean, and Esther Blank Grief. "Men's Speech to Young Children." In *Language, Gender and Society*. See Thorne et al. 1983. 140-50.

Berlin, James. "Rhetoric and Ideology in the Writing Class." *College English*. 50, no. 5 (1988): 477-94.

Bernard, Jessie. *The Sex Game*. New York: Atheneum, 1972.

Berry, Ellen, and Elizabeth Black. "The Integrative Learning Journal (or Getting beyond 'True Confessions' and 'Cold Knowledge')." *Women's Studies Quarterly* 15, no. 3/4 (Fall/Winter 1987): 59-64.

Berthoff, Ann E. *Reclaiming the Imagination: Philosophical Perspectives for Writers and Teachers of Writing*. Upper Montclair, N.J.: Boynton/Cook, 1984.

———. "Dialectical Notebooks and the Audit of Meaning." In *The Journal Book*. See Fulwiler 1987. 11-18.

Bizzell, Patricia. "Cognition, Convention and Certainty: What We Need to Know about Writing." *Pre/Text* 3 (1982): 213-43.

———. "College Composition: Invitation into the Academic Discourse Community." *Curriculum Inquiry* 12 (1982): 191-207.

———. "Composing Processes: An Overview." In *The Teaching of Writing*. See Petrosky and Bartholomae 1986. 49-70.

———. "What Happens When Basic Writers Come to College?" *College English* 37, no. 3 (1986): 294-301.

Bizzell, Patricia, and Bruce Herzberg, eds. *The Rhetorical Tradition: Readings from Classical Times to the Present*. Boston: Bedford Books, 1990.

Blackburn, Regina. "In Search of the Black Female Self: African-American Women's Autobiographies and Ethnicity." In *Women's Autobiography*. See Jelinek 1980. 133-48.

Bleich, David. "Gender Interests in Reading and Language." In *Gender and Reading*. See Flynn and Schweickart 1986. 234-66.

Blodgett, Harriet. *Centuries of Female Days: Englishwomen's Private Diaries*. New Brunswick: Rutgers University Press, 1988.

Blythe, Ronald, ed. *The Pleasures of Diaries: Four Centuries of Private Writing*. New York: Pantheon Books, 1989 .

Bodine, Ann. "Androcentrism in Prescriptive Grammar: Singular 'They,' Sex-Indefinite 'He,' and 'He or She.'" *Language in Society* 4, no. 2 (1975): 129-46.

Bolker, Joan. "Teaching Griselda to Write." *College English* 40, no . 8 (1979): 906-08.

Borker, Ruth. "Anthropology: Social and Cultural Perspectives." In *Women and Language*. See McConnell-Ginet et al. 1980. 26-44.

Boston Woman's Health Book Collective. *The New Our Bodies, Ourselves*. New York: Simon and Schuster, 1984.

Britton, James, Tony Burgess, Nancy Martin, Alex McLeod, and Harold Rosen. *The Development of Writing Abilities (11-18)*. London: Macmillan Education, 1975.

Brodkey, Linda. *Academic Writing as Social Practice*. Philadephia: Temple University Press, 1987.

———. "Modernism and the Scene(s) of Writing." *College English* 49, no. 4 (Apr. 1987): 396-418.

Brodski, Bella, and Celeste Schenk, eds. *Life/Lines: Theorizing Women's Autobiography*. Ithaca: Cornell University Press, 1988.

Brooks, Virginia R. "Sex Differences in Student Dominance Behavior in Female and Male Professors' Classrooms." *Sex Roles* 8 (1982). 683-90.

Brown, Penelope, and Stephen Levinson. "Universals in Language Usage: Politeness Phenomena." In *Questions and Politeness*. See Goody 1978. 56-289.

Bruffee, Kenneth A. "Collaborative Learning and 'The Conversation of Mankind.'" *College English* 46, no . 7 (Nov. 1984): 635-52.

————. "Social Construction, Language, and the Authority of Knowledge: A Bibliographical Essay. " *College English* 48, no. 8 (1986): 773-90.

Bunch, Charlotte, and Sandra Pollack, eds. *Learning Our Ways: Essays in Feminist Education*. Trumansburg: Crossing Press, 1983.

Bunkers, Suzanne L. "'Faithful Friend': Nineteenth Century Midwestern Women's Unpublished Diaries." *Women's Studies International Forum* 10, no. 1 (1987): 7-17.

Butler, Sandra. "Incest: Whose Reality, Whose Theory." In *Feminist Frontiers*. See Richardson and Taylor 1983. 55-60.

Butturff, Douglas, and Edmund L. Epstein, eds. *Women's Language and Style*. Akron, Ohlo: L and S Books, 1978.

Cambridge, Barbara L. "Equal Opportunity Writing Classrooms: Accommodating Interactional Differences Between Genders in the Writing Classroom." *The Writing Instructor* 7, no. (1987): 30-39.

Carpenter, Carol. "Exercises to Combat Sexist Reading and Writing." *College English* 43, no. 3 (Mar. 1981): 293-300.

Carter, Kathryn, and Carole Spitzack, eds. *Doing Research on Women's Communication*. Norwood: Ablex, 1989.

Caws, Mary Ann. "The Conception of Engendering: The Erotics of Editing." In *The Poetics of Gender*. See Miller 1986. 42-62.

Cayton, Mary Kupiec. "Women's Initiation into Academic Discourse Communities." Paper presented at the Conference on College Composition and Communication, St Louis, Mo., March 1988.

————. "Writing as Outsiders: Academic Discourse and Marginalized Faculty." Paper presented at the conference on College Composition and Communication, Chicago, March 1990.

Caywood, Cynthia L., and Gillian R. Overing, eds. *Teaching Writing: Pedagogy,*

Gender and Fquity. Albany: State University of New York Press, 1987.

Chamberlain, Miriam, ed. *Women in Academe: Progress and Prospects.* New York: Russell Sage Foundation, 1988.

Chesler, Phyllis. *Women and Madness.* New York: Doubleday, 1972.

Chiseri-Strater, Elizabeth. "Lost Voices." Paper presented at the Conference on College Composition and Communication, New Orleans, March 1986.

——— . *Academic Literacies: The Public and Private Discourse of College Students.* Portsmouth, N.H.: Heinemann, 1991.

Chodorow, Nancy. *The Reproduction of Mothering: Psychoanalysis and the Sociology of Gender.* Berkeley: University of California Press, 1978.

——— . "Family Structure and Feminine Personality." In *Feminist Frontiers II.* See Richardson and Taylor 1986. 43-58.

Christ, Carol P. "Heretics and Outsiders: The Struggle Over Female Power in Western Religion." In *Feminist Frontiers.* See Richardson and Taylor 1983. 87-94.

Churgin, Jonah R. *The New Woman and the Old Academe: Sexism and Higher Education.* New York: Libra Publishers, 1978.

Cixous, Hélène, and Catherine Clément. *The Newly Born Woman.* Trans. Betsy Wing. Minneapolis: University of Minnesota Press, 1986.

Clifford, John. "Discerning Theory and Politics." *College English* 51, no. 5 (1989): 517-32.

Coates, Jennifer. *Women, Men and Language.* London and New York: Longman, 1986.

Connors, Robert J. Address. "The Feminization of Rhetoric." Conference on "New Directions in Composition Scholarship," University of New Hampshire, Durham, 10 Oct. 1986.

Connors, Robert J., Lisa S. Ede, and Andrea A. Lunsford. *Essays on Classical Rhetoric and Modern Discourse.* Carbondale: Southern Illinois University Press, 1984.

Cooper, Joanne E. "Shaping Meaning: Women's Diaries, Journals and Letters: The Old and The New." *Women's Studies International Forum* 10, no. 1 (1987): 95-99.

Cooper, Marilyn M. "The Ecology of Writing." *College English* 48, no. 4 (1986): 364-75.

Cote, Margaret M. "Now That We Have a Room of Our Own, Are We Throwing Away the Key?" *College English* 44, no. 6 (Oct. 1982): 606-11.

Cozby, Paul C. "Self-Disclosure: A Literature Review." *Psychological Bulletin* 79 (1973): 73-91.

Crawford, Patricia. "Women's Published Writings 1600-1700." In *Women in English Society*. See Prior 1985. 211-31.

Culley, Margo, ed. *A Day at a Time: The Diary Literature of American Women from 1764 to the Present.* New York: Feminist Press at City University of New York, 1985.

Culley, Margo, and Catherine Portuges, eds. *Gendered Subjects: The Dynamics of Feminist Teaching.* Boston: Routledge and Kegan Paul, 1985.

Davis, G. "Women's Frontier Diaries: Writing for Good Reason." *Women's Studies* 14 (1987): 5-14.

Derrida, Jacques. "Freud and the Scene of Writing." *Yale French Studies* 48 (1972): 73-117.

DeSalvo, Louise. *Virgina Woolf: The Impact of Childhood Sexual Abuse on Her Life and Work.* Boston: Beacon Press, 1989.

DiIorio, Judith. "Sex Glorious Sex, The Social Construction of Masculine Sexuality in a Youth Group." In *Feminist Frontiers II.* See Richardson and Taylor 1986. 261-69.

Dinnerstein, Dorothy. *The Mermaid and the Minotaur: Sexual Arrangements and Human Malaise.* New York: Harper and Row, 1976.

Dobbs, Brian. *Dear Diary . . . Some Studies in Self Interest.* London: Elm Tree, 1974.

Donovan, Josephine. "The Silence is Broken." In *Women and Language*. See McConnell-Ginet et al. 1980. 205-18.

Dubois, Betty Lou, and Isabel Crouch, eds. *The Sociology of the Languages of American Women.* San Antonio: Trinity University Press, 1976.

Dunaway, Philip, and Melvin Evans, eds. *Treasury of the World's Greatest Diaries.* Toronto: Doubleday, 1957.

DuPlessis, Rachael Blau. "For the Etruscans." In *New Feminist Criticism.* See Showalter 1985. 271-91.

Eakins, Barbara W., and R. Gene Eakins. *Sex Differences in Human Communication.* Boston: Houghton, 1978.

Edelsky, Carole. "Who's Got the Floor?" *Language and Society* 10 (1981): 383-421.

Elbow, Peter. *Writing Without Teachers.* New York: Oxford University Press, 1973.

Elbow, Peter, and Jennifer Clark. "Desert Island Discourse: The Benefits of Ignoring Audience." In *The Journal Book*. See Fulwiler 1987. 19-32.

Elshtain, Jean Bethke. *Public Man, Private Woman: Women in Social and Political Thought*. Princeton: Prlnceton University Press, 1981.

――――. "Feminist Discourse and its Discontents: Language and Power." *Signs* 7 (1982): 603-21.

Eisenstein, Hester, and Alice Jardine. *The Future of Difference*. Boston: Barnard College Women's Center, 1980.

Emig, Janet. *The Composing Processes of Twelth Graders*. National Council of Teachers of English Research Report 13. Urbana: National Council of Teachers of English, 1971.

――――. *Web of Meaning: Essays on Writing, Teaching, Learning, and Thinking*. Upper Montclair, N.J.: Boynton/Cook, 1983.

――――. "Writing as a Mode of Learning." *College Composition and Communication* 28 (1977): 122-28.

Fader, Dan. *Hooked on Books*. New York: Medallion, 1966.

Faderman, Lillian. *Surpassing the Love of Man: Love Between Women from the Renaissance to the Present*. New York: Morrow, 1981.

Faigley, Lester. "Competing Theories of Process: A Critique and Proposal." *College English* 48, no. 6 (October 1986): 527-42.

Farrell, Thomas J. "The Female and Male Modes of Rhetoric." *College English* 40, no. 8 (1979): 909-21.

Fausto-Sterling, Anne. "The New Research on Women: How Does it Affect the Natural Sciences." *Women's Studies Quarterly* 2 (1985): 30.

Ferguson, Mary Anne. "Feminist Theory and Practice, 1985" *College English* 48, no. 7 (November 1986): 726-35.

Ffeifer, Jules. Cartoon. *The Boston Sunday Globe* 1 Feb. 1981: A31.

Field, Joanna. *A Life of One's Own*. Los Angeles: J. F. P. Tarcher, 1981.

Fiore, Kyle, and Nan Elasser. "'Strangers No More': A Liberatory Literacy Curriculum." *College English* 44, no. 2 (Feb. 1982) 115-28.

Fischer, Christiane, ed. *Let Them Speak for Themselves: Women in the American West 1849-1900*. Hamden, Conn.: Archon, 1977.

Fishman, Pamela. "Conversational Insecurity." In *Language: Social Psychological Perspectives*. See Giles et al. 1980. 127-32.

————. "Interaction: The Work Women Do." In *Language, Gender and Society*. See Thorne et al. 1983. 89-101.

————. "What Do Couples Talk About When They're Alone?" In *Women's Language and Style*. See Butturff and Epstein 1978. 11-22.

Flynn, Elizabeth A. "Gender Difference and Student Writing: Topics and Concerns." Unpublished Paper. Department of Humanities, Michigan Technological University. Houghton, Mich., 1985.

————. "Gender and Reading." In *Gender and Reading*. See Flynn and Schweickart 1986. 267-88.

————. "Composing as a Woman." *College Composition and Communicatlon* 39, no. 4 (1988): 423-36.

Flynn, Elizabeth A., and Patrocinio P. Schweickart, eds. *Gender and Reading: Essays on Readers, Texts, and Contexts*. Baltimore: Johns Hopkins University Press, 1986.

Forten, Charlotte. *The Journal of Charlotte Forten: A Young Black Woman's Reactions to the White World of the Civil War Era*. Ed. and intro. Ray Allen Billington. New York: W. W. Norton, 1981.

Fothergill, Robert A. *Private Chronicles: A Study of English Diaries*. London: Oxford University Press, 1974.

Foucault, Michel. *Power/Knowledge: Selected Interviews and Other Writings, 1972-1977*. Ed. Colin Gordon. New York: Pantheon, 1980.

Fowlkes, Diane L., and Charlotte S. McClure, eds. *Feminist Visions: Toward a Transformation of the Liberal Arts Curriculum*. Alabama: University of Alabama Press, 1984.

Fox-Genovese, Elizabeth. "My Statue, My Self: Autobiographical Writings of Afro-American Women." In *The Private Self*. See Benstock 1988. 63-89.

Frank, Francine Wattman. "Language Planning, Language Reform, and Language Change: A Review of Guidelines for Nonsexist Usage." In *Language, Gender and Professional Writing*. See Frank and Treichler 1989. 105-36.

Frank, Francine Wattman, and Paula Treichler, eds. *Language, Gender and Professional Writing: Theoretical Approaches and Guidelines for Non-Sexist Usage*. New York: MLA, 1989.

Franklin, Penelope, ed. *Private Pages: Diaries of American Women 1830's-1970's*. New York: Ballantine, 1986.

Franzosa, Susan Douglas, and Karen A. Mazza. *Integrating Women's Studies into the Curriculum: An Annotated Bibliography*. Westport, Conn.: Greenwood Press, 1984.

Freed, Richard C., and Broadhead, Glenn J. "Discourse Communities, Sacred Texts, and Institutional Norms." *College Composition and Communication* 38, no. 2 (1987): 154-65.

Freedman, Aviva, and Ian Pringle, eds. *Reinventing the Rhetorical Tradition*. Conway, Ark.: L and S Books, 1980.

Freidan, Betty. *The Feminine Mystique*. Baltimore: Penguin, 1963.

Friedman, Susan Stanford. "Women's Autobiographical Selves: Theory and Practice." In *The Private Self*. See Benstock 1988. 34-62.

Freisinger, Randall. "Cross-Disciplinary Writing Programs: Beginnings." In *Language Connections*. See Fulwiler and Young 1982. 3-14.

———. "Cross-Disciplinary Writing Workshops: Theory and Practice." *College English* 42, no.6 (Oct 1980): 154-66.

Freisinger, Randall, and Bruce Peterson. "Writing Across the Currlculum: A Theoretical Background." *Fforum* 2 (Winter, 1981): 65-67, 92.

French, Emily. *Emily: The Diary of a Hard Worked Woman*. Ed. Janet Lecompte. Lincoln: Nebraska University Press, 1987.

French, Marilyn. "Text as Context." *Women's Studies Quarterly* 16 (1988): 34.

Froula, Christine. "The Daughter's Seduction: Sexual Violence and Literary History." In *Feminist Theory In Practice and Process*. See Malson et al. 1989. 139-63.

Fulwiler, Toby., ed. and intro. *The Journal Book*. Portsmouth, N.H.: Heinemann, 1987.

———. "The Personal Connection: Journal Writing Across the Curriculum." In *Language Connections*. See Fulwiler and Young 1982. 15-32.

Fulwiler, Toby, and Bruce Petersen. "Towards Irrational Heuristics: Freeing the Tacit Mode." *College English* 43, no. 6 (Oct. 1981): 621-29.

Fulwiler, Toby, and Art Young, eds. *Language Connections: Writing And Reading Across the Curriculum*. Urbana, Ill.: National Council of Teachers of English, 1982.

Gabriel, Susan L., and Isiah Smithson, eds. *Gender in the Classroom: Power and Pedagogy*. Urbana: University of Illinois Press, 1990.

Gage, John T. "Why Write?" In *The Teaching of Writing*. See Petrosky and Bartholomae 1986. 8-29.

Gannett, Cinthia. "Gender and Journals: Life as Text and Text as Life in College Composition." Unpublished paper, 1987.

——— . "Sex and the Single Brain: A Neurolinguistic Perspective on Sex Differences in Language and Writing Style." Paper presented at the World Congress of Sociology, Uppsala, Sweden, Aug. 1978.

——— . "Sex Differences in Language Laterality and Verbal Cognition." Master's Paper, University of New Hampshire, May 1976.

——— . "What Can Brain Research Tell Us About Feminine Consciousness and Modes of Expression?" Paper presented at the Annual Conference of the Modern Language Association, New York, Dec. 1976.

——— . "Murray and the Journal: Praxis What You Preach." Paper presented at the Conference on Mind in Society: The Context for Writing, University of New Hampshire, 7-9 October 1988.

——— . *Gender and Journals: Life and Text in College Composition.* Ph.D. diss., University of New Hampshire, May 1987.

——— . "The Stories of Our Lives Become Our Lives." *Feminine Principles in Composition.* Ed. Janet Emig and Louise Weatherbee Phelps. New York: Modern Language Association, 1991 (forthcoming).

Gannett, Cinthia, and Karl Diller. "Process and Pedagogy in Writing: Some Neurolinguistic Considerations." Paper presented at the Conference of the American Association of Applied Linguistics, New York, Dec. 1981.

Garner, Shirley Nelson, Clair Kahane, and Madelon Sprengnether, eds. *The (M)Other Tongue: Essays in Feminist Psychoanalytic Interpretation.* Ithaca: Cornell University Press, 1985.

Gearhart, Sally. "The Womanization of Rhetoric." *Women's Studies International Quarterly* 2, no. 2 (1979): 195-202.

Geertz, Clifford. *The Interpretation of Cultures.* New York: Basic, 1983.

——— . *Local Knowledge.* New York: Basic, 1973.

Gelfand, Elissa D., and Virginia Thorndike Hules. *French Feminist Criticism: Women, Language and Literature.* New York: Garland, 1985.

Gelinas, Denise J. "The Persisting Negative Effects of Incest." *Psychiatry* 46 (Nov 1983): 312-32.

Gere, Anne Ruggles. "Teaching Writing: The Major Theories." In *The Teaching of Writing.* See Petrosky and Bartholomae 1986. 49-70.

Gershuny, H. Lee. "English Handbooks 1979-1985: Case Studies in Sexist and Nonsexist Usage." In *Language, Gender and Professional Writing.* See Frank and Treichler 1989. 95-104.

Gilbert, Sandra M. "Life Studies, or, Speech After Long Silence: Feminist Critics

Today." *College English* 40, no. 8 (1979): 849-63.

Gilbert, Sandra M., and Susan Gubar. *No Man's Land: The Place of the Woman Writer in the Twentieth Century.* Vol. 1: *The War of the Words.* New Haven: Yale University Press, 1988.

Giles, Howard, W. Peter Robinson, and Philip M. Smith, eds. *Language: Social Psychological Perspectives.* New York: Pergamon, 1980.

Gilligan, Carol. *In a Different Voice: Psychological Theory and Women's Development.* Cambridge, Mass.: Harvard University Press, 1982.

——. "Women's Place in Man's Life Cycle." In *Feminist Frontiers II.* See Richardson and Taylor 1986. 31-42.

Gillikin, Dure Jo. "A Lost Diary Found: The Art of the Everyday." In *Women's Personal Narratives.* See Hoffman and Culley 1985. 124-38.

Glastonbury, Marion. "Holding the Pens." In *Inspiration and Drudgery.* 1978. 24-46.

Goodwin, Marjorie Harness. "Directive-Response Speech Sequences in Girls' and Boys' Task Activities." In *Women and Language.* See McConnell-Ginet et al. 1980. 157-73.

Goody, Esther N., ed. *Questions and Politeness: Strategies in Social Interaction.* Cambridge: Cambridge University Press, 1978.

Goswami, Dixie, and Peter Stillman, eds. *Reclaiming the Classroom: Teacher Research as an Agency for Change.* Upper Montclair, N.J.: Boynton/Cook, 1987.

Gordon, Barbara L. "Sex Differences in Composition—What's Different?" Paper presented at the Conference on College Composition and Communication, Atlanta, 19-21 March 1987.

Goulianos, Joan. *By a Woman Writt: Literature from Six Centuries by and about Women.* Baltimore: Penguin, 1973.

Goulston, Wendy. "Women Writing." In *Teaching Writing.* See Caywood and Overing 1987. 19-30.

Gradin, Sherrie. "British Romanticism and Composition Theory: The Traditions and Value of Romantic Rhetoric." Ph.D. diss., University of New Hampshire, May 1990.

Graham, Alma. "The Making of a Non-Sexist Dictionary." In *Language and Sex.* See Thorne and Henley 1975. 57-63.

Graves, Donald. "Sex Differences in Children's Writing." *Elementary English* 50 (Oct. 1973): 1101-06.

————. *Writing: Teachers and Children at Work.* Portsmouth, N.H.: Heinemann, 1983.

Greene, Gayle, and Coppelia Kahn, eds. *Making a Difference: Feminist Literary Theory.* London: Methuen, 1985.

Greif, Esther Blank. "Sex Differences in Parent-Child Conversations. " In *The Voices and Words of Women and Men.* See Kramarae 1980. 253-58.

Griffin, Susan. "Rape: the All-American Crime." In *Feminist Frontiers.* See Richardson and Taylor 1983. 159-67.

————. "Thoughts on Writing: A Diary." In *The Writer on Her Work.* See Sternberg 1980. 107-20.

Grumet, Madelaine R. *Bitter Milk: Women and Teaching.* Amherst: University of Massachusetts Press, 1988.

"Guidelines for Using Journals in School Settings." National Council of Teachers of English Commission on Composition, June 1987. In *The Journal Book.* See Fulwiler 1987. 5-8.

Gusdorf, Georges. "Conditions and Limits of Autobiography." Trans. James Olney. In *Autobiography.* See Olney 1980. 28-48.

Hall, Donald, and D. L. Emblen. *A Writer's Reader.* 3rd ed. Boston: Little, Brown and Company, 1982.

Hall, Roberta, and Bernice R. Sandler. *The Classroom Climate: A Chilly One for Women?* Washington, D.C.: Association of American Colleges/Project on the Status and Education of Women (AAC/PSEW), 1982.

————. *Out of the Classroom: A Chilly Campus Climate for Women?* Washington D.C.: Association of American Colleges/Project on the Status and Education of Women (AAC/PSEW), 1984.

————. *The Campus Climate Revisited: Chilly for Women Faculty, Administrators and Graduate Students.* Washington D.C.: Association of American Colleges/Project on the Status and Education of Women (AAC/PSEW), 1986.

Hampsten, Elizabeth. *Read This Only to Yourself: The Private Writings of Midwestern Women, 1880-1910.* Bloomington: Indiana University Press, 1982.

Harris, Joseph. "The Idea of Community in the Study of Writing." *College Composition and Communication.* 40, no. 1 (1989): 11-22.

Hartman, Joan E., and Ellen Messer-Davidow. *Women in Print I: Opportunities for Women's Studies Research in Language and Literature.* New York: Modern Language Association, 1982.

Hays, Kate F. "Journal Writing with Clients: An Introduction and Case History."

In *Innovations in Clinical Practice: A Source Book.* Vol. 7 (1988): 127-35.

Heath, Gail. "Journals in a Classroom: One Teacher's Trials and Errors." *English Journal* (February 1988): 58-60.

Heath, Shirley Brice. "Literate Behaviors as Interpretation." Paper presented at the Conference on "New Directions in Composition Scholarship," University of New Hampshire, 10 Oct. 1986.

———. *Ways with Words.* New York: Cambridge University Press, 1983.

———. "The Essay and the Routines of Everyday Discourse." Paper Presented at the Conference on College Composition and Communication, Chicago, March 1990.

Heilbrun, Carolyn G. "The Politics of Mind: Women, Tradition and the University." In *Gender in the Classroom.* See Gabriel and Smithson 1990. 28-40.

———. *Writing A Woman's Life.* New York: Ballantine, 1988.

Held, Virginia. "Feminism and Epistemology: Recent Work on the Connection Between Gender and Knowledge." *Philosophy and Public Affairs* 14, no. 3 (1985): 296-307.

Herman, Judith Lewis. *Father-Daughter Incest.* Cambridge, Mass.: Harvard University Press, 1981.

Herman, Judith Lewis, and Lisa Hirschman. "Father-Daughter Incest." *Signs* 2, no. 4 (1977): 735-56.

Hoffmann, Leonore, and Margo Culley, eds. *Women's Personal Narratives: Essays in Criticism.* New York: Modern Language Association, 1985.

Hoffman, Leonore, and Deborah Rosenfelt, eds. *Teaching Women's Literature From a Regional Perspective.* New York: Modern Language Association, 1982.

Hogan, Rebecca. "Diarists on Diaries." *Auto/Biography Studies* 2, no. 2 (Summer 1986): 9-14.

———. "Selected Bibliography of Books and Articles on Diaries and Related Subjects: Selected Sources on Women's Diaries." *Auto/Biography Studies* 2, no. 2 (Summer 1986): 1-6.

The Hopkins Bulletin. "A Look at the Dartmouth Curriculum." 2, no. 7 (March 1989): 1-4.

Hollowell, John, and G. Lynn Nelson. "Bait/Rebait: We Should Abolish the Use of Personal Journals in English Classes." *English Journal* (January 1982): 14-17.

Homans, Margaret. *Bearing the Word: Language and Experience in Nineteenth-Century Women's Writing*. Chicago: Chicago University Press, 1986.

Howe, Florence. "Identity and Expression: Writing Course for Women." *College English* 32, no. 8 (May 1971): 863-71.

———. "A Report on Women and the Profession." *College English* 32, no. 8 (May 1971): 847-53.

———. "Those We Still Don't Read." *College English* 43, no. 1 (Jan. 1981): 12-16.

Huff, Cynthia. *British Women's Diaries*. New York: AMS Press, 1985.

———. "Chronicles of Confinement: Reactions to Childbirth in British Women's Diaries." *Women's Studies International Forum*. 10, no. 1 (1987): 63-68.

Hunter, Paul, and Nadine Pearce. "Writing, Reading and Gender." *Journal of Developmental Education*. 12, no. 1 (Sept. 1988): 20-26.

Inspiration and Drudgery: Notes on Literature and Domestic Labour in the Nineteenth Century. N.p.: Women's Research and Resource Centre, 1978.

Irigaray, Luce. *Speculum of the Other Woman*. Trans. Gillian C. Gill. Ithaca: Cornell University Press, 1985.

Jacobus, Mary. *Women Writing and Writing About Women*. New York: Harper, 1979.

———. *Reading Women: Essays in Feminist Criticism*. New York: Columbia University Press, 1986.

Jelinek, Estelle. *The Tradition of Women's Autobiography: From Antiquity to the Present*. Boston: G. K. Hall, 1986.

———, ed. *Women's Autobiography: Essays in Criticism*. Bloomington: Indiana University Press, 1980.

Jenkins, Mercilee M. "Stories Women Tell: An Ethnographic Study of Personal Experience Narratives in a Women's Rap Group." Paper presented at the Tenth World Congress of Sociology, Mexico City, 1982.

Jones, Ann Rosalind. "Writing the Body: Toward an Understanding of l'Ecriture Féminine." In *Feminist Criticism*. See Newton and Rosenfeldt 1985. 86-104.

Jost, Jean E. "Gender Bias in Composition Classes: A Case of Language." Unpublished essay.

Kagle, Steven. *American Diary Literature: 1620-1799*. Boston: G. K Hall, 1979.

———. *Early Nineteenth Century Diary Literature*. Boston: G. K. Hall, 1986.

———. *Late Nineteenth Century Diary Literature*. Boston: G. K. Hall, 1988.

Kalčik, Susan. ". . . Like Ann's Gynecologist or the Time I Was Almost Raped: Personal Narratives In Women's Rap Groups." *Journal of American Folklore* 88 (Jan.-Mar. 1975): 3-11.

Kamel, Rose. "Women's Studies and the Professional School: A Contradiction in Terms?" *College English* 44, no. 7 (Nov. 1982): 685-91.

Kamholtz, Jonathan Z., and Robin Sheets. "Women Writers and the Survey of English Literature: A Proposal and Annotated Bibliography for Teachers." *College English* 46, no. 3 (Mar. 1984): 278-300.

Kaplan, Cora. *Sea Changes: Culture and Feminism.* London: Verso Press, 1986.

Kelley, Liz. *Surviving Social Violence.* Minneapolis: University of Minneapolis Press, 1988.

Kelley, Mary. *Private Woman, Public Stage: Literary Domesticity in Nineteenth Century America.* New York: Oxford University Press, 1984.

Key, Mary Ritchie. *Male/Female Language.* Metuchen, N.J.: Scarecrow Press, 1975.

Kinneavy, James. *A Theory of Discourse.* Englewood Cliffs, N.J.: Prentice-Hall, 1971.

Kissel, Susan S. "Preparing a Collection of Regional Autobiographical Materials for Use in the Composition Classroom." In *Women's Personal Narratives.* See Hoffman and Culley 1985. 153-61.

Knoblauch, C. H. "Rhetorical Construction: Dialogue and Commitment." *College English* 50, no. 2 (1988): 125-40.

Kolb, Elene. "When Women Got the Word." *New York Times Book Review* 9 July 1989: 1, 28-29.

Kolodny, Annette. "Dancing through the Minefield: Some Observations on the Theory, Practice and Politics of a Feminist Literary Criticism." *Feminist Studies* 6 (1980): 1-25. Rpt. in *The New Feminist Criticism.* See Showalter 1985. 144-67.

————. "A Map for Re-Reading: Gender and the Interpretation of Literary Texts." *New Literary History* 11 (1980): 451-67. Rpt. in *The New Feminist Criticism.* See Showalter 1985. 46-62.

Komarovsky, Mirra. *Blue Collar Marriage.* New York: Random, 1962.

Kramarae, Cheris. "Proprietors of Language." In *Women and Language.* See McConnell-Ginet et al. 1980. 58-68.

————. ed. *Women and Men Speaking.* Rowley, Mass.: Newbury, 1981.

————. ed. *The Voices and Words of Women and Men.* Oxford: Pergamon, 1980.

Kramarae, Cheris, and Paula Treichler. "Power Relationships in the Classroom." In *Gender in the Classroom*. See Gabriel and Smithson 1990. 41-59.

Kramer, Cheris. "Perceptions of Female and Male Speech." *Language and Speech* 20, no. 2 (Apr.-June 1977): 151-61.

Kristeva, Julia. "Woman's Time." Trans. Alice Jardine and Harry Blake. *Signs* 7 (1981): 13-35.

Lacan, Jacques. *Ecrits: A Selection*. Trans. Alan Sheridan. New York: W. W. Norton, 1977.

Lakoff, Robin. *Language and Women's Place*. New York: Harper, 1975.

Landy, Marcia. "The Silent Woman: Towards a Feminist Critique." *The Authority of Experience*. Ed. Arlyn Diamond and Lee R. Edwards. Amherst, Mass.: University of Massachusetts Press, 1977.

Langland, Elizabeth, and Walter Gove, eds. *A Feminist Perspective in the Academy*. Chicago: University of Chicago Press, 1981.

Language and Gender Working Party. *Alice in Genderland: Reflections on Language, Power, and Control*. England: David Green, 1985.

LeFevre, Karen Burke. *Invention as a Social Act*. Edwardsville, Ill.: Southern Illinois University Press, 1987.

Lerner, Gerda. *The Creation of Patriarchy*. New York: Oxford University Press, 1986.

Lewis, Robert. "Emotional Intimacy Among Men." *Journal of Social Issues* 34 (1978): 108-21.

Lifshin, Lyn, ed. *Ariadne's Thread: A Collection of Contemporary Women's Journals*. New York: Harper and Row, 1982.

Lorde, Audre. "The Transformation of Silence in Language and Action." Paper presented at the Lesbian Literature Panel, Annual Conference of the Modern Language Association, Chicago, Dec. 1977.

Lowenstein, Sharyn Sondra. "The Personal Journal-Journal Keeper Relationship as Experienced by the Journal Keeper: A Phenomenological and Theoretical Investigation." Ph.D. diss., Boston University, 1982.

———. "A Brief History of Journal Keeping." In *The Journal Book*. See Fulwiler 1987. 87-98.

MacKay, Donald G. "Prescriptive Grammar and the Pronoun Problem." In *Language, Gender and Society*. See Thorne et al. 1983. 38-53.

Macrorie, Ken. *Telling Writing*. Rochelle Park, N.J.: Hayden, 1970.

————. Foreword. *The Journal Book*. See Fulwiler 1987. i-iii.

Maglin, Nan Bauer. "'Full of Memories:' Teaching Matrilineage." *College English* 40, no. 8 (1979): 889-98.

Mahl, Mary R., and Helene Koon. *The Female Spectator: English Women Writers Before 1800*. Bloomington: Indiana University Press, 1977.

Mallon, Thomas. *A Book of One's Own: People and Their Diaries*. New York: Penguin, 1984.

Malson, Micheline, R. Jean F. O'Barr, Sarah Westphal-Wihl, and Mary Wyer, eds. *Feminist Theory in Practice and Process*. Chicago: Chicago University Press, 1989.

Marcus, Jane. "Invincible Mediocrity: The Private Selves of Public Women." In *The Private Self*. See Benstock 1988. 114-46.

Marks, Elaine, and Isabelle de Courtivron, eds. and intro. *New French Feminisms: An Anthology*. 1980. New York: Schocken Books, 1981.

Martin, Jane Roland. *Reclaiming a Conversation: The Ideal of the Educated Woman*. New Haven, Conn.: Yale University Press, 1985.

Martyna, Wendy. "Beyond the He/Man Approach: The Case for Nonsexist Language." In *Language, Gender and Society*. See Thorne et al. 1983. 25-38.

Mason, Mary Grimley. "The Other Voice: Autobiographies of Women Writers." In *Autobiography*. Olney 1980. 207-35.

Mason, Mary Grimley, and Carol Hurd Green. *Journeys: Autobiographical Writings by Women*. Boston: G. K. Hall, 1979.

Matthews, William. *American Diaries: An Annotated Bibliography of American Diaries Written Prior to the Year 1861*. Berkeley: University of California Press, 1945.

————. *British Diaries: An Annotated Bibliography of British Diaries Written Between 1442 and 1942*. Berkeley: University of California Press, 1980.

McConnell-Ginet, Sally. "Linguistics and the Feminist Challenge." In *Women and Language*. See McConnell-Ginet et al. 1980. 3-25.

————. "The Sexual (Re)Production of Meaning: A Discourse Based Theory." In *Language, Gender and Professional Writing*. See Frank and Treichler 1989. 35-50.

McConnell-Ginet, Sally, Ruth Borker, and Nelly Furman, eds. *Women and Language in Literature and Society*. New York: Praeger, 1980.

McKay, Nellie Y. "Nineteenth Century Black Women's Spiritual Autobiographies: Religious Faith and Self-Empowerment." In *Interpreting Women's Lives*. See Personal Narratives Group 1989. 139-54.

Meese, Elizabeth . "Archival Materials: The Problem of Literary Reputation." In *Women in Print I*. See Hartman and Messer-Davidow 1982. 37-46.

——— . *Crossing the Double-Cross: The Practice of Feminine Criticism*. Chapel Hill: University of North Carolina Press, 1986.

Meisenhelder, Susan. "Redefining 'Powerful' Writing: Toward a Feminist Theory of Composition." *Feminist Education/Journal of Thought* 20, no. 3 (1985): 184-95.

Melichar, Don. "A Leap of Faith: The New Right and Secular Humanism." *English Journal* (October 1983): 55-57 .

Mendelson, Sara Heller. "Stuart Women's Diaries and Occasional Memoirs." In *Women in English Society 1500-1800*. See Prior 1985. 181-210.

Merriam, Eve. *Growing Up in America: Ten Lives*. Boston: Beacon Press, 1987.

Miller, Casey, and Kate Swift. *Words and Women: New Language in New Times*. Garden City, N.Y.: Doubleday, 1976.

Miller, Nancy, ed. *The Poetics of Gender*. New York: Columbia University Press, 1986.

Min-zhan, Lu. "From Silence to Words: Writing as Struggle." *College English* 49, no. 4 (Apr. 1987): 437-48.

Mitchell-Kernan, Claudia. "Signifying." In *Mother Wit from the Laughing Barrel*. Ed. A. Dundes. Englewood Cliffs, N.J.: Prentice-Hall, 1973.

Moffat, Mary Jane, and Charlotte Painter, eds. *Revelations: Diaries of Women*. 1974. New York: Vintage Books, 1975.

Moffett, James. *Teaching the Universe of Discourse*. Boston: Houghton Mifflin, 1968.

Moi, Toril. *Sexual/Textual Politics: Feminist Literary Theory*. London: Methuen, 1985.

Montaigne, Michel de. *Essays*. Middlesex: Penguin, 1975.

Morgan, Bob. "Three Dreams of Language; Or, No Longer Immured in the Bastille of the Humanist Word." *College English* 49, no. 4 (Apr. 1987): 449-58.

Morris, Adelaide. "Locutions and Locations: More Feminist Theory and Practice, 1985." *College English* 49, no. 4 (April 1987): 465-75.

Morris, Ivan, ed. and trans. *The Pillow Book of Sei Shonagon*. New York: Penguin, 1967.

Mueller, Janel M. "Autobiography of a New 'Creatur': Female Spirituality, Self-hood, and Authorship, *The Book of Margery Kemp*." In *Women in the Middle Ages and the Renaissance*. See Rose 1986. 155-72.

Mulchahy, G. A. "Sex Differences in Patterns of Self-Disclosure Among Adolescents: A Developmental Perspective. *Journal of Youth and Adolescence* 4 (1973): 343-56.

Murray, Donald. "Write before Writing." *College Composition and Communication* 29 (December 1978): 375-82.

———. *A Writer Teaches Writing*. 2nd ed. Boston: Houghton Mifflin, 1985.

Myers, Greg. "Texts as Knowledge Claims: The Social Construction of Two Biologist's Articles." *Social Studies of Science* 15 (1985): 593-630.

Myers, Sandra. *Westering Women and the Frontier Experience, 1800-1915*. Albuquerque: University of New Mexico Press, 1982.

———. ed. *Ho for California! Women's Overland Diaries from the Huntington Library*. San Marino, Cal.: Huntington Library Press, 1980.

Neilsen, Lorrie. *Literacy and Living: The Literate Lives of Three Adults*. Portsmouth, N.H.: Heinemann, 1989.

Newkirk, Thomas. *Only Connect: Uniting Reading and Writing*. Upper Montclair, N.J.: Boynton/Cook, 1986.

Newton, Judith and Deborah Rosenfeldt, eds. *Feminist Criticism and Social Change: Sex, Class and Race in Literature and Culture*. New York: Methuen, 1985.

Nilsen, Alleen Pace. "Grammatical Gender and its Relationship to the Equal Treatment of Males and Females in Children's Books." Ph.D. diss., University of Iowa, 1973.

Nilsen, Alleen Pace, Haig Bosmajian, H. Lee Gershuny, and Julia P. Stanley, eds. *Sexism and Language*. Urbana: National Council of Teachers of English, 1977.

Nin, Anaïs. *The Diary of Anaïs Nin: Volume One 1931-1934*. Ed. Gunther Stuhlmann. New York: Swallow Press and Harcourt, 1966.

Nussbaum, Felicity. "Eighteenth-Century Women's Autobiographical Commonplaces." In *The Private Self*. See Benstock 1988. 147-72.

Odell, Lee, and Dixie Goswami, eds. *Writing in Nonacademic Settings*. New York: Guilford, 1985.

Olney, James, ed. *Autobiography: Essays Theoretical and Critical*. Princeton: Princeton University Press, 1980.

———— . *Metaphors of Self: The Meaning of Autobiography.* Princeton: Princeton University Press, 1972.

Olsen, Tillie. *Silences.* New York: Delacorte/Seymour Lawrence, 1979.

Ong, Walter. *Fighting for Life.* Ithaca: Cornell University Press, 1981.

The Compact Edition of the Oxford English Dictionary: Complete Text Reproduced Micrographically. Vol. 1. New York: Oxford University Press, 1971.

Pagels, Elaine H. "What Became of God the Mother? Conflicting Images of God in Early Christianity." *Signs* 2, no. 2 (1976): 293-303.

Parsons, Ann. "Teaching Writing Instructors About Language and Gender." Unpublished essay.

Partnow, Elaine, ed. *The Quotable Woman: From Eve to 1799.* New York: Facts on File Publications, 1985.

Pascal, Roy. *Design and Truth in Autobiography.* London: Routledge and Kegan Paul, 1960.

Penelope, Julia, and Susan J. Wolfe. "Consciousness as Style: Style as Aesthetic." In *Language, Gender and Society.* See Thorne et al. 1983. 125-39.

Pepys, Samuel. *The Diary of Samuel Pepys.* Ed. Robert Latham and William Matthews. Vol. 1: *1660.* Berkeley and Los Angeles: University of California Press, 1970.

Perry, Donna, M. "Making Journal Writing Matter." In *Teaching Writing.* See Caywood and Overing 1987. 151-56.

Personal Narratives Group, eds. *Interpreting Women's Lives: Feminist Theory and Personal Narratives.* Bloomington: Indiana University Press, 1989.

Peterson, Linda H. "Gender and Autobiographical Writing: The Implications for Teaching." Unpublished essay.

Petrosky, Anthony R., and David Bartholomae, eds . *The Teaching of Writing: Eighty-Fifth Yearbook of the National Society for the Study of Education.* Chicago: University of Chicago Press, 1986.

Pigott, Margaret B. "Sexist Roadblocks in Inventing, Focusing, and Writing." *College English* 40, no. 8 (1979): 922-27.

Pomerleau, Cynthia S., "The Emergence of Women's Autobiography in England." In *Women's Autobiography.* See Jelinek 1980. 21-38.

Ponsonby, Arthur. *English Diaries.* London: Methuen, 1923.

Presnell, Michael. "Narrative Gender Differences: Orality and Literacy." In *Doing Research on Women's Communication.* See Carter and Spitzack 1989. 118-36.

Prior, Mary, ed. *Women in English Society 1500-1800*. London: Methuen, 1985.

Progoff, Ira. *At a Journal Workshop*. New York: Dialogue House, 1975.

Purves, Alan C. "The Teacher as Reader: An Anatomy." *College English* 46, no. 3 (Mar. 1984): 259-65.

Rainer, Tristine. *The New Diary: How to Use a Journal for Self-Guidance and Expanded Creativity*. Los Angeles: J. P. Tarcher, 1978.

Ranieri, Paul W. "Gender and Composing at the College Freshman Level: A Developmental Approach." Unpublished essay.

Reither, James A. "Writing and Knowing: Toward Redefining the Writing Process. " *College English* 47, no. 6 (Oct . 1985): 620-28.

Rich, Adrienne. *The Dream of a Common Language: Poems 1974-1977*. New York: W. W. Norton, 1978.

———. *On Lies, Secrets, and Silence: Selected Prose: 1966-78*. New York: Norton, 1979.

———. *Of Woman Born: Motherhood as Experience and Institution*. London: Virago, 1977.

Richardson, Laurel, and Verta Taylor. *Feminist Frontiers: Rethinking Sex, Gender, and Society*. New York: Random House, 1983.

———. *Feminist Frontlers II: Rethinking Sex, Gender and Society*. New York: Random House: 1986.

Ritchie, Joy S. "Beginning Writers: Diverse Voices and Individual Identity." *College Composition and Communication*. 40, no. 2 (May 1989): 152-73.

Robbins, Susan. "Gender and Agency in Indo-European Languages." Paper presented at the Ninth World Congress of Sociology, Uppsala, Sweden, 14-20 Aug. 1978.

Robinson, Lillian S. "Treason Our Text: Feminist Challenges to the Literary Canon." In *New Feminist Criticism*. See Showalter 1985. 105-22.

Rodenas, Adriana Mendez. "Tradition and Women's Writing: Toward a Poetics of Difference." In *Engendering the Word*. See Berg et al. 1989. 29-50.

Rodiman, F. Robert. "Shattered Children." Rev. of *Soul Murder: The Effects of Childhood Abuse and Deprivation*, by Leonard Shengold. *New York Times Review of Books* 17 Dec. 1989: 14-15.

Rohman, D. Gordon, and Albert O. Wlecki. *Prewriting: The Construction and Application of Models for Concept Formation in Writing*. Health, Education, and Welfare Project No. 2174. East Lansing: Michigan State University, 1964.

Rorty, Richard. *Philosophy and the Mirror of Nature.* Princeton: Princeton University Press, 1979.

Rose, Mary Beth, ed. and intro. *Women in the Middle Ages and the Renaissance: Literary and Historical Perspectives.* Syracuse, N.Y.: Syracuse University Press, 1986.

Rose, Mike, ed. *When a Writer Can't Write: Studies in Writer's Block and Other Composing Process Problems,* New York: Guilford, 1985.

Rosenblatt, Paul C. *Bitter, Bitter Tears: Nineteenth Century Diarists and Twentieth Century Grief Theorists.* Minneapolis: University of Minnesota Press, 1983.

Rosenfeldt, Deborah. "The Politics of Bibliography." In *Women in Print I.* See Hartman and Messer-Davidow 1982. 11-36.

Rubenstein, Roberta. *Boundaries of the Self: Culture, Gender and Fiction.* Urbana: University of Illinois Press, 1987.

Rubin, Donnalee. "The Characteristics and Implications of Gender-Based Reading Differences When Teachers Read Student Texts." Unpublished paper, April 1985.

———. "Gender Patterns: Reading Student Texts." Unpublished essay.

Russ, Joanna. *How to Suppress Women's Writing.* Austin: University of Texas Press, 1983.

Russell, Diana E. H. *The Secret Trauma: Incest in the Lives of Girls and Women.* New York: Basic Books, 1986.

Sadker, Myra, and David Sadker. "Confronting Sexism in the College Classroom." In *Gender in the Classroom.* See Gabriel and Smithson 1990. 176-88.

Sandborn, Jean. "Blocked by the Academic Essay: Case Studies of 'Misfits.'" Paper presented at the Conference on College Composition and Communication, Atlanta, 19-21 March 1987.

Sanderson, Catherine. "Writing About Gender: Sexual Politics and Student Perceptions." In *Gender and Writing.* Unpublished essay.

Sanford, Mollie Dorsey. *Mollie: The Journal of Mollie Dorsey Sanford in Nebraska and Colorado Territories, 1857-1866.* Lincoln: University of Nebraska Press, 1976.

Sankovitch, Tilde. "Inventing Authority of Origin: The Difficult Enterprise." In *Women in the Middle Ages and the Renaissance.* See Rose 1986. 227-45.

Sargent, Alice, ed. *Beyond Sex Roles.* St. Paul, Minn.: West, 1977.

Sarton, May. *Journal of a Solitude.* 1973. New York: Norton, 1984.

Sartre, Jean-Paul. *What Is Literature?* Trans. Bernard Frechtman. Gloucester, Mass.: Peter Smith, 1978.

Sattel, Jack. "Men, Inexpressiveness, and Power." In *Language, Gender and Society.* See Thorne et al. 1983. 119-24.

Schilb, John. "The Usefulness of Women's Nontraditional Literature in the Traditional Literature-and-Composition Course." In *Women's Personal Narratives.* See Hoffman and Culley 1985. 115-23.

Schinto, Jean. "Private Lives: Why We Keep Diaries." *Boston Globe Magazine* 8 November 1987: 22-38.

Schlafly, Phyllis, ed. *Child Abuse in the Classroom.* Alton, Ill. Père Marquette Press, 1984.

Schlissel, Lillian. *Women's Diaries of the Westward Journey.* New York: Schocken, 1982.

Schmitz, Betty. *Integrating Women's Studies into the Curriculum: A Guide and Bibliography.* New York: The Feminist Press, 1985.

Schneider, J., and Sally Hacker. "Sex Role Imagery and the Use of the Generic Man." *American Sociologist* 8, no. 1 (Feb. 1973): 12-18.

Schulz, Muriel. "Man (Embracing Woman): The Generic in Sociological Writing." Paper presented at the Ninth World Congress of Sociology, Uppsala, Sweden, 14-20 Aug. 1978.

———. "The Semantic Derogation of Women." In *Language and Sex.* See Thorne and Henley 1975. 64-75.

Schweickart, Patrocinio P. "Reading Ourselves: Toward a Feminist Theory of Reading." In *Gender and Reading.* See Flynn and Schweickart 1986. 31-62.

Scott-Maxwell, Florida. *The Measure of My Days.* New York: Penguin, 1979.

Segel, Elizabeth. "'As the Twig Is Bent . . .': Gender and Childhood Reading." In *Gender and Reading.* See Flynn and Schweickart 1986. 165-86.

Seitz, Cheryl Glenn. "Muted Voices: Women in the History of Rhetoric from Antiquity through the Renaissance." Ph.D. diss. proposal, University of Ohio, 1987.

Shakeshaft, Charol. "A Gender at Risk." *Phi Delta Kappan* (Mar. 1986): 499-503.

Sherry, Ruth. *Studying Women's Writing: An Introduction.* London: Edward Arnold, 1988.

Shields, David. *A History of Personal Diary Writing in New England 1620-1745.* Ann Arbor, Mich.: University Microfilms, 1982.

Shonagon, Sei. *The Pillow Book of Sei Shonagon*. Ed. and trans. I Morris. Harmondsworth, U.K.: Penguin, 1977.

Showalter, Elaine. *A Literature of Their Own*. Princeton, N.J.: Princeton University Press, 1977.

———. *The New Feminist Criticism: Essass on Women, Literature, and Theory*. NY: Pantheon, 1985.

Silviera, Jeanette. "Generic Masculine Words and Thinking." In *The Voices and Words of Women and Men*. See Kramarae 1980. 165-78.

Simons, George. *Keeping Your Personal Journal*. New York: Paulist Press, 1978.

Sklar, Elizabeth S. "Sexist Grammar Revisited." *College English* 45, no. 4 (Apr. 1983): 348-58.

Slevin, James F. "Connecting English Studies." *College English* 48, no. 6 (1986): 543-50.

Smith, Carol H. "Review: The Literary Politics of Gender." *College English* 50, no. 3 (March 1988): 318-22.

Smith, Dorothy. "A Peculiar Eclipsing: Women's Exclusion from Man's Culture." *Women's Studies International Quarterly* 1, no. 4 (1978): 281-96.

Smith-Rosenberg, Carroll. "The Female World of Love and Ritual: Relations Between Women in Nineteenth-Century America." In *Feminist Frontiers II*. See Richardson and Taylor 1986. 229-49.

Smithson, Isaiah. "Investigating Gender, Power, and Pedagogy." In *Gender in the Classroom*. See Gabriel and Smithson 1990. 1-27.

Solomon, Barbara Miller. *In the Company of Educated Women*. New Haven: Yale University Press, 1985.

Spacks, Patricia Meyer. *The Female Imagination*. New York: Alfred A. Knopf, 1975.

———. "Selves in Hiding." In *Women's Autobiography*. See Jelinek 1980. 112-32.

Spanier, Bonnie, Alexander Bloom, and Darlene Boroviak, eds. *Toward a Balanced Curriculum: A Sourcebook for Initiating Gender Integration Projects*. Cambridge, Mass.: Schenkman, 1984.

Spector, Judith A., ed. "Gender Studies: New Directions for Feminist Criticism." *College English* 43, no. 4 (Apr. 1981): 374-78.

———. *Gender Studies: New Directions in Feminist Criticism*. Bowling Green, Ohio.: Bowling Green University, Popular Press, 1986.

Spellmeyer, Kurt. "A Common Ground: The Essay in the Academy." *College English* 51, no. 3 (March 1989): 262-76.

Spender, Dale. "Journal on a Journal." *Women's Studies International Forum*. 10, no. 1 (1987): 1-5.

―――. *Man Made Language*. London: Routledge and Kegan Paul, 1980.

―――. *Mothers of the Novel: 100 Good Women Writers Before Jane Austen*. New York: Pandora, 1986.

―――. *The Writing or the Sex? or Why You Don't Have to Read Women's Writing to Know it's No Good*. New York: Pergamon, 1989.

Spender, Lynn. *Intruders on the Rights of Men: Women's Unpublished Heritage*. London: Pandora, 1983.

Spengemann, William. *The Forms of Autobiography: Episodes in the History of A Literary Genre*. New Haven: Yale University Press, 1980.

Spretnak, Charlene. *Lost Goddesses of Early Greece: A Collection of Pre-Hellenic Myth*. Boston: Beacon Press, 1984.

Stanley, Julia. "Gender Marking in American English." In *Sexism and Language*. See Nilsen et al. 1977. 44-76.

Stanley, Liz, and Sue Wise. *Breaking Out: Feminist Consciousness and Feminine Research*. Boston: Routledge and Kegan Paul, 1983.

Stannard, Una. *Mrs. Man*. San Francisco: Germain Books, 1977.

Stanton, Domna C., ed. *The Female Autograph*. New York: Literary Forum, 1985.

Sterling, Dorothy, ed. *We Are Your Sisters: Black Women in the Nineteenth Century*. New York: W. W. Nortoll, 1984.

Sternberg, Janet, ed. and intro. *The Writer on Her Work*. New York: W. W. Norton, 1980.

Stimpson, Catharine R. Intro. *Feminist Issues in Literary Scholarship*. See Benstock 1987. 1-6.

Stone, Merlin. *When God was a Woman*. New York: Harcourt Brace Jovanovich, 1976.

Strodtbeck, Fred, Rita M. James, and Charles Hawkins. "Social Status in Jury Deliberations." *American Sociological Review* 22 (1957): 713-19.

Summerfield, Geoffrey. "Not in Utopia: Reflections on Journal-Writing." In *The Journal Book*. See Fulwiler 1987. 33-40.

Swacker, Marjorie. "The Sex of the Speaker as a Sociolinguistic Variable . " In *Language and Sex*. See Thorne and Henley 1975. 76-83.

―――. "Women's Verbal Behavior at Learned and Professional Conferences."

In *The Sociology of the Languages of American Women*. See Dubois and Crouch 1976. 155-60.

Taylor, Sheila Ortiz. "Women In a Double Bind: Hazards of the Argumentative Edge." *College Composition and Communication* 29 (1978): 387.

Thomas, Trudelle. "Book of One's Own: A History of the Student Journal as a Pedagogical Tool." Paper presented at the Conference on College Composition and Communication, Seattle, Wash., March 1989.

————. "Women's Diaries of the Westward Movement: A Methodological Study." *Forum: A Women's Studies Quarterly* (1984): 7-11.

Thorne, Barrie. "Claiming Verbal Space: Women's Speech and Language in College Classrooms." Paper presented at the Research Conference on Educational Environments and the Undergraduate Woman, Wellesley College, Sept. 1979.

Thorne, Barrie, and Nancy Henley, eds. *Language and Sex: Difference and Dominance*. Rowley, Mass.: Newbury House, 1975.

Thorne, Barrie, Cheris Kramarae, and Nancy Henley, eds. *Language, Gender and Society*. Rowley, Mass.: Newbury House, 1983.

Tilford, Elinor. "Nothing Ever Happens as Interesting as a Story." *English Journal* 29 (Spring 1940): 563-71.

Todd, Janet. *Gender and Literary Voice*. New York: Holmes and Meier, 1980.

Treichler, Paula A. "From Discourse to Dictionary: How Sexist Meanings are Authorized." In *Language Gender and Professional Writing*. See Frank and Treichler 1989. 51-79.

Treichler, Paula A., and Kramarae, Cheris. "Women's Talk in the Ivory Tower." *Communications Quarterly* 31, no. 2 (1983): 118-32.

Ulrich, Laurel Thatcher. *A Midwife's Tale: The Life of Martha Ballard, Based on her Diary, 1785-1812*. New York: Alfred A. Knopf, 1990.

————. "The Significance of Trivia: The Diaries of Martha Moore Ballard, 1785-1812." Address to the Women's History Symposium on "Women's Diaries: What They Tell Us and How We Can Use Them," Strawberry Banke Museum, Portsmouth, N.H., 7 March 1987.

Voss, Norine. "'Saying the Unsayable': An Introduction to Autobiography." In *Gender Studies*. See Spector 1986. 218-33.

Vygotsky, Lev. *Thought and Language*. Cambridge, Mass.: Massachusetts Institute of Technology Press, 1962.

Walters, Anna. "Self Image and Style: A Discussion Based on Estelle Jelinek's

*The Tradition of Women's Autobiography from Antiquity to the Present."
Women's Studies International Forum* 10, no. 1 (1987): 85-93.

Walters, Margaret. "The Rights and Wrongs of Women: Mary Wollstonecroft,
Harriet Martineau, Simone De Beauvoir." In *The Rights and Wrongs of
Women*. Ed. Juliet Mitchell and Ann Oakley. Baltimore: Penguin, 1976.

Wandor, Micheline, ed. *On Gender and Writing*. London: Pandora Press, 1983.

Wann, Louis, ed and intro. *Century Readings in the English Essay*. New York:
Appleton-Century Crofts, 1939.

Warshay, Diana W. "Sex Differences in Language Style." In *Toward a Sociology
of Women*. Ed. Constantina Safilios-Rothschild. Lexington, Mass.: Xerox
College, 1972. 3-9.

Washington, Mary Helen. *Invented Lives: Narratives of Black Women*. New York:
Doubleday, 1987.

Waugh, Susan. "Women's Shorter Autobiographical Writings: Expression, Identity, and Form." In *Women's Personal Narratives*. See Hoffman and Culley
1985. 144-52.

Weaver, Elissa. "Spiritual Fun: A Study of Sixteenth Century Tuscan Convent
Theater." In *Women in the Middle Ages and the Renassiance*. See Rose 1986.
173-206.

Weintraub, Karl J. "Autobiography and Historical Consciousness." *Critical
Inquiry* 1 (June 1975): 821-48.

West, Candace, and Don H. Zimmerman. "Women's Place in Everyday Talk:
Reflections on Parent-Child Interaction." *Social Problems* 24 (1977): 521-28.

————. "Small Insults: A Study of Interruptions in Cross-Sex Conversations
Between Unaquainted Persons." In *Language, Gender and Society*. See
Thorne et al. 1983. 103-18.

Whitehead, Ann. "Sexual Antagonism in Herefordshire." In *Dependence and
Exploitation in Work and Marriage*. See Barker and Allen 1976. 169-203.

Wiesner, Merry E. "Women's Defense of their Public Role." In *Women in the
Middle Ages and the Renaissance*. See Rose 1986. 1-28.

Willy, Margaret. *Three Women Diarists*. Ed. Geoffrey Bullough. London: Long-
mans, Green and Company, 1964.

Wittig, Monique. *Les Guérillères*. Trans. David Le Vay. New York: Avon, 1969.

Wolfe, Susan J. "The Reconstruction of Word Meanings: A Review of the Scholarship." In *Language, Gender and Professional Writing*. See Frank and Treichler 1989. 80-94.

Woolf, Virginia. *A Room of One's Own.* 1929. New York: Harcourt, 1981.

———. *The Diaries of Virginia Woolf.* Ed. Anne Olivier Bell. 5 vols. New York: Harcourt Brace Jovanovich, 1977-1984.

———. *Women and Writing.* 1st American edition. New York: Harcourt, 1980.

Young, Art, and Toby Fulwiler, eds. *Writing Across the Disciplines: Research into Practice.* Upper Montclair, N.J.: Boynton/Cook, 1986.

Zimmerman, Don, and Candace West. "Sex Roles, Interruptions and Silences in Conversation." In *Language and Sex.* See Thorne and Henley 1975. 105-29.

Index

Coding
    privacy and, 25, 26, 209
    Samuel Pepys' diaries, 124
Cognitivism, language and, 5
Cole, Mary, 36
Collaboration, 76-79
College English, 204
Coming of Friars, The (Jessop), 107
Coming to voice, 15-18, 49, 207
    women's student journals and,
        178-179
*Common-Place Book of the Fifteenth
    Century, A*, 109
Commonplace books, 24, 34, 109, 112
    men's student journals as, 165-166
Community, 7-9. *See also* Academic
    discourse communities; Discourse
    communities
"Competing Theories of Process: A
    Critique and a Proposal"
    (Faigley), 3
Competition, in men's conversation,
    71-79
Complex thought, journals and, 197-
    198
"Composing as a Woman" (Flynn), 10
Composition
    feminism and, 2-11
    social constructionism and, 2-11
Connors, Robert, 182, 194-195
Consciousness-raising groups, 80
Consensus, 76-79
Constitutive power of language, 31
Constructionism, social. *See* Social
    constructionism
Conversation. *See also* Discourse;
    Speaking among men and
    women, 71-72, 76-79
    cooperation in, 71-72, 76-79
    interruptions in, 73-74
    management of, by men, 72-79
Cooley, Elizabeth Ann, 145
Cooper, Annie, 144
Cooperation, in women's
    conversation, 71-72
Cooper, Marilyn, 6

Coupling, of personal and academic
    learning, 29-30
Cowper, Lady, 132
Creation of Patriarchy, The (Lerner),
    61-62
Culley, Margo, 125, 127, 129, 133,
    137, 142
Cultural literacy, 37

Dartmouth, *The Hopkins Bulletin*, 37
Darwin, Charles, 112
Davis, Varina Howell, 121
*Day at a Time, A: The Diary Literature
    of American Women from 1764 to
    the Present* (Culley), 125
Daybooks
    vs. journals, 23-25
    men's student journals as, 156, 163
    women's student journals as, 170-
        171
Dear Diary (Dobbs), 111
Death, journal keeping and, 140-141
De Beauvoir, Simone, 47
De Courtivron, Isabelle, 45, 46
De France, Marie, 71
De Jars, Marie, 51
DeSalvo, Louise, 146
Descriptive writing, in women's
    student journals, 169
Des Roches, Madeleine, 71, 87
"Development of the Essay in
    English, The" (Wann), 111-112
Dialectical notebooks, 31
"Dialectical Notebooks and the
    Audit of Meaning" (Berthoff), 31
Diaries. *See also* Academic journals;
    Journals; Student journals
    blank books for, 101, 114-115,
        130
    derivation of term, 105-107
    domestic, 126-127, 132-133
    feminization of, 193, 197
    freewriting, 20, 23, 26
    vs. journals, 21, 26-27, 29, 34, 39-42,
        99-100, 148, 149, 181-182, 188

Curriculum) movement, 27-32
Walker, Mary Richardson, 129
Wallada, 94
Walpole, Horace, 91
"Wanderings: Misreadings,
    Miswritings, Misunderstandings"
    (Bartholomae), 198
Wann, Louis, 111-112
Warwick, Countess of, 128-129
Ways with Words (Heath), 8
Webb, Beatrice, 143-144
Weeton, Ellen, 131
Wesley, John, 110
West, Candace, 74, 75-76
"When Women Got the Word"
    (Kolb), 86
Wife battering, 81-82
Wilde, Oscar, 68
"Wild zone"
    in journals, 149, 189
    in women's discourse, 195
Willis, Winifred, 144
Winnileodas (songs for a friend), 65
Wister, Sally, 119
Wittig, Monique, 51, 60
Wlecke, Albert O., 22, 25, 196
Wolfe, Susan J., 147-148
Wolfe, Virginia, 207
Wolthius, Lois, 37
"Womanization of Rhetoric, The"
    (Gearhart), 200
Women
    academic, 12-14, 195
    attitudes toward journal writing
        by, 27, 172-177, 180-182, 184-187
    black, silence and, 82
    defined in relation to men, 57, 60
    demands on, 13-14
    as diarists, 117-120, 125
    education of, 86-88
    as garrulous, 68-71
    as gossipers, 68
    identification with mother by, 49
    journal-writing experience, 182-187
    language and, 43-48
    marginality of, 11, 13, 17, 204

"marriage plot" and, 14
nurturer role, 48-49
personal-style pedagogy and, 195-196
silence of, 15, 53(fig.), 58-60, 64, 68-71, 82
surnames, 57
terms referring to, 57-58
Women of Academe: Outsiders in the Sacred Grove (Aisenberg and Harrington), 13
Women's discourse
    classroom speaking, 79-81, 199
    conversation patterns, 71-72
    difficulty in finding a voice, 15-18
    macropolitical and institutional sanctions on, 61-66
    marginality of, 11, 13, 17, 204
    mutedness of, 51-54, 125-129, 189, 199
    silencing of, 58, 61-66, 81-85, 179
    speech, 61-68, 71-72, 76-81, 199
    "wild zone" in, 149, 189, 195
Women's journals
    destruction of, 121-123
    dominance and mutedness in, 125-129
    legacy of, 148-159,188-190
    as letters, 133-136
    preservation of, 120-124
    privatization of, 130, 192
    public and private, 129-132
    purposes of, 133-136, 148-149
    self and, 136-145
    sexual violence and, 38-39, 146-147, 179
    social and domestic purposes of, 132-133
    "wild zone" in, 149, 189
    women's uses of, 147-148
Women's rights, women as defenders of, 71
Women's student journals
    attitudes toward, 172-177, 180-182, 184-187
    characteristics, topics, uses and